ELECTIONSBYDESIGN

ELECTIONS

BY DESIGN

PARTIES AND
PATRONAGE IN
RUSSIA'S
REGIONS

BRYON MORASKI

NORTHERN
ILLINOIS
UNIVERSITY
PRESS

© 2006 by Northern Illinois University Press

Published by the Northern Illinois University Press, DeKalb, Illinois   60115

Library of Congress Cataloging-in-Publication Data

Moraski, Bryon.

Elections by design : parties and patronage in Russia's regions / Bryon Moraski.— 1st ed.

p. cm.

Includes bibliographical references and index.

ISBN-13: 978-0-87580-355-5 (clothbound : alk. paper)

ISBN-10: 0-87580-355-5 (clothbound : alk. paper)

1. Subnational governments—Russia (Federation) 2. Representative government and

representation—Russia (Federation) 3. Russia (Federation)—Politics and government—

1991- I.Title.

JN6699.A88M67 2006

324.6'3094709049—dc22

2005029738

CONTENTS

LIST OF TABLES

PREFACE

Although a number of works have been published on institutional choice in recent years, our understanding of the politics behind institutional choice lags behind our comprehension of the consequences of different institutional arrangements. This gap has led to a plethora of works that warn against certain institutions and promote the adoption of others. Yet political institutions are not created in a laboratory, and very little evidence exists to suggest that they are designed for such altruistic reasons as consolidating democracy, promoting economic development, or engendering popular satisfaction with government. An investigation of parliamentary electoral systems at the regional level in states in transition, like Russia, drives this latter point home while simultaneously providing greater insight into the politics governing institutional decisions. For example, even though studies of institutional choice at the national level focus on political bargaining between political parties, it is not always safe to assume that political parties are the main actors structuring the decisions made during such negotiations. In Russia's regions, political parties were extremely weak throughout the 1990s; in fact, the design of regional electoral systems often came before the advent of functioning party systems (to the extent that such systems have even emerged). Accordingly, this book's theoretical framework for understanding institutional choice is based in part on the individual interests and preferences of political actors comprising different branches and levels of government. While political parties are not ignored, they dominate neither the assumptions nor the hypotheses guiding the work.

The book's emphasis on the design of subnational institutions also fills an important gap in the existing literature on institutional choice. Prior works have regularly overlooked institutional choice at the regional level in transitional states. Likewise, the political effects of regional institutions have received relatively little attention when compared to the body of research on the consequences of national-level institutions. Yet democratization is a multi-layered phenomenon. And, while information on national institutions may be more readily available, this does not necessarily mean that the political consequences of national institutions will have a greater influence on whether democratic politics takes root in previously uncultivated soil. One could argue that democratic regressions and authoritarian revivals occur precisely because democratic reforms at the national level stall when confronted with persisting institutional and behavioral legacies of the old regime at lower levels of government. Indeed, a popularly elected and democratically oriented national leader may resort to undemocratic practices when confronted with corrupt or incompetent politicians at the regional and local levels. Thus, I contend that the study of transitions from authoritarian rule should more deeply consider the effects that regional institutions have on the process of democratization. At the same time, I believe we must study the origins of these institutions if we are to adequately understand their effects.

Just as the theoretical contentions guiding this book bridge different topics in comparative politics, the empirical analyses mix different methodologies. Actually, the genesis of the book occurred in 1997, when as a graduate student at the University of Iowa, I realized that post-Soviet Russia provided scholars a unique opportunity for studying institutional choice. The regions of the Russian Federation constitute a relatively large population of polities experiencing the trials and tribulations of transition, if not democratization. Yet, as a group, these regions also exhibit less variation than nation-states in terms of cultural heritages, historical experiences, and international influences, which often serve as intervening variables capable of frustrating cross-national analyses. As my study of institutional choice progressed, however, I became painfully aware of the impediments associated with acquiring quality data across 89 regional polities in a transitional state. Upon encountering these difficulties, the benefits of mixing methodological approaches became evident. In fact, after several months of research on the topic, I had decided that a comparative study of four to six regions would be all that was possible. However, thanks to the pioneering work of various scholars of Russian politics, to which this book is greatly indebted, I managed to cobble together a set of data that allowed my initial vision of mixing statistical analyses with detailed case studies to become a reality.

In addition to the wide range of scholars that I cite throughout the book, I am also indebted to various individuals who shaped the project at different stages in its development. I begin with John Ishiyama, one of my undergraduate mentors at then Northeast Missouri State University. John's contagious enthusiasm for the study of democratization and electoral institutions motivated me to consider graduate school and greatly influenced my approach to the study of political science. Likewise, I am grateful to the faculty in the Department of Political Science at the University of Iowa, where I completed my Ph.D. My zeal for comparative politics would have gone to waste had it not been for the excellent training, support, and encouragement I received from various instructors during my years there. I am particularly grateful to my dissertation committee: Vicki Hesli, Jae-On Kim, Gerhard Loewenberg, William Reisinger (chair), and Charles Shipan. As a group, they pushed me to formulate and complete the dissertation that would eventually evolve into this book.

The work also benefited from the insightful comments of several other scholars. When the case studies were still in the initial stages, the suggestions of Philip Roeder and Christopher Nevitt helped improve them. The statistical analyses, meanwhile, benefited from observations by Renée Johnson and Judith Kullberg. Equally valuable were the criticisms of numerous anonymous reviewers, who read pieces of the larger project while I was submitting article-length manuscripts for publication. These criticisms not only greatly influenced the final manuscript but also convinced me that its arguments would be best served as a book rather than a series of articles. On a related note, much of the empirical analysis in chapter 3 was originally published in *Europe-Asia Studies* (see "Electoral System Design in Russian *Oblasti* and Republics: A Four Case Comparison" (2003) 55(3): 437–68; http://www.tandf.co.uk).

While I was searching for a press, Michael Gorham, Thomas Remington, Daniel Smith, and Philip Williams took the time to read either my prospectus or first chapter. I am grateful to each for expressing interest in the project as well as for urging me to think about its larger implications. Prior to finding a press, Robert Moser and John Ishiyama read the book manuscript in its entirety. Both reacted positively, encouraged me to persist with the work, and offered their own words of wisdom. Fortunately, the editor of Northern Illinois University Press, Mary Lincoln, greeted the manuscript with a similar level of enthusiasm. I want to thank her for carefully reading my prospectus and locating two extremely diligent and knowledgeable anonymous reviewers. I greatly appreciate the time and effort both reviewers dedicated to the manuscript. As always, however, any errors or shortcomings of the work are my own.

Research for the book would not have been possible without significant financial support from several sources. I owe Margaret Mills in the Russian Department at the University of Iowa for twice thinking of me when funding to study intensive Russian became available through the Social Science Research Council. Likewise, I am indebted to the University of Iowa's Stanley Foundation for a pre-dissertation fellowship, its Graduate Council for a T. Anne Cleary International Dissertation Fellowship, and its Center for Russian, East European, and Eurasian Studies for three academic-year fellowships. The University of Florida's Department of Political Science also awarded me a departmental research grant in 2002, which I used to collect some final pieces of data. Meanwhile, Joe Aufmuth in the University of Florida's Government Documents Department helped me create the book's map.

I also would like to acknowledge the kindness, patience, and support of the friends and acquaintances I made in Russia. While there are too many people to list by name, I would be remiss to neglect Nikolai Petrov at Moscow's Carnegie Center, who shared with me some preliminary data on Russia's regional electoral systems, and the staff in the Moscow office of the International Foundation for Election Systems, who assembled various publications on regional election laws for me in 1998. Information from both sources proved critical in providing me a better sense of what questions I could reasonably expect to answer.

On a personal note, I would like to express my gratitude to my family for their continual love and support. I feel extremely fortunate to have the opportunity to publicly thank those I love for all they have given me and for forgiving my tendency to take them for granted as I occasionally focused too much on my career. Of course, the one person to whom I am most indebted is my wife, Jayne. Over the years, my chosen path has demanded more of her than I think either of us ever imagined, yet she has demonstrated only patience and love while only asking for the same in return. The book is dedicated to her.

NOTE ON TRANSLITERATION

Throughout the book I use the Library of Congress system for transliterating the Russian alphabet. Some words and many geographic names, however, appear in their more commonly found English-language spellings as opposed to what the LC system of transliteration would produce (e.g., Yeltsin rather than El'tsin, Chechnya instead of Chechnia, and Buriatia not Buriatiia).

ELECTIONSBYDESIGN

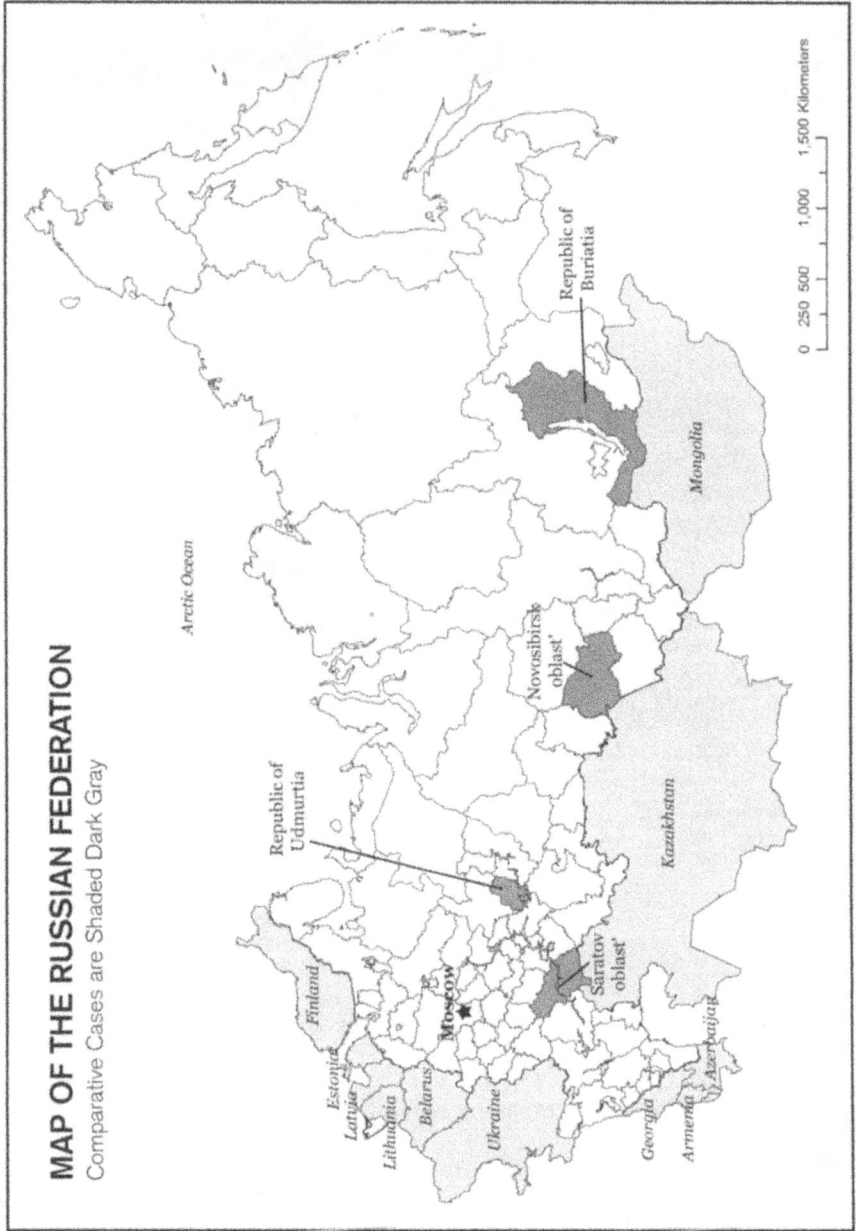

MAP OF THE RUSSIAN FEDERATION
Comparative Cases are Shaded Dark Gray

Republic of Buriatia

Mongolia

Novosibirsk' oblast'

Kazakhstan

Republic of Udmurtia

Saratov' oblast'

Arctic Ocean

Finland

Estonia

Latvia

Lithuania

Belarus

Ukraine

Moscow

Georgia

Armenia

Azerbaijan

0   250 500   1,000   1,500 Kilometers

ONE— THE RULES OF THE GAME

During a visit to Izhevsk—the capital of the republic of Udmurtia—in 1999, I had the opportunity to attend a gathering of several Russian experts on public policy. During a conversation with two of these experts, I asked their opinion about the choice of electoral systems in Russia's 89 federal subjects. I specifically noted the contrast between the initial electoral system in Saratov oblast—where 10 of the 35 parliamentary deputies were elected in a single regionwide district using party lists—and the system in their republic—where only one representative was elected per electoral district. One Russian acquaintance offered a straightforward explanation for the divergence: Saratov oblast had political parties, the republic of Udmurtia did not. While initially intuitive, this reply proves controversial for two reasons. First, it raises the issue of endogeneity: Do electoral systems determine the development of party systems, or does the existence of parties determine the choice of electoral systems? Second, it suggests that party development had advanced far enough in some Russian regions to actually determine the design of institutions, yet many political observers disagree about the level of party development in Russia during the 1990s. Therefore, what at first seems like a straightforward answer in fact raises only new questions. How does electoral system choice reflect party development where the party system itself is undeveloped? Does the number of parties competing shape an electoral system's proportionality? Or, does the level of party organization determine the proportionality of an electoral system? Is it possible, instead, that electoral system design reflects the level and nature of elite competition rather than the party system per se?

This book examines the choice of regional parliamentary electoral systems in Russia. Although it is certainly a work about the choice of specific institutions in a specific context, it has two larger and more fundamental goals. First, it seeks greater insight into how institutional decisions are made. Second, it strives to explicate the consequences these initial institutional decisions can have on transitions from authoritarian rule. In pursuing these goals, the book considers the following questions: What factors determined the proportionality of Russia's regional parliamentary electoral systems? Specifically, why did some regions adopt more proportional parliamentary electoral systems than other regions did? What roles did party development and elite competition play in the design of these parliamentary electoral systems? What influence did the federal government exert over these decisions? What have been the political consequences of parliamentary electoral systems? How have the regional parliamentary electoral systems contributed to the current state of Russian democracy?

WHY ELECTORAL SYSTEM CHOICE?

Why is it important to understand the politics of institutional choice? The initial selection of political institutions sets the rules by which the game of politics will be played. Because political institutions substantially shape how politicians work with one another, which policies they address, and how they seek to resolve political conflict, the initial period of institutional design emerges as a critical juncture for transitional states. Struggles to claim or retain control over valuable resources generally accompany the collapse of the old order, and these struggles raise the stakes when designing new political institutions. Moreover, since the creation of political institutions is a complicated and labor-intensive task, institutional decisions generally produce a significant degree of inertia, which makes future alterations to the institutional framework difficult.

One particularly important institutional decision for a new democracy is the selection of the parliamentary electoral system, which translates popular votes into parliamentary seats. The choice of a parliamentary electoral system entails important implications for the future of a democratizing regime because different electoral systems have different advantages and disadvantages. Proportional representation (PR) systems allow smaller parties representing specific societal interests a better chance to attain seats in parliament (e.g., Bogdanor 1984; Hoag and Hallet 1926; Lakeman 1974). However, majoritarian systems, like single-member-district (SMD) plurality systems (described in detail below), consistently inhibit party fragmentation. Just as such electoral systems help reduce the number of political parties effectively competing across most electoral districts, they also tend to yield stable single-party governments that can carry through a policy program. In addition, plurality systems better reflect changes in public preferences from one election to the next: Where candidates need a majority (or just a plurality) of the vote to win elections, a small shift in the distribution of votes can create a significant shift in the distribution of parliamentary seats (Hermens 1941; Hain 1986).

Electoral systems, then, determine the degree to which elections fulfill different visions of democracy. Majoritarian systems are designed to concentrate political power at the expense of underrepresenting smaller groups in society. However, these systems also make it easier for "the people" (i.e., voters) to hold policymakers accountable for their decisions. PR systems are designed to represent a wider cross-section of the public. However, these systems make it more difficult for the people to hold policymakers accountable, since policies result from a complex bargaining process among multiple interests (Powell 2000). While changes in electoral system design certainly occur, the initial selection of electoral rules and their corresponding effects on politics often limit the range of alterations to the institutional framework (see Birch et al. 2002, 20–22). For example, shifting from an SMD system to a PR system (or vice versa) provides the most effective means for altering the degree of electoral proportionality, yet such changes have rarely been attempted. Instead, altering the features of electoral systems within one of the two systems has been more common (Lijphart 1994, 143).

Since electoral system choice can have important implications for the direction of democracy, the period during which electoral systems are being designed may be a tense time for a democratic transition. However, plenty of room exists for negotiation and compromise among different political actors with diverging interests: "The number of electoral systems is, in principle, infinite; [although] the number of systems that democratic engineers and reformers have proposed is much smaller" (Lijphart 1994, 1). The infinite range of theoretical possibilities and the large number of operational electoral systems undermine attempts to make electoral system choice a zero-sum game. For example, institutional designers must determine the average district magnitude of the system (M), that is, how many seats should be allocated per district. If they choose to allocate only one seat per electoral district, then they must also decide whether the seats will be distributed on the basis of plurality rule (i.e., first past the post), majority rule (using second ballots when necessary), or preference voting (e.g., the alternative vote system in which voters can rank candidates). Meanwhile, if the designers choose to allocate multiple seats per district, they need to determine how many seats should be distributed in each district, including whether each district should possess the same number of seats. There are also questions about which mathematical formula should be used to allocate seats in these multimember districts—divisor or quota methods (for an exceptionally lucid explanation of these options, see Riedwyl and Steiner 1995, 360–63). Likewise, decisions must be made as to whether political parties need to win a minimum level of support (i.e., pass a legal threshold) to gain representation in parliament.

Perhaps the most important feature of a parliamentary electoral system is its average district magnitude, which has been shown to most directly influence the proportionality of the system (Monroe and Rose 2002; Rae 1967; Taagepera and Shugart 1989). The divergence between the large number of votes cast in a district and the comparatively small number of parliamentary seats being allocated per district creates a relationship between district magnitude and proportionality in which higher magnitudes produce greater levels of proportionality. The logic behind the relationship is straightforward. When more seats are allocated, a better fit between the percentage of votes for a party and the percentage of seats for that party can be achieved (see Taagepera and Shugart 1989, 112–14).

District magnitude also serves as a fundamental electoral feature for differentiating among parliamentary electoral systems. Single-member-district (SMD) systems, like the system used to elect the U.S. House of Representatives, are systems in which each legislator represents a different district. Since only one seat is allocated from each district, the district magnitude equals one. At the extreme opposite, SMD systems are proportional representation (PR) systems, like those in Israel and the Netherlands, in which voters elect all members of parliament through a single, nationwide district, making the district magnitude equal to the number of seats in parliament. In these cases, a high district magnitude and a large assembly size yield a high degree of proportionality between vote and seat shares. Not all PR systems have district magnitudes equal to the number of seats in their parliament, however. Falling in between SMD systems and these "pure" PR systems are PR systems that divide the country into several multimember districts (districts that elect two or more legislators). Although a multi-member-district (MMD) system can allocate all of the seats in each district to the party that wins a plurality of votes in that district, most allocate seats on a more proportional basis. Meanwhile, some systems—like the one governing elections to the lower house of Russia's national parliament—mix SMDs with PR.

While average district magnitude itself exists along an interval scale, it is equally important to note that the political consequences of electoral systems tend to mirror this interval scale. Specifically, electoral studies have repeatedly emphasized the importance of district magnitude rather than types of electoral systems in assessing the political consequences of electoral systems, regardless of whether those consequences fall on political parties or voters.

In advanced industrial democracies, less proportional electoral systems (those with lower district magnitudes) consistently exclude smaller parties from representation in parliament. Rae (1967) and Taagepera and Shugart (1989) emphasize that lower district magnitudes reduce the number of parties at higher rates. Thus, the lower the district magnitude, the less proportional the electoral system and the fewer political parties winning represen-tation in parliament. Meanwhile, Cox (1997) contends that district magni-tude (M) sets an upper limit on the number of parties at M+1. In other words, district magnitude determines the carrying capacity of the electoral system, but the number of cleavages in society determines the actual num-ber of parties.

In advanced industrial democracies, less proportional electoral systems (those with lower district magnitudes) also consistently encourage voters to cast their votes strategically by selecting parties with better electoral prospects. While Duverger (1954) contends that proportional representa-tion systems relieve voters from the constraints of strategic voting, this relief does not directly coincide with the type of electoral system (Cox 1997). Voters in certain PR systems regularly vote strategically. It is only when district magnitudes exceed five that strategic voting becomes infea-sible, for the voter lacks the information necessary to accurately assess the electoral environment.

As this discussion suggests, electoral systems have been shown to have a direct impact on party systems and voting behavior (Birch 2003; Gabel 1995; Golder 2003; Ishiyama 1993; Katz 1980; Kim and Ohn 1992; Riker 1982; Sartori 1994). In addition, because electoral systems determine levels of political inclusion and exclusion, their consequences also have been ex-amined with regard to ethnic representation (Barkan 1995; Horowitz 1985, 1991; Lijphart 1986; Mitchell 1995; Ordeshook and Shvetsova 1994; Reynolds 1995), as well as the representation of women (Golosov 2001; Reynolds 1999; Rule and Zimmerman 1994; Matland and Studlar 1996). That is, more proportional systems increase the chances that smaller parties representing specific societal interests will attain seats in parliament and, therefore, provide at least the perception that a wider range of societal groups has access to the political process.

Ultimately, then, while electoral system choice is often regarded as a de-cision between a plurality-rule system and a proportional representation system, its consequences operate along a continuum that is often defined in terms of district magnitude. Thus, depicting electoral system decisions as a choice between plurality and proportional representation systems exag-gerates the difference between the two categories and underestimates the level of variation within proportional representation systems. For example, an electoral system that elects ten deputies through a single regionwide dis-trict is substantively different from one that elects ten deputies through five two-member districts. Although both may fall into the category of propor-tional representation systems, the difference in proportionality between the two is greater than the difference in proportionality between a system that elects ten deputies through five two-member districts and one that uses ten single-member districts. Therefore, rather than focusing on types of elec-toral systems, this book conceptualizes electoral system choice as occur-ring along a continuum of options and compares the features of different electoral systems. At the same time, while the work recognizes that electoral system designers confront a plethora of decisions, it places special emphasis on average district magnitude because of its current pride of place in the electoral system literature.

WHY RUSSIA'S REGIONS?

In the context of electoral systems research, a comparative study of electoral system design in the 89 administrative units (*sub"ekty* in Russian, but most commonly translated as "regions" in English) of the Russian Federation represents an intriguing and unusual opportunity. Although previous works examining electoral system choice have produced important insights as to how such institutional decisions are made (Birch et al. 2002; Benoit 2002, 2004; Benoit and Schiemann 2001; Boix 1999; Geddes 1995, 1996; Lijphart 1992; Kaminski 1999; Shugart 1997), these works focus on the national level, which in turn provides the opportunity for intervening variables and rival explanations. These intervening variables include disparate institutional legacies and different international environments. Such variation can arise even within a specific geographic region that has many shared legacies.

In Central and Eastern Europe, in particular, the type of communist regime in power determined key elements of the democratic transition, which in turn shaped institutional design (Kitschelt 1995; Kitschelt et al. 1999). Patrimonial communist regimes (like Belarus, Russia, and Ukraine) exhibited lower opportunities for intra-elite competition, popular interest articulation, and rational bureaucratic institutionalization. As a result, opposition groups in these states were weak, and elites from the old regime were able to preemptively change institutions in their own favor. Not surprisingly, these elites preferred rules that personalized power—like single-member-district electoral systems—allowing them to capitalize on preexisting patron-client networks. In other communist regimes, however, political competition and interest articulation were also low, but rational bureaucratic institutionalization was high. Due to their highly structured and inflexible nature, these bureaucratic-authoritarian systems (e.g., the former Czechoslovakia and the former German Democratic Republic) imploded, giving the democratic opposition the power to choose institutions that depersonalized power. Finally, some communist regimes (e.g., Hungary and Poland) combined rational bureaucratic institutionalization with intermediate levels of competition and interest articulation, which they permitted in exchange for basic compliance. These communist states were likely to experience negotiated transitions that in turn produced institutions with mixed personalized and depersonalized characteristics. From this perspective then, one advantage of examining electoral system design at the regional level within the Russian Federation is that such a focus holds constant important intervening variables, like previous regime type.

The study of electoral system choice in Russia's regions also provides an opportunity for new theoretical insights. Most studies of institutional choice emphasize political bargaining among political parties (see, for example, Benoit and Hayden 2004; Colomer 2005; Mozaffar and Vengroff 2002). However, an investigation of electoral system choice at the subnational level in Russia differs from these works by examining institutional decisions in an environment where the notion of political parties as organizations endogenously structuring politics (as described by Aldrich 1995) has been hotly debated. For example, Hough (1998, 688) portrays the initial incarnation of post-Soviet parties as "highly personalistic and ephemeral." Meanwhile, Rose (2000) depicts a tendency for Russian parties to "float" above society, often supplying candidates and policy rather than responding to voter demands. On the other hand, several scholars have dedicated significant energy to demonstrating the importance of parties to Russian politics (Fish 2003; Miller et al. 2000; Moser 2001). Given the issue of endogeneity between electoral system choice and party dynamics, Russia's regions provide an excellent opportunity to test whether electoral system choice reflects party development in cases where the party system itself is relatively undeveloped—that is, where party formation has occurred largely from scratch. Specifically, electoral system design in Russia's regions permits one to examine how electoral systems are designed in places where political competition is, at best, weakly structured along party lines.

An examination of electoral system choice at the regional level is also an important issue in its own right. Since lower levels of government operate in closer proximity to the people, the design of these institutions substantively shapes the direction of politics in democratizing countries. If new subnational institutions operate effectively and produce consensus and cooperation, they will increase the legitimacy of the larger system as the masses learn to trust democratic institutions from the ground up. However, ineffective subnational institutions plagued by political conflict and graft can quickly squander public faith in the new system of government, regardless of success at the national level. As Jeffrey Hahn (1997a, 130) notes, "it is hard to imagine a successful transition to democracy taking place only at the national level. Indeed, it seems more reasonable to argue that the democratization of national political institutions without corresponding changes taking place locally would be a prescription for disaster." Thus, the choice of institutions and their operation serve as critical litmus tests measuring the breadth and depth of political change in new democracies. They indicate the degree to which political elites have embraced ideas of cooperation and consensus rather than antagonism and exclusion.

Russia's regions, in particular, have emerged as major players, sometimes undermining national policy and at other times appearing to guide it. Following the August 1998 ruble devaluation, one regional leader after another announced radical measures for addressing the crisis and protecting their regions from its fallout. For example, many regions restricted export of their agricultural products, violating federal laws guaranteeing the free movement of goods and services (Lapidus 1999). This kind of defiance has been far from unusual. Throughout the mid-1990s, various Russian regions defied the center through such acts as refusing to send conscripts into federal service and asserting the right to establish their own currency (Treisman 1997).

While increased liberty since the end of communism has permitted Russia's regions to defy the federal government, it has also granted them the opportunity to serve as proving grounds for new methods of governmental administration (Tucker 1995). Lessons from the regions have not necessarily been good for Russian democracy, however. In 1996, the governor of Sverdlovsk oblast, Eduard Rossel', sought to undermine the power of local governments in the region by creating six new "administrative districts" headed by gubernatorial appointees (Slider 2004, 159). In hindsight, this move appears to foreshadow President Putin's reorganization of the federal structure to gain greater control over the regions through the introduction of seven federal administrative districts headed by presidential representatives. Likewise, Yeltsin's decision to resign from the presidency in order to hold early elections and to increase the electoral prospects of his chosen successor resembles an electoral ploy known as the "Belgorod alternative" used in that region's May 1999 gubernatorial election (Moses 2002, 907).

Generally speaking, regional politics has not necessarily aided the cause of Russian democracy. In fact, observers frequently comment that effective governance in Russia has been subverted through political machinations in its regions. Despite a few key exceptions—like Novgorod oblast (see Petro 2004)—the regions are depicted as fiefdoms suffering from electoral "clanism" in which political segmentation has impeded the development of western-style federalism: "An essentially neo-feudal, corporatist-oligarchical system has evolved in the country, in which republican and, to a lesser extent, regional princes and barons determine the rights, privileges, and rules of the game for their underlings" (Smirnov 2001, 526). The influence of the regions on Russian democracy has led Sakwa (2002, 5) to note that "regionalism was the great under-rated force of early postcommunist Russian politics," because most scholarly attention focused on civil society and political parties.

As the actions of Russian president Vladimir Putin indicate, Russian politics in the twenty-first century will depend on the direction of politics in the country's regions. A top priority of the Putin administration has been to establish greater control over Russia's federal structure. The creation of the seven federal districts to oversee activities in the regions has been just one element of Putin's plan to reestablish a vertical hierarchy of executive power. In addition, Putin charged his presidential representatives with ensuring that regional laws conform to Russia's federal constitution, and his administration has actively promoted or denounced different candidates in key gubernatorial elections. However, while Putin was able to bring national institutions quickly to heel in his first administration (see Shevtsova 2003), he has struggled with gaining control over the regions. The difficulties have ranged from an inability to regularly supply heat for Russia's Far East (Slider 2004) to a failure to effectively influence gubernatorial election outcomes (Moraski and Reisinger 2006).

The problems associated with governing Russia's regions are often explained as resulting from a combination of Soviet-era cultural legacies and a weakened federal center during the Yeltsin era that was willing to trade political autonomy for national unity (see Kahn 2002; Kirkow 1998; Söderland 2003; Treisman 1999). Yeltsin's willingness to embark upon bilateral treaties with more powerful regions actually encouraged weaker regions to press for greater autonomy. As provisions for autonomy spread, cultural traditions emphasizing local patronage were bolstered. Although political culture and federal policies help explain the state of politics in Russia's regions, they do not tell the whole story. The choice of subnational institutions, specifically the design of regional parliamentary electoral systems, also may explain the rise of regional fiefdoms. The decision by Russia's federal government to add party-list proportional representation to the regional parliamentary electoral systems suggests that some Russian elites may share this perspective.

In July 2002, Russia's national legislature reversed the large degree of electoral system experimentation in the regions when it mandated uniform electoral systems for all of the regional parliaments within the federation. The new law directed the 89 subjects of the Russian Federation to elect their regional members of parliament in the same manner as deputies to the lower house of the Russian parliament (the Duma) were elected. Thus, regional parliaments were required to employ mixed electoral systems in which half of the regional deputies were elected through single-member districts and half through party-list proportional representation.[1] Despite initial protests from the regions, the federal government's plan to mandate uniform electoral systems appears to be on its way to full implementation. These actions illustrate the federal government's recognition that regional parliamentary electoral systems have had important political implications on the direction of Russian politics. As Golosov (2004, 262) notes, "The first years of Putin's centralizing efforts demonstrated that intra-elite conflict could not be induced in the regions externally. Electoral system reform emerged as the only feasible way to stimulate party formation by regulating the demand side of the political marketplace."

Despite this clear indication that the initial choice of regional parliamentary electoral systems has influenced the direction of post-Soviet politics in Russia, no one has sought to systematically analyze the politics behind these initial decisions. Perhaps this oversight stems from the fact that the federal government, specifically the Yeltsin administration itself, is considered to have designed the parliamentary electoral systems in the majority of the regions. During the 1993 constitutional crisis, President Yeltsin issued a decree recommending that regions adopt single-member-district electoral systems. In practice, however, the regions enjoyed substantial liberty over the choice of their electoral systems. Thus, the question that emerges is: Why did some regions defy the presidential decree, while many obeyed it?

Before outlining a theoretical framework for understanding parliamentary electoral system design at the subnational level in the Russian Federation (chapter 2), the remainder of this chapter outlines the institutional and historical setting in which these decisions were made. This discussion will clarify key contextual differences relating to the distribution of power among different actors in Russia's 89 regions and the influence of these actors on institutional choice.

SETTING THE STAGE FOR INSTITUTIONAL REFORM

The 1993 constitutional crisis between Russia's president and its national parliament set the stage for the reform of the executive and legislative branches of government in Russia's regions. The origins of the 1993 constitutional crisis can be traced back to Boris Yeltsin's first year as president.

As the elected president of Russia, Boris Yeltsin began consolidating his position even before the collapse of the Soviet Union in December 1991. In November 1991, he convinced the Russian parliament (the Russian Congress of People's Deputies) to grant him emergency powers for one year. These powers included the ability to decree legislation, form a cabinet, and make governmental appointments. Although the emergency powers were designed to increase presidential control over economic reform and federal policy, the Russian parliament retained the prerogative to strip the president of these powers as well as the constitutional authority to impeach the president with a two-thirds vote (Willerton 1994, 45).

Following the acquisition of emergency powers, Yeltsin assumed the position of prime minister and appointed to key governmental posts several academics who promoted radical economic reform (like Egor Gaidar and Gennadii Burbulis). Not only did these reformers think that they could lift the Russian economy out of its dire straits; they also hoped to capitalize on the defeat of conservative forces in the August 1991 coup attempt. These radical reformers believed that the best way to minimize the inevitable economic hardship associated with the transition to a market economy was to move as quickly as possible. Shortly after the resignation of Gorbachev on 25 December 1991, Yeltsin plunged ahead with radical economic change under the heading of "shock therapy." On 2 January 1992, he introduced the first step of this economic program: the end of price controls on most goods. As expected, enormous increases in prices and inflation as well as significant drops in the living standard accompanied price liberalization.

Although initial economic reforms were enacted without significant public protest, they were bitterly criticized in the Russian parliament by the Supreme Soviet's chairman, Ruslan Khasbulatov and by Russian vice president Aleksandr Rutskoi (both had been excluded from the president's inner circle despite supporting Yeltsin during the August 1991 coup attempt). Coalitions of bureaucrats pressed for restrictions on the president's power. During May and June 1992, parliamentary criticism and growing public discontent eventually forced Yeltsin to appoint more moderate politicians to leading posts in the Russian government. The most important appointment was Viktor Chernomyrdin, a former head of the Soviet Union's natural gas industry. At the same time, however, Yeltsin reaffirmed the course of reform by appointing Egor Gaidar acting prime minister (Sakwa 1996, 75).

As the president's economic program began privatizing more than 200,000 state-run enterprises, Khasbulatov and Rutskoi moved closer and closer to Yeltsin's hard-line opponents in parliament. By the seventh session of the Russian Congress in December 1992, the Congress not only appeared poised to reject the confirmation of acting prime minister, Gaidar, but opened debate on legislation designed to more clearly delineate the relationship between the cabinet and the parliament. To win support for Gaidar's confirmation, Yeltsin offered the Supreme Soviet the right to confirm several important cabinet ministers (security, foreign affairs, internal affairs, and defense). Despite this concession, however, the Congress voted to reject Gaidar's nomination. A furious Yeltsin responded by demanding a national referendum that would dissolve the Congress and adopt a new constitution. With the executive and legislative branches at odds, the chairman of Russia's Constitutional Court negotiated an arrangement in which both sides accepted Viktor Chernomyrdin as a compromise candidate for prime minister and agreed to an April 1993 referendum that would decide the principles of a new constitution (Remington 1994, 75–76).

Despite the replacement of Gaidar and the dilution of shock therapy, the constitutional crisis continued to intensify, "reaching a fever pitch at the intermittent convocations of congress" (Colton 1998, 5). In March 1993, continued dissatisfaction with Yeltsin's reform program led the Supreme Soviet of the Congress of People's Deputies to annul the decision to hold the April referendum. The Congress also gave itself the power to suspend presidential decrees (subject to approval from the Constitutional Court) and gave the cabinet the power to initiate legislation. It also restated the constitutional principle that the president did not possess the power to disband constitutionally elected bodies such as the Congress (or its smaller functioning body, the Supreme Soviet) (Roeder 1993, 91–92). Yeltsin retaliated by announcing on television that he would issue a decree establishing a system of "special presidential rule." He also announced that he would use this opportunity to introduce a new constitution and new electoral laws. However, due to divisions within the national security ministries and the firm opposition of parliament, presidential rule failed to materialize. Nevertheless, the Russian Congress responded with a vote to impeach Yeltsin—a proposal that fell 72 votes short of the two-thirds requirement (Remington 1994, 64).

Following the impeachment vote, the two sides finally agreed to hold a referendum in April to resolve the constitutional impasse. However, the April 1993 referendum set constitutional principles aside and asked voters to evaluate the president, his administration's policies, and the need for new presidential and parliamentary elections. Although the results revealed more support for Yeltsin than for the Russian parliament (for results by region see Clem and Craumer 1993), Yeltsin was unable to take advantage of this popular support to end the impasse. Instead, the rift between the two branches deepened. Yeltsin attempted to bypass the parliament with the creation of a broadly representative Constitutional Assembly in the summer of 1993; meanwhile, the parliamentary leadership extended its control over regional and local soviets in preparation for another attempt to remove President Yeltsin from office.

In September 1993, the federal constitutional conflict reached its climax. Yeltsin declared that the parliament was making reform impossible, and, on 21 September, he issued a series of decrees lacking constitutional foundation but offering a solution to the political gridlock. He disbanded the parliament, stripped all deputies of their legal mandates, and set new federal parliamentary elections for December 1993.[2] The president's breach of his constitutional power produced a standoff in which demonstrators opposing Yeltsin's decrees confronted riot troops that had surrounded the parliamentary building. The standoff ended on the weekend of 3–4 October in an armed confrontation between the police backing the president and the paramilitary units opposing him. While elements of the conflict between the federal executive and the legislative branches were mirrored in the regions, various demands for sovereignty accompanying the collapse of the Soviet Union complicated the distribution of governmental power in the regions.

VARIATIONS IN SOVEREIGNTY AND REFORM

The Soviet Union itself employed a complex, federal façade that masked a highly centralized state. Under Gorbachev, however, this façade came to life as demands for sovereignty and independence emanated from various ethnonational identities. Eventually, the Soviet Union disintegrated along ethnic lines as its 15 union republics—each named after and representing one of the major nationalities comprising the Soviet Union—gained independence (for an ethnonational analysis of the Soviet Union's collapse, see Beissinger 2002).

The complex system of Soviet "federalism" did not end with the union republics, however. The core of the Soviet Union and its acknowledged successor, the Russian Soviet Federated Socialist Republic (RSFSR), was itself a multinational state with numerous ethnonationally defined administrative units within its borders. The most prominent of these units were the "autonomous soviet socialist republics."[3] Although union republics received independence in 1991, these administrative units of lower status did not, and despite "solid claims based on population size (the Tatars) or cultural uniqueness (the Chechens), these and other potentially deserving ethnonationalist groups were left frustrated" (Kempton and Clark 2002, 2). As a result, the Russian Federation consists of 89 regions with various appellations stemming from the Soviet era. Twenty-one are republics and 10 are autonomous okrugs (districts). While regions in both of these categories are named after particular ethnic groups, the republics comprise about one-sixth of the population and around 28% of the territory in the Russian Federation. The 10 okrugs, on the other hand, are sparsely populated and more predominantly Russian. The remaining regions are even more clearly ethnically Russian. They include 49 oblasts (provinces), 6 krais (territories), 2 cities of federal status (Moscow and St. Petersburg), and one autonomous oblast.[4]

Important differences between Russia's republics and its others regions became evident as the Soviet Union crumbled. With few exceptions, only Russia's republics declared sovereignty from the Soviet Union in 1990. And, in 1991, several of Russia's autonomous republics—Adygeia, Kabardino-Balkaria, Marii El, Mordovia, Tatarstan, Chechnya, and Sakha—elected "presidents" to head executive branches that operated independent of their republican parliaments (see Hahn 1997b; McFaul and Petrov 1998).

After the Soviet Union collapsed, President Yeltsin sought to mitigate the rising tide of regionalism through the Federal Treaty of March 1992. This treaty was intended to outline the rights of Russia's regions and the center, with a primary concern being economic issues, like subsidies and taxes. However, the ethnic republics were particularly aggressive in demanding that they retain special status, and they rejected the idea of equality with other regions. As a result, three versions of the treaty were actually signed— one with the leaders of the republics, one with the autonomous okrugs and autonomous oblast, and one with the oblasts, krais, and cities of federal status. During this process, the republics acquired greater power and more responsibilities than other regions. According to the treaty, "the national republics were recognized as state entities, which joined the Russian Federation with all of the ensuing consequences" (Shlapentokh et al. 1997, 100). That is, unlike other regions, the republics would enjoy complete authority, both legislative and executive, in their borders, and the republics were the only regions permitted to ratify their own constitutions. The remaining 68 regions were to adopt charters *(ustavy)*. As Kahn notes (2002, 6), such distinctions are not merely terminological: "Republics present these and other differences as hallmarks of their state sovereignty. Republics enshrine in their constitutions rights to republican citizenship, with attendant privileges and duties. There is no such thing as oblast citizenship." Likewise, these differences have had direct impacts on institutional design: While most regions in Russia have chief executives with independent mandates, two republics—Dagestan and Udmurtia—were governed by parliamentary-style executives throughout the 1990s.[5]

In contrast to the sovereignty enjoyed by the republics, the Russian federal government, and the Russian president in particular, was much more assertive in other regions. In 1991, President Yeltsin urged the Russian Congress of People's Deputies to propose the popular election of independent chief executives at the regional and local levels. The new executives were mayors at the city level and governors, as opposed to presidents, in the republics. Popularly elected governors were intended to replace the executive committees existing under the Soviet system that were elected by and accountable to the regional legislatures (or soviets). Initially, reformers hoped that the direct election of these executives would install democratically oriented politicians, who could not be removed by the more conservative regional soviets. However, the absence of support for the democratic movement in the regions during the August 1991 coup attempt led Yeltsin to question the ability of reform-oriented governors to win popular elections. As a result, in October 1991, Yeltsin asked the Russian Congress of People's Deputies to declare a one-year moratorium on the popular election of subnational executives (Hahn 1997a, 139). When the Russian parliament agreed, Yeltsin acquired the power to appoint governors in regions other than the republics.

One consequence of Yeltsin's attempts to solidify control in the country by appointing governors was increased opposition from the deputies in these regional soviets. In 1992 and 1993, the political conflict between Russia's national executive and the legislative branches of government extended into the regions. Elites in the regional legislatures with strong ties to the old regime clashed with Yeltsin's appointed governors, who were drawn largely from the ranks of the democratic reform movement. In many of these regions, legislators viewed Yeltsin's gubernatorial appointments as an infringement on their power. As a result, appointed governors often faced an uncooperative legislative branch.

Surprisingly, despite the hostility between Yeltsin and the Russian parliament throughout 1992, the moratorium on gubernatorial elections was not lifted as planned. Instead, Yeltsin consistently postponed gubernatorial elections as the appointments became tools by which the president could assert his influence in the regions. Russia's Chief State Inspector, Valerii Makharadze, cited devotion to the cause of the president as the most important qualification of the gubernatorial appointments, followed by professional competence and the ability to command support from a sizable portion of the local population (Roeder 1993, 90–91).[6] Not only did Yeltsin's decisions to postpone gubernatorial elections stoke interbranch rivalries in the regions, it also increased the legitimacy of the conservative legislative deputies since the deputies were popularly elected in March 1990 (Hahn 1994, 210–13).

At the seventh session of the Congress of People's Deputies in December 1992, the national parliament sought to counter presidential influence in the regions and declared that gubernatorial elections would be held if regional soviets insisted on them (Hahn 1997a, 140). In April 1993, an initial round of gubernatorial elections occurred in eight oblasts and krais.[7] In none of them did regional voters support the head of administration appointed by Yeltsin (Gel'man 2000b, 94). These defeats came at a critical juncture in Russia's political transition because they coincided with the escalating conflict between President Yeltsin and the Russian parliament. As a result, Yeltsin only gradually permitted gubernatorial elections following the 1993 constitutional crisis and then only where he expected his preferred candidate to win. It was not until the second half of 1995 that Yeltsin allowed the popular election of governors in the majority of Russia's regions.

The difference between the liberty granted to the ethnic republics and Yeltsin's intervention in other regions was perhaps most evident during the 1993 federal constitutional crisis. At the time of the 1993 crisis, Yeltsin had appointed 58 of the 68 regional executives (McFaul and Petrov 1998, v1, 602–5). In addition to the eight governors elected in April 1993, the Presidium of Russia's Supreme Soviet established directly elected mayors in Moscow and Leningrad in 1991 (Gel'man 2000b, 91). When the conflict culminated in the forceful dissolution of the Supreme Soviet in October 1993, Yeltsin not only reaffirmed his right to appoint governors (Debardeleben 1997, 168), but also replaced disloyal appointees. For example, Yeltsin removed the governor of Belgorod oblast—Vladimir Berestovoi—and the governor of Novosibirsk oblast—Vitalii Mukha—for supporting the federal parliament during the crisis. Yeltsin also demonstrated a willingness to replace popularly elected governors with loyal appointees: On 5 October 1993, Yeltsin removed the governor of Amur oblast—Aleksandr Surat, who had been elected in April 1993—for supporting the Russian parliament during the crisis. Likewise, the governor of Briansk oblast, Iurii Lodkin (also elected in April 1993), opposed Yeltsin's actions during the crisis and was removed from his post ("Soobshaet press-sluzhba Prezidenta RF," 6 October 1993). By contrast, Yeltsin never attempted to remove republican presidents, regardless of their level of opposition. In fact, many republics had yet to create an executive branch independent of the republican legislatures by the time of the 1993 October crisis.[8]

Yeltsin's influence during the 1993 constitutional crisis in the nonrepublic regions of Russia extended beyond the executive branch. After shelling the White House, Yeltsin took steps to eliminate the main sources of conservative opposition in these regions. First, Yeltsin disbanded the soviets in the city of Moscow and in Moscow oblast for allegedly supporting the president's opponents (Slider 1996, 249).[9] He then dissolved local soviets and recommended the dissolution of regional soviets. Article 5 of presidential decree #1617 specifically stated that in any instance where a soviet dissolved itself or failed to meet the necessary quorum to function, the authority of the representative organs was to be temporarily allocated to the executive branch of government ("Ukaza Prezidenta . . ." 13 October 1993).

Based on expert accounts of the political events at the time, more than half of the soviets (40 out of 68) were dissolved by the governor or dissolved themselves following the 1993 crisis (McFaul and Petrov 1998, v2).[10] Half of the legislatures that were dissolved had openly condemned Yeltsin's actions during the crisis while most of the other legislatures took more neutral positions.[11] Interestingly, not every legislature that explicitly condemned Yeltsin's actions was dissolved. Twelve soviets in these regions openly opposed Yeltsin, but remained active after the crisis. Two of the most notable of these soviets were Amur and Briansk oblasts, where Yeltsin removed elected governors.

In contrast to the parliaments in other regions, the parliaments in all but one republic remained active immediately after the 1993 crisis. In the republic of Sakha (also known as Yakutia) the constitutional crisis led to the dissolution of the regional legislature prior to the design of the new electoral system. The president of Sakha, Mikhail Nikolaev, supported Yeltsin during the October conflict while members of the soviet opposed Yeltsin's actions. Following Yeltsin's victory, Nikolaev convinced the deputies of the Supreme Soviet to dissolve the assembly (McFaul and Petrov 1998 v2, 326). Meanwhile, in the republic of Marii El, the soviet dissolved itself following the 1993 crisis, but only after adopting the law governing elections to its new representative branch.[12]

As this discussion suggests, Russia's federal context prior to and after the collapse of the Soviet Union placed different regions on different paths with regard to institutional design. For example, Yeltsin's first major decree, "On the Reform of Representative Bodies of Power and Bodies of Local Self-Government in the Russian Federation," ordered the creation of new regional legislatures with the number of deputies ranging between 15 and 50 ("Ukaz Prezidenta . . ." 13 October 1993). In a subsequent decree, on 22 October, Yeltsin stated that these new legislatures should hold elections between December 1993 and March 1994 (Semenova 1993). Then, on 27 October, Yeltsin urged the cities of federal status, plus the krais, oblasts, and okrugs to adopt first-past-the-post, single-member-district systems ("Ukaz Prezidenta . . ." 3 November 1993). While these decrees set clear guidelines for the new regional legislative elections, they were not evenly binding across all regions within Russia. Specifically, thanks to the influence of the vice premier Sergei Shakhrai, the decrees essentially served as recommendations for the republics to consider (Slider 1996, 250). This decision confirmed the Yeltsin administration's willingness to permit republics greater leverage in the arena of self-governance due to the belief that special conditions there required greater flexibility. As a result, 8 out of 20 republics (Chechnya is not included due to the civil war in the republic at the time) created assemblies with membership above 50.[13] The republics of Bashkortostan, Dagestan, Tatarstan, and Udmurtia all created legislative assemblies with one hundred or more deputies. By contrast, none of the other 68 regions created an assembly exceeding the number of deputies outlined in Yeltsin's decree.

Deviation from Yeltsin's recommendations was not limited to the republics, however. In practice, political and bureaucratic realities often determined parliamentary election dates, with some elections being held as late as December 1995. Although 14 out of 20 republics held their new legislative elections after March 1994, so too did 8 of the 68 remaining regions (McFaul and Petrov 1998 v1; 602–5). Various regions also diverged from the president's prescribed formula of single-member-district plurality elections: The city of St. Petersburg, for example, added a runoff system, as did the republics of Buriatia, Chuvashia, North Ossetia, Sakha, and Tatarstan (Slider 1996, 253–54). Many other regions employed multimember districts (see chapter 3). In sum, then the design of parliamentary electoral systems in Russia's regions occurred across a relatively large number of cases and produced substantively different systems.

The study of how electoral systems influence party systems has been criticized for treating these institutions as exogenous, when in fact the characteristics of party systems themselves can determine electoral system choice. While scholars of electoral system choice have begun to address this issue by explicitly incorporating party preferences into the design process, levels of party development vary dramatically over time and space. Transitions from authoritarian rule that will occur in the near future are likely to take place in states where the soil for democracy—including the development of political parties—will be less than fertile (as the U.S.-imposed transitions in Afghanistan and Iraq poignantly demonstrate). Accordingly, the institutional choices made in Russia's regions, at a time when political parties were quite weak and the potential for external intervention (in this case, from the federal government) was quite high, could provide a more useful framework for understanding institutional decisions in future transitioning states.

The following chapter considers how institutional decisions, in general, and electoral system choice, in particular, vary by context. It then draws directly on the historical setting in Russia's regions to develop a series of hypotheses for explaining the design of the parliamentary electoral systems there. Chapter 3 uses a statistical examination of electoral system design in 86 of Russia's 89 regions to assess the validity of these hypotheses.[14] Chapter 4 utilizes comparative analysis to dig deeper into the politics of institutional decisions, and chapter 5 discusses the implications of electoral system decisions with an emphasis on party development in Russia and the representation of different types of politicians in the regional parliaments. Chapter 6 considers the importance of these findings for new democracies, in general, and Russian federalism, in particular.

TWO— BEYOND SELF-INTEREST

Institutions are not
necessarily or even
usually created to be
socially efficient; rather
they, or at least the formal rules, are created to
serve the interests of
those with the bargain-
ing power to devise
new rules.

—Douglass North

(1990, 16)

North's description of institutional
choice has implicitly or explicitly guided an
array of works seeking to understand institutional decisions in new as well as established
democracies (e.g., Boix 1999; Frye 1997; Gel'-
man 2004; Ostrow 2000). Although the contention that institutional decisions reflect the
interests of those making them provides a
broad generalization, some readers may find
the statement obvious, if not trivial. The contention is not trivial, however, if rather than
being viewed as an explanation, it is seen as
an assumption to be used to develop testable
hypotheses. In other words, the statement
merely provides a valuable point of departure. It says nothing about what the designers' interests are; instead, one must develop
specific hypotheses about the interests of institutional designers based on the circumstances in which the institutions have been
designed as well as the types of institutions
being created. Likewise, the statement that
designers choose institutions that serve their
interests only risks being tautological if one
lacks specific hypotheses about who designed
the institutions and why. North is not con-
tending that institutions necessarily work to
the advantage of their designers, only that
they are created to do so. Institutional decisions can produce unexpected consequences,
especially when institutional designers operate in an atmosphere of uncertainty. Or, in
the terminology of game theorists, institutions are more likely to produce surprising
outcomes when the institutions are designed

in a one-shot game, when the players making the decision lack sufficient information on one another (and other potential players), or when many players are involved in the decision-making process.

To understand how interests—specifically, self-interest—drive institutional design, this book blends rational choice institutionalism with historical institutionalism. Rational choice institutionalism provides the micro-causal link between strategic bargaining and institutional outcomes but does not offer the tools to ascertain who the actors are or how they get to the bargaining table. Historical institutionalism, meanwhile, reveals which actors are at the table, their preferences, and their underlying power asymmetries but lacks the micro-foundations for explaining the bargaining process (Luong 2002, 38–39). Blending the two approaches, therefore, presents a more accurate depiction of how institutional decisions are made than using either approach in isolation.[1]

By focusing on Russia's regions, this book also applies North's axiom of institutional choice to a new context consisting of a relatively large number of cases in order to understand how such institutional decisions manifest themselves under various power arrangements. The work is driven by the belief that the best way to understand political phenomena, like the politics of institutional choice, is to examine them in multiple contexts. It assumes that only with greater illustration of different dynamics by which this seemingly simple axiom operates can an adequate explanatory framework be developed.

ELECTORAL SYSTEM CHOICE IN DIFFERENT CONTEXTS

The collapse of communism in Eastern Europe emerged as one of the most important political events of the twentieth century as it signaled the climax of the "third wave" of democratization (Huntington 1991). For scholars and policy makers, the political and economic transitions provided a new forum for witnessing institutional transformations as some countries sought to build democracy and capitalism from scratch. To a certain extent, competitive multiparty elections in postcommunist Europe marked the introduction (or in some cases, reintroduction) of universal suffrage. Although citizens did vote during communist times, the elections generally listed only a single candidate and the 99% turnout rates symbolized the ritualization of voting as well as its impotence. Since the "right to vote" implies, by definition, the choice of whether to vote or not, only with the revolutions of 1989–1990 and the subsequent collapse of the Soviet Union did suffrage become truly universal in the region.

In a way, electoral system choice in postcommunist Europe resembled institutional decisions in Western Europe at the beginning of the twentieth century. In the states of Western Europe, a wave of newly mobilized voters that threatened the positions of established parties accompanied the introduction of universal suffrage. The convergence of pressures from established parties seeking to protect their weakened political positions after the extension of suffrage and the rise of new parties seeking to assert their growing popular support produced a proliferation of proportional representation electoral systems (Lipset and Rokkan 1967, 32). Similarly, institutional choice in postcommunist Europe reflected the decision calculus of political elites, who assessed their electoral expectations and promoted institutions that granted them a competitive advantage for attaining or maintaining power.

Despite similarities in the motives of institutional designers across geographic regions and time periods, institutional decisions reflect their specific historical and institutional contexts. While changes to the electoral systems in advanced democracies can be traced to the strategic decisions of ruling parties to maximize their representation in parliament, certain aspects of these decisions do not necessarily apply to developing countries. For example, unlike politicians in developed democracies, politicians in new democracies are less able to predict the future structure of electoral competition. Also, political parties in new democracies are less likely to be full-scale national parties (Boix 1999, 622). Such differences were certainly evident in Eastern Europe, where opposition parties lacked both the organization and the electoral experience to make realistic assessments about their electoral prospects. Similarly, a deep popular distrust of all organizations called "parties," as well as a low opinion of parliaments and politicians, created a political environment that emphasized personalities over parties (Lijphart 1992, 213–15). Meanwhile, in contrast to electoral system decisions in Western Europe, universal suffrage in Eastern Europe was completed under communism and, therefore, preceded the design of democratic institutions. Likewise, while expansions of suffrage had considerable consequences for politics in Western Europe, they were in no way akin to the devastating upheavals experienced in Eastern Europe in 1989 and after (Birch et al. 2002, 7–9). Thus, the disappearance of Soviet invasion as an external threat and the lack of their own internal legitimacy weakened the electoral position of communist parties to an extent that was greater than all political parties—especially the ruling communist parties—anticipated.

Comparisons between the institutional decisions in Eastern Europe and those in Latin America also highlight the significance of contextual differences. In Eastern Europe and Latin America, the dominant parties of the old regime preferred majoritarian electoral systems while smaller parties and parties with uncertain electoral prospects preferred more proportional systems. However, democratization in Latin America has differed significantly from democratization in Central and Eastern Europe. Specifically, while postcommunist Europe resembled Latin America in that it possessed an urban-rural divide, the countries of Eastern Europe possessed neither the opportunity to rejuvenate political parties from the past nor a history of class-based politics. Both of these made party development easier in Latin America than in postcommunist Europe. According to Geddes

(1996, 30), these different postauthoritarian contexts—rather than differences in the norms or motivations of the political elites—help explain differences between the institutional decisions in Eastern Europe and those in Latin America.[2]

The relationship between context and institutional choice entails more than just institutional legacies. It also involves the level of information available to the institutional designers, which can reflect the timing of the decision itself. While the electoral prospects of institutional framers at the national level in Eastern Europe shaped their preferences, these preferences changed over time. Where institutional decisions were made prior to the first round of open elections, both the communists and their challengers overestimated public support for communist parties. As a result, members of communist parties preferred plurality electoral systems, because plurality systems would allow these members of the old regime to run as individuals unhampered by the party label. At the same time, communist candidates expected to capitalize on their parties' existing organization and patronage at the local level. Meanwhile, noncommunist parties in Eastern Europe were uncertain about their electoral prospects, and this uncertainty led them to promote proportional representation systems in early transitions as a means to gain at least some representation in the new parliaments. Therefore, many opposition parties underestimated their own strength and often settled for less in the institutional negotiations than they might have had the assessments on both sides been more accurate (Geddes 1995).

The first round of elections in Central and Eastern Europe substantially changed the level of uncertainty in the transitional political environment. While the communists in Albania, Bulgaria, and Ukraine benefited from majority voting in their first competitive elections, the communists in Croatia, Hungary, Macedonia, Poland, and Slovenia received fewer seats under majoritarian systems than they would have had they adopted party-list proportional representation systems. In Czechoslovakia, the communists did not object to opposition demands for proportional representation and managed to win the second-largest share of seats in parliament (Jasiewicz 1998, 177–78).

The timing of the institutional decisions became important, because as elections inside each country and in other ex-communist countries occurred, all parties made more accurate assessments of the communists' strength. The poor showing of communists in the early elections of Eastern Europe meant that communists elsewhere suddenly became uncertain about their electoral prospects. At the same time, uncertainty remained for opposition groups, since they were unable to predict which of them would survive the upcoming elections and prosper. As a consequence, institutions designed or redesigned following the first round of elections reflected this uncertainty, and proportional representation, which protects small parties from annihilation, became the preferred choice (Geddes 1995, 264–65).

In sum then, while parliamentary electoral system decisions can result from negotiations among key political actors, the institutional preferences of these key political actors can vary by context. Institutional preferences reflect the different levels of political experience, the different degrees of political organization, and the different amounts of information that the institutional designers possess.

Electoral system choice also depends on who the key political actors are. For example, electoral system choice may result from a bargaining game between one set of actors (representing the old regime) seeking to maintain some degree of power and another set of actors (representing the new opposition) striving to acquire a solid foothold in the new parliament. However, neither of the two camps necessarily represents a unified party. Since the rank-and-file members of a political party delegate authority to their party leaders, party members (not party leaders) may ultimately shape institutional design. In this context, electoral system choice could depend on the level of party discipline that rank-and-file party members are willing to accept (Shugart 1997).

Likewise, while the design of parliamentary electoral systems can be cast in terms of expectations among actors likely to compete under the new rules, parliamentary electoral system decisions could just as easily depend on the preferences of other actors (see also Birch et al. 2002, 14–16). For example, the executive branch may play an instrumental role in the design of a parliamentary electoral system if it possesses the power to veto institutional decisions or enjoys the power to make the decision unilaterally through decree. Similarly, institutional choice at the subnational level may reflect federal politics. In some cases, national legislation may present specific guidelines that structure the design of regional institutions. In other cases, national politicians may seek to shape subnational institutional decisions out of a belief that certain institutions will allow them to expand their political influence. These possibilities suggest a wide range of theoretical contexts in which parliamentary electoral systems can be designed.

The remainder of this chapter considers the specific historical context in which Russia's regional parliamentary electoral systems were designed. It presents specific hypotheses based on who the institutional designers were, what interests likely drove their decisions, and how relationships among these actors determined electoral system design.

ELITE POLITICS AND WEAK PARTIES

The following discussion draws on insights from Russia's post-Soviet context to explain the design of Russia's first regional parliamentary electoral systems by considering: 1) the positions of the institutional designers, 2) their political orientations, 3) their beliefs as to how politicians with different orientations would perform under different electoral systems, and 4) the degree to which the institutional designers were accountable to the

Russian president. Since institutional decisions are essentially elite decisions—even when popular input is sought or decisions are subject to popular referenda—the arguments focus on elite politics. However, while previous work on electoral system choice emphasizes the role political parties play in structuring elite negotiations, the nature of politics in Russia's regions forces theorizing beyond interparty relations, since political parties were, at best, weak actors in the regions.

A distinguishing characteristic of Russia's transition from communism has been the weakness of its party system. Both the 1936 and 1977 Soviet constitutions asserted that all organized activity must conform to the substantive goals of the state.[3] The resulting consolidation of political power into the hands of a single entity—the Communist Party of the Soviet Union—undermined party system development and interest group formation throughout the 1990s. In other words, the opening of society and the introduction of multicandidate elections under Gorbachev failed to remedy the historical absence of civil society. Opposition groups during the Gorbachev era struggled to establish collective identities with clear programs for action. Instead, these groups spent much of their time and energy on inconsequential problems as their members became divided over semantics or interpretations of current events. Thus, political inexperience limited the formation of new political organizations, because it became necessary to invent and assemble the most basic elements of political identity entirely from scratch (Fish 1995).

Weak party development in Russia can also be traced to certain aspects of Russia's transition itself. The delay of free, multiparty elections placed specific limits on the development of a healthy party system. The March 1990 elections that selected the Russian Congress of People's Deputies as well as regional and city soviets were held well before alternative parties were legalized. As a result, the opposition in Russia consisted of broad, loosely organized citizen committees and voters' clubs, and their activities were limited primarily to promoting candidates who seemed progressive. So, while new organizations participated in campaigns, they lacked the right to actually nominate their own candidates. These 1990 elections shaped regional party development in the long term, for the deputies elected therein entered the soviets largely unbeholden to political parties or other societal organizations. At the same time, the attention of political entrepreneurs who were able to win election was quickly directed away from the task of party building toward higher-profile work within the legislatures: "The soviets therefore quite naturally depleted movement organizations of potential sources of talent and energy" (Fish 1995, 133).

This discussion is not to imply that political parties were irrelevant to Russian politics in the early 1990s. On the contrary, Hough (1998, 673) notes that the chaotic formation of political parties during the 1993 Duma election surprised even the most pessimistic of observers. Likewise, parties of various ideological orientations proved active in Russia's regions between

1991 and 1994. Small democratic parties included the Republican Party, the Social Democrats, the Christian Democrats, the Cadets, and the Free Democratic Party of Russia. After the Communist Party regained legal status in 1992, various leftist parties also emerged in the regions, including the Communist Party of the Russian Federation, the Russian Communist Workers' Party, and the All-Union Communist Bolshevik Party. While nationalist parties were more rare, the success of the Liberal Democratic Party of Russia in the 1993 Duma elections makes them notable as well (McAuley 1997, 326). Still, when parliamentary electoral systems were designed in Russia's regions during the early 1990s, Russia's party system was undeveloped by conventional standards.

LaPalombara and Weiner (1966, 6) outline four components of a political party that distinguish it from "a loosely knit group of notables with limited and intermittent relationships to local counterparts." These components include 1) a continuity in organization, such that the organization's life span does not depend on the life span of current leaders; 2) a manifest and presumably permanent local organization with regularized communication between local and national branches; 3) leaders at both the national and local levels who are consciously determined to capture and hold onto decision-making power; and 4) a concern within the organization to attract popular support. Only the Communist Party of the Russian Federation came close to fulfilling this classic definition of a political party, largely thanks to its reliance on preexisting local organizations (Hough 1998, 673). Accordingly, almost none of the national political organizations besides the Communist Party competed in the first regional parliamentary elections. Rather, political competition at the regional level was among local interests, including "the administration, particular business interests, ex-deputies, sometimes left-patriotic candidates, and plenty of independent candidates" (McAuley 1997, 298).

Even by the late 1990s, most national political parties failed to meet LaPalombara and Weiner's definition of a political party. In January 1998, of the 3,481 deputies elected to 83 of Russia's regional legislatures, only 635 (18.4%) were members of national political parties (Ross 2002, 39). Perhaps more importantly, Badovskii and Shutov (1997, 36) point out that party labels themselves were poor indicators of elite preferences throughout the early to mid-1990s: "The most distinctive feature of the new elites in Russia's regions is their relatively vague political and ideological orientation." Terms like "communist" and "democrat" tended to lose their meaning in the regions, since they rarely reflected personal political or ideological views but instead indicated an affiliation with a group supporting a specific person among the national or regional leadership. Thus, while scholars, like Brown (1998, 28), argue that local political parties have played various roles in Russia—including the structuring of electoral competition—they also admit that strict factional or party discipline is rarely manifested in the regional assemblies.

The lack of party development in Russia actually led Gel'man and Golosov (1998, 32) to consider one Russian region with relatively competitive parties to be a deviant case: "in contrast to nearly all other regions, Sverdlovsk oblast has developed a set of sustainable political organizations whose competition can be viewed as a pivotal factor of the political process." However, Gel'man and Golosov also find that the holding of free elections itself promoted party development in Sverdlovsk. In other words, the initial design of the parliamentary electoral systems tended to come before the advent of functioning party systems, to the extent that such systems have emerged at all.

Still, one may argue that if political parties are likely to influence any institutional decision, they should affect electoral system design, even where they are largely undeveloped. Accordingly, when possible, the impact of political parties on electoral system design is examined here, both in terms of the influence of general party development in the regions and the potential links among certain parties and the regional elite. At the same time, however, this work also relies on a broader categorization of political elites to estimate the political orientations of potential institutional designers, as well as their preferences, in order to overcome the limitations associated with generalizing across Russia's regions on the basis of party development. Specifically, it differentiates primarily between members of the old regime (or insiders) and political newcomers (or outsiders). Classifying Russian politicians as political insiders or outsiders is certainly a simplification of reality. Lukin (1999a, 100) wisely warns against stereotyping Russian political actors during this period into two groups: conservatives and reformers, or supporters of the old and promoters of the new. And, as the case studies in chapter 4 demonstrate, rival "insider" factions in Russia's regions clearly competed with one another during the period under investigation, just as political newcomers consisted of politicians of various ideological orientations. Still, dividing Russia's regional elite into members of the old regime and political newcomers provides a useful starting point for developing a theoretical model of electoral system choice in the regions. Even if this division poorly estimates the political orientations of different institutional designers, it permits one to develop straightforward, reasonable hypotheses about their beliefs regarding the electoral prospects of different politicians under different systems. In addition, this initial bifurcation captures the political relationship between different institutional designers in the regions and the Russian president.

MULTIPLE ACTORS, MULTIPLE MOTIVES

What factors guided the preferences of politicians responsible for designing Russia's regional parliamentary electoral systems? I argue that the electoral system preferences of politicians are driven first and foremost by a desire for power. This approach differs significantly from some rational choice

models employed in other contexts, which have depicted institutional decisions as the first stage in a two-stage game over policy. These scholars suggest that disagreements over the choice of institutions emerge whenever
there are disagreements about the policies that different institutions will
produce (e.g., Brady and Mo 1990; Garrett 1992; Tsebelis 1990).

Although an assumption that ties political interests to policy outcomes
is intuitive (especially for stable democratic polities), many of the assumptions associated with these models fall short when applied to transitions
from authoritarian rule. For example, Bawn (1993) not only assumes that
party preferences are defined over policy outcomes; she also assumes that
parties have enough information to predict future vote shares and the institutional preferences of other participants. The lack of party development in
Russia's regions, as well as the uncertainty about which policies would allow Russia to best navigate its transition from communism, undermines
the utility of such assumptions for understanding electoral system design
in Russia's regions. As a result, I not only assume that institutional designers select institutions that advance their self-interests; I also argue that
these self-interests can be defined in terms of the desire to acquire and
maintain political power rather than to achieve specific policy outcomes
(see also Luong 2002).

Defining the self-interest of institutional designers in terms of power relations is attractive for three reasons. First, describing politics as a struggle
to gain and maintain power fits quite well with existing empirical work on
the transitions from communism (Benoit 2003; Frye 1997; Jasiewicz 1993;
Lijphart 1992; Kaminski 1999, 2002; Moraski and Loewenberg 1999). These
works have shown that various institutional decisions in Eastern Europe
emanated from attempts among different actors to gain a comparative advantage over their political rivals. Second, conceptualizing institutional designers as power-seeking actors overlaps nicely with another theoretically
powerful assumption, that politicians are driven by the electoral motive.
Since electoral system design represents a political decision that overtly influences election results, it stands to reason that the electoral system preferences of individuals expecting to compete under the new rules of the game
will reflect personal considerations as to which institutions best advance
their electoral prospects. In other words, electoral incentives guide the decisions of future competitors for parliamentary seats because the fates of
these actors in future elections will likely determine their access to political
power. Of course, constituent interests and policy issues also concern
prospective legislators, but winning elections remains the goal that must be
achieved if other ends are to be entertained (Mayhew 1974, 16).

Third, an emphasis on power politics is attractive because it indicates
how electoral interests can produce temporary alliances during the politics
of institutional design. While individuals with similar political backgrounds, experiences, and connections will not necessarily agree on specific
policy programs in an atmosphere of political uncertainty, such individuals

can recognize that they have common interests in the construction of the electoral system. The design of the electoral system governing Duma elections at the federal level in Russia provides an excellent example. Although policy goals may help explain why Yeltsin decreed a mixed electoral system to govern the first Duma election in 1993, they do not help explain why legislative deputies maintained the system for the 1995 Duma election. Despite reduced uncertainty regarding the consequences of alternative electoral systems, the incumbent deputies and factions in the parliament maintained the electoral system that elected them even at the expense of their policy interests. In other words, Duma deputies with disparate policy orientations recognized their shared interest as incumbents and maintained an electoral system that worked against their policy goals but kept them in power (Remington and Smith 1996).

Developing testable hypotheses about electoral system choice in Russia's regions based on these assumptions requires some delineation of the multiple actors shaping the decisions, as well as the expected motivations of these individuals. As outlined in chapter 1, the distribution of power in Russia's regions varied systematically between ethnic republics and other regions in Russia. President Yeltsin and the Russian Supreme Soviet agreed to establish chief executives (or "governors") in the nonrepublic regions. Yeltsin also used his position as head of the new Russian state to make the initial appointments of these governors and to manipulate the timing of the gubernatorial elections in order to increase the likelihood that reform-minded politicians would hold these positions. Thus, the creation of governors with mandates independent of the legislative branch produced a potentially combative environment between two branches of the regional governments with opposing political orientations. Although the federal government did not create independent chief executives in Russia's republics, the possibility for divided government still existed in these regions since several republics elected "presidents" as they struggled to attain greater sovereignty while the Soviet state was crumbling around them.

In addition to the appointment of governors and the election of presidents across the regions, a second contextual factor affected the design of the regional parliamentary electoral systems: the 1993 federal constitutional crisis. The 1993 constitutional crisis extended the executive-legislative conflict at the federal level to Russia's regions, especially to the 68 nonrepublic regions. Yeltsin's decrees during the crisis also potentially altered the balance of power in these regions. In some of the regions, Yeltsin removed disloyal governors. In others, the regional parliaments dissolved themselves. Then, the Yeltsin administration outlined specific recommendations for institutional reform, although it is not clear to what extent politicians in these regions followed his recommendations.

Within this complicated context then, perhaps the most obvious hypotheses relate to the electoral system preferences of those actors in the regional legislative branch. Drawing on the assumption that parliamentary deputies in Russia's regions seek power through election, a central hypothesis of this investigation is that, during the process of parliamentary electoral system design, regional legislators who represented the old regime (or insiders) were likely to have preferred less proportional electoral systems, *ceteris paribus*. This hypothesis stems from the Soviet legacy of patronage in Russia and the competitive advantage that patron-client ties would grant to regional insiders in SMD elections.

The extensive power of the Communist Party defined the Soviet period. The communist system not only vested political power in a small group of people rather than in a set of impersonal rules, the Communist Party controlled society itself through the nomenklatura system in which the party administered appointments to the leading positions in society from factory directors to rectors of institutes. Since party officials either pursued careers in the party apparatus or moved in and out of key posts in government administration, industry, culture, and education, it was commonplace for politicians in the Soviet Union to form personal alliances of loyalty and protection (see Miller 1989 and McAuley 1997). In this system, reciprocal accountability between two tiers of actors—political leaders and bureaucrats—dictated the bureaucratic institutional order: Political leaders needed the support of bureaucratic constituencies to implement policy and bureaucrats needed to maintain the confidence of their policy-making patrons to remain in office. These relationships demanded subordination and fostered a patronage system in which political rivalries in the upper echelons of power shaped rivalries at lower levels (Roeder 1993; Willerton 1992).

While the breadth of the Communist Party's power produced patron-client relationships that permeated the economic and political realms of the Soviet Union, its hierarchical structure added depth to these patronage networks. At the regional level, party leaders were responsible for the collection of taxes, feeding the population, and maintaining law and order. Meanwhile, the existence of huge enterprises created powerful directors whose funding and orders came from Moscow. Thus, regional and local party leaders relied on strong relationships with the directors of key industries to ensure the attainment of regional targets and the provision of housing and local services. These closely knit, personal networks shaped political advancement and were used to protect regional interests against demands from Moscow (McAuley 1997, 14–15).

Ultimately then, official relationships during the Soviet period produced informal, interpersonal networks that operated on the basis of reciprocal favors. Factors such as common service with an important individual in a particular geographic region, one's succession of job assignments, and ascriptive traits (like ethnic identity and gender) became the determinants of recruitment and mobility as opposed to factors such as education and merit (Barghoorn and Remington 1986). At the same time, the Soviet system itself lacked the mechanisms to moderate the politics of personality and patronage: Members of the nomenklatura operated beyond the reach of the law since the prosecution of a member of the nomenklatura required the approval of the Communist Party itself (Harasymiw 1969, 495).

Attempts to transform the system during and after perestroika only reinforced the utility of personalized patronage. Roeder (1993), for example, notes that reciprocal accountability in the Soviet bureaucracy limited the government's ability to adapt its institutions to social change. Gorbachev's reforms altered the Soviet political order, but the pervasiveness of the Soviet bureaucracy maintained the importance of patronage networks. Soviet politicians used these patronage networks to build localized political machines that could undermine national policies and allow local politicians to enrich themselves (Willerton 1992, 14). As a result, the same political elites who enjoyed privileges from patron-client ties during the Soviet era were a consistent threat to the reform process following Soviet rule. The institutional features of state-run economies, in particular, produced some of the most adamant opponents to reform as managers sought to retain their powerful economic positions in state-owned industries (Crawford and Lijphart 1995). Meanwhile, the absence of a strong rule of law maintained patron-client relationships among economic elites: Throughout the 1990s, managers of Russian enterprises continued to rely on personal connections when handling disputes and, when one-on-one negotiations failed to resolve a problem, sought the aid of political patrons (Hendley 1997, 241–43).

Given this sociopolitical context, it seems logical that members of the old Soviet nomenklatura would have preferred single-member districts when confronted with the question of designing new regional parliamentary electoral systems. Not only did the Soviet era employ single-member districts to "elect" legislative deputies in the regions, but insiders were also likely to believe that they could capitalize on the vestiges of the Soviet electoral network. In other words, members of the nomenklatura, who maintained their ties to the Communist Party, probably expected to benefit from its preexisting political machine at the local level. It was reasonable to expect such personal and professional connections could operate as the grassroots organization that would be necessary to perform well in smaller geographic districts where a single seat was to be allocated to the candidate receiving the most votes.

In addition, SMD systems would not force insiders to identify themselves with a political party. Indeed, nonpartisanship was a very attractive option for Russian candidates, because party labels identifying one's self as pro-reform or anti-reform automatically alienated a large proportion of voters (Moser 1997). Therefore, SMD systems allowed regional insiders to obscure their link to the Soviet regime in the minds of voters who were dissatisfied with the old order. At the same time, however, where regional voters held a strong allegiance to the Soviet system, the use of SMDs did not keep insiders from emphasizing their political backgrounds and ties to the old regime while campaigning.

As mentioned previously, these arguments are not intended to suggest that former members of the nomenklatura did not come into conflict with one another in the electoral arena or that they shared common policy goals. To the contrary, the rise of rival "clans" or "cliques" representing different segments of the old regional elite is well-documented (see Badovskii and Shutov 1997; Wedel 1996). McAuley (1997, 143) emphasizes that electoral politics in certain regions emerged as hotly contested battles among clans:

> Unlike the election campaign in many parts of the country, Krasnodar's 1993 race was bitterly fought. It was not between parties but between candidates put forward by different "clans", now a visible feature of the political landscape. The combination of a conservative and unsettled community, a small democratic opposition, and powerful individuals with organized backing, all bitterly opposed to one another, made for a sharply contested election in December 1993 and again the following autumn when the local elections were finally held.

Likewise, Lukin (1999a, 1999b) argues that Russia's political system is better characterized as "electoral clanism" than as electoral democracy. In his view, elections in Russia neither select public officials according to the law within a framework of checks and balances, as in a liberal democracy, nor do they select a powerful charismatic authority to occupy a position above factional struggles and to rule in the name of the majority, as in a delegative democracy. Instead, Russian elections merely resolve "disputes among post-totalitarian clans that generally operate outside the law or in a situation of legal confusion" (1999a, 108).

The concept of "electoral clanism" entails different connotations, including the possibility of politics revolving around kinship or tribes (see Collins 2002). In post-Soviet Russia, the term generally refers to elites who consolidated bureaucratic power within their areas of competence (soviets, ministries, government agencies, industries, etc.) after the collapse of the Soviet Union. These elites capitalized on their positions of power and used preexisting patron-client ties to create a personalized base of political support. To the extent that these bureaucratic struggles manifested themselves in electoral politics, I use the term "faction" in place of clan.

The rise of rival factions among political insiders presents the possibility that their bureaucratic and patronage structures could serve as the organizational foundation for party systems. For example, Gel'man and Golosov (1998) explain Sverdlovsk's "deviant" party formation as the result of rival regional elites utilizing latent social cleavages to advance their electoral prospects. This finding supports Grumm's (1958) argument that the societal roots of multiparty systems preceded the adoption of PR electoral systems in Western Europe. Likewise, Cox (1997, 221) notes that the consequences of electoral systems depend on the composition of society: "a polity can tend toward bipartism either because it has a strong [that is, dispropor-tional] electoral system or because it has few cleavages. Multipartism arises as the joint product of many exploitable cleavages and a permissive elec-toral system." In other words, while intra-elite cleavages do not necessarily translate into meaningful party competition, they can seize upon societal cleavages to advance their electoral interests. What is important for this study, however, is not only that such behavior might set into motion the development of a party system; these intra-elite divisions themselves may also influence electoral system choice.

In Russia's regions, the number of elite factions and the intensity of fac-tional rivalries may have influenced the design of the regional parliamen-tary electoral systems. Where a small number of rival elites competed with one another, the fact that these elites owed their power and influence to legacies from the old regime made proportional representation unlikely. In fact, it is plausible that personal and political differences were set aside during the design of the electoral system in such settings, as rivals recog-nized a common interest in creating rules of the game that would work to their mutual advantage. In these cases, the design of the electoral sys-tem may have even been uneventful, although the elections themselves would likely be fiercely fought. Where the number of nomenklatura fac-tions was substantial, more proportional electoral systems were likely. More proportional electoral systems were also probably likely where elite divisions mobilized or resembled deep societal cleavages, like ethnic dif-ferences. As Rokkan (1970) notes, PR systems can be adopted as a way to preserve national integrity by stemming the tide of unrest among under-represented minorities.

Under certain circumstances, then, members of the old regime in Rus-sia's regions may have deviated from the choice of SMD electoral systems to promote a more proportional alternative. First, where the number of nomenklatura factions was higher, one should expect regional insiders to have questioned the relative advantages of SMDs, given the number of competitors with similar backgrounds and orientations. Second, to the de-gree that the opposition had formed political parties, one should expect re-gional insiders to have questioned the relative advantages of SMDs, given their opponents' level of organization. In these instances, regional insiders may have hedged their bets and adopted more proportional electoral sys-tems. Third, where regional insiders were concerned about the representa-tion of national minorities in their borders or where ethnic cleavages shaped elite divisions among insiders, more proportional electoral arrange-ments should have been more likely. However, one should also suspect that, rather than promoting electoral systems that clearly emphasize party organization—like party-list PR in a regionwide district—members of the old regime were still likely to have preferred electoral systems that would continue to benefit personal networks and patronage. These systems are SMD-majority or electoral systems with relatively low district magnitudes.

SMD-majority systems would permit competition between rival insiders in the first round of elections and the formation of insider-led alliances in the second round, thus maintaining the existing power structure in the regions. Creating electoral districts with low magnitudes would permit the equivalent of multiple patrons per geographic district without necessarily structuring electoral competition around political parties.

Although an assessment of the regional political context and the prospects for electoral success suggests that legislative insiders were likely to have preferred SMD systems *ceteris paribus*, what factors shaped the preferences of legislative outsiders? Given the finding that federal deputies in the Duma maintained Russia's 1993 electoral system because that was the system that elected them (Remington and Smith 1996), were outsiders in the regional legislatures also likely to prefer an SMD system because that was the system that placed them in office? Just as an assessment of the political context prior to the first round of regional parliamentary elections led legislative insiders to prefer SMDs, a similar assessment probably led legislative outsiders to prefer more proportional electoral systems.

When Gorbachev initiated his policy of *demokratizatsiia*, the goal was not "democratization" in the western sense of the term. Rather, the hope was that greater choice and greater openness, even in very limited versions, would encourage ordinary citizens to help in the reform effort, especially in the economic arena. While the election of a new Soviet parliament in 1989 (the 2,250-member Congress of People's Deputies) provided Soviet voters a choice among candidates, the electoral law emphasized the continuing political monopoly of the Communist Party. One-third of the seats to the Congress of People's Deputies was reserved for the Communist Party. In addition, the electoral commissions that supervised the nomination and registration of candidates were the same electoral commissions that had supervised Soviet elections for decades, and these commissions were dominated by local party officials (Remington 1994, 67).

Like the 1989 election of the Soviet Congress of People's Deputies, the March 1990 Russian Republic elections and the election of local soviets employed single-member districts that required candidates to receive more than 50% of the votes cast, with no less than 50% of eligible voters participating. Because it was likely that no one would emerge victorious in a district with several competing candidates, provisions were made for runoffs and repeat elections, which in turn created the possibility of endless elections. Unlike the 1989 election, however, no seats were automatically allocated to the Communist Party, and there were no requirements that candidates be approved at the pre-election meetings of the district election commissions. In addition, while candidates could only be nominated at the workplace in 1989, in 1990 they could also be nominated by officially registered public organizations and at places of residence (Hahn 1997a, 134).

Nevertheless, as in 1989, the 1990 electoral laws were expected to favor the communists and work against political newcomers. Regional party machines had indirect control over the formation of electoral districts, and the election commissioners were members of the old regional executive committees (Helf and Hahn 1992, 512). In addition, the majority of seats to the regional soviets were located in rural areas, and rural voters proved much more likely to vote for members of the old regime. Finally, since campaign expenses were paid by the state, local party officials enjoyed an overwhelming advantage in resources (Hahn 1997a, 135–36). Thus, the success of noncommunist forces under this system was not only somewhat of a surprise, but it is reasonable to assume that the noncommunists (or outsiders) attributed their success to the political mood of the voters and to their own political efforts, as opposed to the electoral system. Among the political outsiders, democratic candidates in particular performed well, thanks to the popularity of their ideas and their willingness "to stand outdoors campaigning in the cold for days on end, handing out literature" (Remington 1994, 70).

As Russia's transition progressed, regional outsiders also probably realized that they could not rely on the preceding levels of voter support that had allowed them to win SMD elections in 1990. Following the 1989–1990 period, most Russians experienced sharp disappointment with the changed regime, and in more recent elections, voters actually have preferred candidates with proven credentials (Remington 1999, 113). Thus, the window of opportunity for outsiders narrowed significantly between 1990 and 1993, as the revolutionary zeal of the democratic transition waned and gave way to the trials of privatization. Accordingly, legislative outsiders in Russia's regions likely believed that they won representation in the March 1990 elections despite the electoral system rather than thanks to it.

Two additional reasons probably encouraged legislative outsiders in Russia's regions to prefer more proportional parliamentary electoral systems. First, legislative outsiders likely recognized that they lacked both the established patron-client relationships and the strong local organization to win parliamentary seats in an electoral system that would require a plurality of votes in geographically delineated districts. At the same time, outsiders also were likely to realize that party name recognition could provide a distinct advantage in party-list PR elections, especially where the party names had gained recognition at the national level, or where their party consisted of nationally known individuals.

Thus far, the discussion of electoral system preferences has been limited to politicians composing one branch of government—the regional legislature. However, independent chief executives (either governors or presidents) were likely to have played a key role in the design of regional electoral systems in Russia. In those regions of Russia where independent executives were in office at the time the electoral system was designed, the law designing the electoral system was subject to their approval. For example, where President Yeltsin appointed governors, the president's decrees in 1993 granted these heads of administration the power to veto assembly decisions and to require a two-thirds vote by the assembly to override a veto (Gel'man 2000b, 95–97). In these instances, then, one could reasonably expect the political interests of the regional executive branch to have influenced electoral system design.

The political motives of independent executives in Russia's regions regarding the design of a parliamentary electoral system are not as evident as the motives of members of parliament. Unlike legislators, executive preferences were likely shaped by competing motivations. First, executives probably preferred electoral systems that would elect legislators who were close to them ideologically. Governors and presidents may have preferred an electoral system that facilitated the election of like-minded politicians, because the election of such deputies would create a political environment more favorable to their preferred policies. In these cases, if the ideology of the chief executive was proximate to outsiders, then one should expect the governor or president to have promoted the adoption of a more proportional electoral system. If the ideology of the chief executive was proximate to insiders, then one should expect the governor or president to have promoted the adoption of a less proportional electoral system.

A second potential influence on the motives of regional executives was the relationship these executives had with the Russian president at the time, Boris Yeltsin. Where Yeltsin appointed the chief executives, the executives should have been more likely to design electoral systems that corresponded with Yeltsin's decree. In fact, such behavior was more likely where the consequences of the different electoral options were uncertain. Research on institutional design at the national level in Russia stresses the lack of information and uncertainty that existed even during the design of the federal electoral system:

> Both Yeltsin's team and his opponents, however, lacked reliable information about their prospects under various schemes. The referendum of April 1993 revealed patterns of support for and opposition to President Yeltsin and his government's reform policy. Elections of governors in a few regions during the same year gave some indication of voters' preferences. Neither these, however, nor the election of deputies in 1989 and 1990 and the presidential election of 1991 gave any concrete evidence of the levels of local or national support for the current array of political parties, blocs, and movements. (Smith and Remington 2001, 98)

Thus, recommendations emanating from the federal executive were likely to be an influential factor in the decision calculus of regional executives. In other words, regional executives were likely to have promoted single-member-districts systems either because they felt a significant degree of allegiance or accountability to the Russian president, or because they took his recommendation as an indication that SMDs would elect like-minded legislative deputies.

With the passage of time, however, the two factors shaping the electoral system preferences of Yeltsin's appointees probably came into conflict with each other. Both the 1993 national parliamentary election and other regional parliamentary elections helped decrease the degree of uncertainty associated with the design of new parliamentary electoral systems. Russia's 1993 Duma election revealed that parties with strong patron-client ties and strong local organization (i.e., parties comprised of insiders) were more successful in the SMD half of the election than those parties that lacked such local ties. It also revealed that politicians and parties lacking local organizations were still able to win parliamentary seats in the party-list PR segment of the election (Moser 1995). These outcomes support the contention that regional insiders should have preferred SMD systems. Likewise, legislative outsiders participating in electoral system decisions after the Duma election had greater cause to prefer more proportional electoral systems in the first round of truly competitive parliamentary elections despite having been elected under SMDs in 1990.

The 1993 Duma election and elections to regional parliaments, therefore, revealed that the President's recommendation of SMD-plurality was not necessarily in the best interest of reform-oriented executives. Yet, appointed governors were probably more liberal than their regional soviets and, all else being equal, should have preferred more proportional electoral systems that would have favored the election of political outsiders (i.e., legislators more likely to have a similar political orientation). In Russia's regions, then, appointed governors with a voice in the design of the regional parliamentary electoral systems were pulled in opposing directions.

While different institutions may have different consequences for institutional designers, institutional designers do not necessarily weigh these different consequences equally. Different institutions not only produce specific outcomes with different levels of certainty; some outcomes are simply more important to institutional designers than others. For example, while legislators may have various political goals, how an electoral system will influence their electoral prospects becomes of primary concern to them when they design this institution, because the outcome will directly influence legislative representation (Smith and Remington 2001, 22–24). From this perspective then, the preferred electoral system of appointed governors probably depended on the degree to which these governors believed the design of the electoral system would influence the ideology of the future parliament, as well as the degree to which they believed President Yeltsin would reprimand them for promoting something other than SMD-plurality. With regard to the latter consideration, the passage of time probably diluted the sense of urgency associated with the 1993 constitutional crisis. As a result, gubernatorial disobedience was probably less damaging to President Yeltsin, and the threat of removal was also probably less likely. In sum then, the passage of time provided reform-oriented executives with information that would encourage them to deviate from federal recommendations, and it may also have granted Yeltsin appointees more room to maneuver.

ROOM FOR NEGOTIATION

Given the potential for different actors with multiple motivations to participate in the design of parliamentary electoral systems across Russia's regions, the likelihood of political bargaining among these actors seems high. Of course, the degree to which political bargaining and compromise was necessary depended on the configuration of governmental power in the regions. Where the regional parliament controlled the design of the electoral system, the decision should have reflected the balance of power among parliamentary insiders and outsiders, with some consideration of the level of intra-elite conflict and party development in the region. Where regional executives designed the electoral systems, electoral system choice should have reflected the ideology of the executive, the relationship between the executive and President Yeltsin, and the timing of electoral system decisions.

In many of Russia's regions, however, both branches of the regional government were in office when the new parliamentary electoral system was designed. In places where both the executive and regional legislators influenced the design of the electoral system, the decision should reflect bargaining between the two branches of government, with the balance of power among political insiders and outsiders in parliament serving as the determining factor. Specifically, although an independent executive with formal veto power could require legislators to consider his preferences, the viability of a veto threat depended on the size and orientation of the majority in parliament. In places where the executive was reform oriented, the smaller the percentage of insider-oriented legislators the greater the likelihood that a veto threat could force the parliament to pass a bill acceptable to the executive or to incorporate the institutional preferences of legislative outsiders as a means of overcoming the threat. Both instances should have yielded more proportional systems. However, where insiders enjoyed larger majorities in parliament, the influence of a veto threat was diminished, and the insiders would have enjoyed greater leverage over the institutional decision.

Just as the potential for political bargaining over the parliamentary electoral system was high in many Russian regions, the range of electoral system features available to the institutional designers also granted room for compromise. Electoral system design provides plenty of creative opportunities to balance multiple goals. Electoral engineers can adopt mixed systems that elect a specific number of deputies through single-member districts and another set of deputies through party-list proportional representation. They can also select systems that elect all deputies through several multimember districts (districts that elect two or more representatives each) or systems that mix single-member districts with multimember districts. Therefore, although the preferences of the different institutional designers probably focused initially on different types of electoral systems (such as SMDs or party-list PR), one should expect more complicated electoral systems where political bargaining and the need to compromise were more likely.

CONCLUSION

This chapter describes how the context of Russia's transition influenced the design of parliamentary electoral systems in its regions. Przeworski (1986) asserts that the domination of one political actor during a democratic transition leads to an institutional arrangement that reproduces this dominance, while uncertainty about political outcomes is conducive to more consensual institutional structures. The theory presented here develops this account of institutional decisions by emphasizing how the range of political actors, their corresponding preferences, and the negotiation among them can produce a variety of institutional decisions. Yeltsin's attempt to solidify his support in Russia instigated greater political competition in the regions, where the distribution of executive and legislative powers became a primary issue of debate. The initiation of this debate and the subsequent passage of the 1993 federal constitution arguably had positive implications for Russian democracy in the regions, since the timing of the two events allowed the design of regional institutions to be made in a more competitive setting. If the federal government had granted the regions the power to design their own electoral institutions immediately following the collapse of the Soviet system, then the old Soviet elite would have certainly dominated institutional design, and the new institutions would have replicated their dominance to a degree even greater than that which materialized.

THREE— THE POWER TO CHOOSE

Institutional designers at all levels enjoy a wide range of options when designing parliamentary electoral systems. Within Eastern Europe and the former Soviet Union, different electoral features have been combined in a multitude of fashions. Countries like the Czech Republic, Estonia, Latvia, Moldova, Poland, and Romania have employed proportional representation with varying district magnitudes, electoral formulas, and legal thresholds. Other countries like Albania, Armenia, Lithuania, Macedonia, and Ukraine began the 1990s by electing new parliaments through single-member districts but since have adopted some degree of proportional representation as well. Meanwhile, countries like Belarus, Croatia, Kazakhstan, Kyrgyzstan, Serbia, Tajikistan, Turkmenistan, and Uzbekistan have relied solely on single-member-district elections, often with the use of runoff elections (Shvetsova 1999).

Within the regions of the Russian Federation there has been a substantial amount of experimentation with electoral rules. Based on the districting options, electoral formulas, and candidate nomination procedures, five types of electoral systems can be identified as governing the first parliamentary elections in Russia's regions. The majority of Russian regions relied on single-member-district-plurality (SMD-plurality) elections, but others (like the republic of Buriatia) used runoff elections —SMD-majority. Meanwhile, some regions (like Amur oblast) employed multimember-district-plurality (MMD-plurality) elections in which more than one seat was allocated per district and candidates receiving the greatest percentages of votes won the seats. Still others combined MMD-plurality elections alongside SMD-plurality elections. Finally, Saratov oblast and the republics of Marii El and Tuva increased electoral proportionality by allocating a portion of seats through party-list PR in a single regionwide district alongside SMD-plurality.

Tables 3.1 and 3.2 describe the electoral systems governing the first regional parliaments across Russia's regions. As these tables reveal, electoral system design in Russia's regions was not constrained to a choice between single-member districts, party-list proportional representation, or a simple mixture of the two. Regional institutional designers employed a variety of districting options to introduce different degrees of proportionality. At the same time, there seems to have been some limit on the degree to which the institutional designers deviated from the recommendation of SMD-plurality emanating from the center. In no region, including the republics, did politicians adopt a pure party-list PR system for electing their parliaments.

Due to the wide range of electoral systems in Russia's regions, it is difficult to capture the various electoral possibilities with a single dependent variable. However, electoral scholars have consistently asserted that district magnitude is the most important indicator of whether a system distributes parliamentary seats in a manner proportional to the distribution of the popular vote (see chapter 1). Therefore, to compare across electoral systems, electoral scholars generally use the average district magnitude, which is the average number of seats distributed across all districts within a specific electoral system.

The average district magnitude of the parliamentary electoral systems in Russia's regions emerges as a logical dependent variable for several reasons. First, a core assumption of the theory is that while institutional designers may have considered different types of electoral systems, the array of electoral options available and the presence of multiple actors with competing motivations should have yielded more variation in terms of electoral system proportionality than in terms of the types of electoral system. Second, as tables 3.1 and 3.2 demonstrate, the parliamentary electoral systems in Russia's regions vary most visibly in terms of their electoral districting. Average district magnitude, therefore, represents a dependent variable that captures the large degree of variation that exists across Russia's regional electoral systems without allowing too much relevant information to be lost (Golosov 1999, 1349). A third benefit of focusing on average district magnitude is that it acts as "a truly continuous continuum expressed in, and measured by, natural numbers" (Sartori 1986, 53), which lends it to ordinary least squares regression analysis.

Although calculating the average district magnitude is the simplest method for expressing the different district magnitudes of an electoral system as a single index, the use of a simple average has limitations. Specifically, while two electoral systems may have the same average district magnitude, they also may have different implications for political

TABLE 3.1 **ELECTORAL SYSTEMS GOVERNING THE FIRST PARLIAMENTARY ELECTIONS IN THE REPUBLICS**

Region	No. of Seats per District x No. of Districts	Electoral Formula	Weighted Average District Magnitude	Assembly Size	Election Date
1. Adygeia	1x27, 2x9	Plurality	1.4	45	Dec-95
2. Altai	1x27	Plurality	1	27	Dec-93
3. Bashkortostan*			1.79	190	Mar-95
Lower Chamber	1x40	Plurality	1	40	
Upper Chamber	2x74	Plurality	2	148	
4. Buriatia	1x65	Majority, runoff	1	65	Jun-94
5. Chechnya	—		—	—	—
6. Chuvashia	1x47	Majority, runoff	1	47	Mar-94
7. Dagestan[a]	1x121	Majority, runoff	1	121	Mar-95
8. Ingushetia	1x27	Plurality	1	27	Feb-94
9. Kabardino-Balkaria*			2	72	Dec-93
Lower Chamber	1x36	Plurality	1	36	
Upper Chamber	3x12	Plurality	3	36	
10. Kalmykia[b]	1x18, 9x1	Plurality, Presidential List	3.67	27	Oct-94
11. Karachaevo-Cherkesia	1x73	Plurality	1	73	Jun-95
12. Karelia*			1.59	61	Apr-94
Lower Chamber	1x25	Plurality	1	25	
Upper Chamber	2x18	Plurality	2	36	
13. Khakassia	1x75	Plurality	1	75	Dec-96
14. Komi	1x50	Plurality	1	50	Jan-95
15. Marii El	1x22, 8x1	Plurality, Party-list PR	2.13	30	Dec-93
16. Mordovia	1x75	Plurality	1	75	Nov-94
17. North Ossetia	1x75	Majority, runoff	1	75	Mar-95
18. Sakha (Yakutia)*			1	56	Dec-93
Lower Chamber	1x21	Majority, runoff	1	21	
Upper Chamber	1x35	Majority, runoff	1	35	
19. Tatarstan	1x130[a]	Majority, runoff	1	130	Mar-95
20. Tuva (Tyva)	1x27, 5x1	Plurality, Party-list PR	1.625	32	Dec-93
21. Udmurtia	1x100	Plurality	1	100	Mar-95

* Indicates a republic with a bicameral parliament. The analysis employs the cumulative weighted average district magnitude (in bold) for republics with two legislative chambers.
[a] Dagestan had an exceptionally complex electoral system. In 1995, 121 seats were allocated via majority voting with a second round if necessary. Forty-eight seats were open to all candidates, but 73 were reserved for candidates of a certain ethnic group, educational background, or gender (i.e., female) (Kisriev and Ware 2001).
[b] In Kalmykia, President Iliumzhinov created a "presidential list" to elect nine candidates. Each candidate from his list only had to receive 15% of the vote in the nine-seat, multimember district (with a turnout of 35%) to win election (McFaul and Petrov 1998 v2, 152; Slider 1996, 254).
Data were compiled from various sources including McFaul and Petrov (1998), Slider (1996), the Central Election Commission (1998), and the home page of the Russian Social Institute of Election Law (http://www.roiip.ru/regions/index.htm). Some of the initial electoral systems were subsequently modified (see Golosov 1999, 2004).

TABLE 3.2 **ELECTORAL SYSTEMS GOVERNING THE FIRST PARLIAMENTARY ELECTIONS IN THE REMAINING 68 REGIONS**

Region	No. of Seats per District x No. of Districts	Electoral Formula	Weighted Average District Magnitude	Assembly Size	Election Date
1. Aginskoe-Buriat (okrug)	1x15	Plurality	1	15	Mar-94
2. Altai (krai)	1x50	Plurality	1	50	Apr-94
3. Amur (oblast)	2x15	Plurality	2	30	Oct-94
4. Arkhangel'sk (oblast)	1x41	Plurality	1	41	Dec-93
5. Astrakhan (oblast)	1x25	Plurality	1	25	Mar-94
6. Belgorod (oblast)	1x21	Plurality	1	21	Mar-94
7. Briansk (oblast)	3x9	Plurality	3	27	Mar-94
8. Cheliabinsk (oblast)	1x15	Plurality	1	15	May-94
9. Chita (oblast)	1x21	Plurality	1	21	Mar-94
10. Chukotka (okrug)	1x9, 3x2	Plurality	1.8	15	Mar-94
11. Evenk (okrug)	1x23	Plurality	1	23	Mar-94
12. Irkutsk (oblast)	1x45	Plurality	1	45	Mar-94
13. Ivanovo (oblast)	1x23	Plurality	1	23	Mar-94
14. Jewish autonomous (oblast)	1x15	Plurality	1	15	Mar-94
15. Kaliningrad (oblast)	1x21	Plurality	1	21	Mar-94
16. Kaluga (oblast)	1x40	Plurality	1	40	Mar-94
17. Kamchatka (oblast)	1x3, 4x4, 2x2	Plurality	3.26	23	Mar-94
18. Kemerovo (oblast)	1x35	Plurality	1	35	Mar-94
19. Khabarovsk (krai)	1x25	Plurality	1	25	Mar-94
20. Khanty-Mansi (okrug)	1x17	Plurality	1	17	Mar-94
21. Kirov (oblast)	1x48	Plurality	1	48	Mar-94
22. Komi-Permiak (okrug)	1x15	Plurality	1	15	Mar-94
23. Koriak (okrug)	1x8	Plurality	1	8	Mar-94
24. Kostroma (oblast)	1x15	Plurality	1	15	Mar-94
25. Krasnodar (krai)	8x1, 7x6	Plurality	6.32	50	Nov-94
26. Krasnoiarsk (krai)	1x11, 2x5, 3x1, 5x2	Plurality	2.65	34	Mar-94
27. Kurgan (oblast)	1x25	Plurality	1	25	Mar-94
28. Kursk (oblast)	1x45	Plurality	1	45	Mar-94
29. Leningrad (oblast)	1x25	Plurality	1	25	Mar-94
30. Lipetsk (oblast)	1x38	Plurality	1	38	Mar-94
31. Magadan (oblast)	1x17	Plurality	1	17	Mar-94
32. Moscow city[a]	1x35	Plurality	1	35	Dec-93
33. Moscow (oblast)[a]	1x50	Plurality	1	50	Dec-93
34. Murmansk (oblast)	3x4, 2x4, 1x5	Plurality	2.28	25	Mar-94
35. Nenets (okrug)	1x10, 5x1	Plurality	2.33	15	Mar-94
36. Nizhnii Novgorod (oblast)	1x45	Plurality	1	45	Mar-94

TABLE 3.2 **CONTINUED**

Region	No. of Seats per District x No. of Districts	Electoral Formula	Weighted Average District Magnitude	Assembly Size	Election Date
37. Novgorod (oblast)	1x27	Plurality	1	27	Mar-94
38. Novosibirsk (oblast)	1x49	Plurality	1	49	Mar-94
39. Omsk (oblast)	1x30	Plurality	1	30	Mar-94
40. Orel (oblast)	1x50	Plurality	1	50	Mar-94
41. Orenburg (oblast)	1x47	Plurality	1	47	Mar-94
42. Penza (oblast)	1x32, 4x1, 3x1, 2x3	Plurality	1.53	45	Jan-94
43. Perm (oblast)	1x40	Plurality	1	40	Mar-94
44. Primore (krai)	1x39	Plurality	1	39	Oct-94
45. Pskov (oblast)	1x21	Plurality	1	21	Jan-94
46. Riazan (oblast)	1x19	Plurality	1	19	Mar-94
47. Rostov (oblast)	1x45	Plurality	1	45	Mar-94
48. Sakhalin (oblast)	4x4	Plurality	4	16	Mar-94
49. Samara (oblast)	1x25	Plurality	1	25	Mar-94
50. Saratov (oblast)	1x25, 10x1	Plurality, Party-list PR	3.57	35	May-94
51. Smolensk (oblast)	1x24, 2x3	Plurality	1.2	30	Mar-94
52. Stavropol (krai)	1x25	Plurality	1	25	Mar-94
53. St. Petersburg	1x50	Majority, runoff	1	50	Mar-94
54. Sverdlovsk (oblast)	4x7	Plurality	4	28	Apr-94
55. Taimyr (okrug)	1x11	Plurality	1	11	Mar-94
56. Tambov (oblast)	2x15	Plurality	2	30	Mar-94
57. Tiumen (oblast)	1x25	Plurality	1	25	Mar-94
58. Tomsk (oblast)	1x21	Plurality	1	21	Mar-94
59. Tula (oblast)	1x29	Plurality	1	29	Dec-93
60. Tver (oblast)	1x33	Plurality	1	33	Mar-94
61. Ul'ianovsk (oblast)	1x25	Plurality	1	25	Dec-95
62. Ust-Ordynskoe Buriat (okrug)	1x15	Plurality	1	15	Mar-94
63. Vladimir (oblast)	1x21	Plurality	1	21	Mar-94
64. Volgograd (oblast)	1x32	Plurality	1	32	Dec-93
65. Vologda (oblast)	1x15	Plurality	1	15	Mar-94
66. Voronezh (oblast)	1x45	Plurality	1	45	Mar-94
67. Yamalo-Nenets (okrug)	1x21	Plurality	1	21	Mar-94
68. Yaroslavl' (oblast)	1x23	Plurality	1	23	Feb-94

---

[a] Indicates electoral systems designed by the federal executive.

Data were compiled from various sources including McFaul and Petrov (1998), Slider (1996), the Central Election Commission (1998), and the home page of the Russian Social Institute of Election Law (http://www.roiip.ru/regions/index.htm). Some of the initial electoral systems were subsequently modified (see Golosov 1999, 2004).

representation and party development. For example, an electoral system with one 100-seat district and 100 SMDs has an average district magnitude roughly equal to two [(100 x 1) + (1 x 100)/ 101 = 1.98], but the election outcome under such a system may differ significantly from a system where all the districts are two-seat districts (Taagepera and Shugart 1989, 127). In particular, small parties are not likely to receive parliamentary seats in an election that employs only two-seat districts, but these same small parties can expect to win seats in the 100-seat district of the mixed electoral system. The different electoral outcomes are especially important for developing democracies, like Russia, with a fledgling party system and many new and small parties. While a two-member-district system limits the electoral prospects of new and small parties, a mixed system like the one described provides greater opportunities for representation. Since electoral system designers clearly consider the representation of new and small parties, the dependent variable of a study analyzing electoral system choice should capture how different methods of electoral districting can produce different electoral outcomes even when systems have the same average district magnitude.

To provide some indication of the different outcomes of electoral systems with different district compositions but similar average district magnitudes, the analysis uses a measure that weights the district magnitudes of an electoral system by squaring them. Thus, a second dependent variable examined in the statistical analysis is the weighted average district magnitude (WADM) of the electoral system that was used to govern the first legislative election in each region. WADM is calculated by summing the squared district magnitudes of an electoral system and then dividing the sum by the total number of seats:

$$WADM = [\Sigma(M^2)]/N$$

where WADM is the weighted average district magnitude, M is the magnitude of each individual district, and N is the number of seats in the assembly (Coppedge 1997).[1]

WADM provides a nice measure of the different levels of proportionality associated with the varying electoral systems in Russia's regions. For electoral systems in which all of the districts have the same magnitude, WADM is equal to that magnitude. For example, in 1993, Arkhangel'sk oblast allocated 41 seats through 41 SMDs; as a result, WADM equals one. However, for electoral systems in which different districts have different magnitudes, WADM takes into account the greater levels of proportionality associated with the districts of larger magnitudes. For example, in Taagepera and Shugart's example of a 200-seat parliament with one 100-seat district and 100 SMDs, WADM yields a value of 50.5 and indicates a greater level of proportionality than the average district magnitude value of 1.98.[2] Likewise, in 1994, Krasnodar krai allocated eight seats through a single, regionwide electoral district and 42 seats through seven six-member districts. As a result, the WADM score of 6.32 reflects how the different magnitudes were weighted, while also indicating the greater level of proportionality associated with this electoral system in comparison to the one used in Arkhangel'sk.[3]

The weighted average district magnitude was calculated for each regional electoral system, except the republic of Chechnya. Of the 88 cases, 67 used only single-member districts to elect their first regional parliaments, although Moscow city and Moscow oblast are not included in the actual analysis, since the federal executive decreed their electoral systems specifically. The minimum value for the variable, WADM, is 1.0 while the maximum value is 6.32 (which describes the electoral system in Krasnodar krai).[4]

Two problems emerge with the use of WADM, however. First, given the limited number of cases with average district magnitudes above one, the use of the weighted measure may exaggerate the level of variation in the dependent variable. To address this concern, the simple average is also used as a dependent variable in the statistical analysis, and the results of the analyses for the two measures are compared given their corresponding shortcomings. Second, a reliance solely on average district magnitude or WADM fails to distinguish between the decision to use a plurality formula versus a runoff system in SMDs. Since two SMD systems exist with the same average district magnitude but different electoral formulas, the question is how to explain the adoption of different electoral formulas in regions that made the same electoral districting decision. Lijphart's (1994) effective threshold is one attempt to combine both electoral formula and district magnitude into a single measure. Unfortunately, this measure suffers from inappropriate assumptions for transitional polities and, ultimately, fails to adequately distinguish among clearly different electoral system decisions in Russia's regions.[5] Thus, the question of differentiating between different electoral formulas is set aside for now and revisited closer to the end of the chapter.

Besides district magnitude and electoral formula, another potential dependent variable exists when examining electoral system choice: assembly size. Assembly size can influence the proportionality of an electoral system by setting limits on how accurately a large number of popular votes can be translated into a smaller number of parliamentary seats. For example, if four parties win 41%, 29%, 17%, and 13% of the vote, the allocation of these seats cannot be distributed in a highly proportional manner if the election is to a legislature with only five seats. The proportionality improves for a ten-seat legislature and can approach perfect proportionality (at least in theory) for a 100-seat legislature (Lijphart 1994, 12–13). While assembly size is generally correlated with population size (see Taagepera and Shugart 1989, 173–83), the circumstances under which Russia's regional electoral systems were designed appear to have undermined this relationship: Republics that tend to have smaller population sizes generally adopted substantially larger assembly sizes than other more populous regions. With these issues in mind, the following statistical analysis employs four dependent variables: average district magnitude, WADM, assembly size, and, eventually, electoral formula.

CORRELATES OF ELECTORAL SYSTEM DESIGN

Chapter 2 outlines four factors that likely shaped electoral system design in Russia's regions: 1) the institutional designers' political positions, 2) the designers' political orientations, 3) the beliefs the designers held as to how politicians with different orientations would perform under different electoral systems, and 4) the relationship between the institutional designers and the Russian president.

The most difficult explanatory factor to capture across each region is the designers' political orientation. Even though chapter 2 makes the simplifying assumption of distinguishing between political insiders and outsiders, distinguishing between these categories in Russia's regional parliaments is a difficult task. One approach for estimating the distribution of legislative insiders and outsiders is to use information from published electoral results, noting which elected deputies were affiliated with the Communist Party of the Soviet Union, and any additional information on their previous occupations. Unfortunately, official data for each regional deputy in each regional soviet are not available, although unofficial data were collected and are used in the following chapter for deputies elected in four of the regions. In the place of such data for the entire population of Russia's regions, this analysis relies on an indicator of insider influence in the regional soviets that reflects the political climate at the time the soviets were elected.

During the 1990 regional soviet elections, the opposition in Russia's regions consisted of broad, loosely organized citizen committees and voters' clubs. The activities of these committees and clubs were limited primarily to promoting candidates who seemed progressive, and although these organizations participated in the election campaigns, they lacked the right to actually nominate candidates. According to Fish (1995, 194–95), this electoral environment not only impeded the nomination of reform-oriented candidates in rural areas but also undermined opportunities for sincere voting among rural residents. For example, since local elites maintained control over the means of coercion and the provision of goods and services, workers in small towns and rural areas were often "requested" to nominate directors of enterprises whom they relied upon for food, housing, and other essential items. Although urban residents surely felt pressure from the workplace, residents of larger cities enjoyed access to alternative sources of scarce goods and greater anonymity. As a result, members of the old regime enjoyed more electoral support from rural voters, because rural residents not only voted as they were told but also often voted in electoral districts without a democratic alternative.

With this in mind, I use a measure of political competition in the re-gions in March 1990 to estimate outsider influence in the regional soviets. The average number of candidates per territorial district in each region competing in the March 1990 elections to the Russian Congress of People's Deputies estimates the ability of the Communist Party to limit the nomina-tions of opposition candidates within a region.[6] Since the regional soviet elections were held in March 1990 as well, the number of candidates com-peting for representation to the Russian parliament from a region also should indicate variation in competition levels in regional parliamentary elections. To the extent that higher levels of competition at the time reflect greater electoral opportunities for the opposition, political outsiders should have enjoyed more representation in the provincial soviets where political competition was higher.[7] As expected, there is a high correlation between the average number of candidates to the Congress of Peoples' Deputies and the percentage of rural residents in the regions. The Pearson's r for the two is -0.43, which is significant at the .01 level for a two-tailed test. This suggests that more rural regions did indeed experience fewer candidates competing for rep-resentation in their districts for seats to the new Russian parliament.[8]

While the preceding measure seeks to capture the general political orien-tation of the regional soviet, the analysis likewise investigates the impact of the political orientation of the chief executives on electoral system choice. As argued in chapter 2, executives are likely to prefer electoral systems that elect like-minded politicians, all else being equal. To estimate the political orientation of governors and presidents in Russia's regions, the executives were coded in terms of whether they openly opposed Yeltsin's actions dur-ing the 1993 constitutional crises (-1), openly supported Yeltsin (1), or made no clear preference publicly (0).[9] Regions where governors openly op-posed Yeltsin and were subsequently replaced by Yeltsin (i.e., Amur, Bri-ansk, and Novosibirsk) score ones for political orientation. Since President Yeltsin appointed governors, and even removed those who were elected but disloyal, the political orientation of the executive should matter more in the republics than in other regions. Accordingly, a dichotomous variable, called Republic, is included in the analysis to control for this important contextual difference.

Just as the executive orientations and their degree of accountability to the Russian president were likely to have shaped their electoral system pref-erences, changing levels of uncertainty over time also likely influenced re-gional executives. For governors, in particular, greater information on the consequences of different electoral systems helped justify a divergence from Yeltsin's recommendations. Accordingly, chief executives who designed their electoral systems later probably made different decisions from those who designed their systems earlier. To introduce this changing level of un-certainty, the number of months between the first legislative elections in a region and the December 1993 Duma election is included in the analysis.[10] As months passed, regional executives were likely to have designed new parliamentary electoral systems with a greater understanding of the consequences of these systems in their regions. Since the timing of the decision may have been less relevant to the republics than to other regions, the dichotomous variable, Republic, again controls for contextual variations by region type.

A key contention of the argument so far is that the willingness and opportunity of regional politicians to defy decrees emanating from the federal executive shaped electoral system decisions in the regions. In an analysis of center-periphery relations, Treisman (1999, 122–28) discovers two factors that led governors to adopt positions counter to the Russian president at different points during the early 1990s. First, a chief executive was more likely to oppose Yeltsin publicly where the support for the Russian president was declining. Specifically, when examining the 1993 constitutional crisis, Treisman finds that regional executives were more likely to denounce Yeltsin's actions in places where the percentage of the regions' voters expressing confidence in Yeltsin during the April 1993 referendum was lower than the vote for Yeltsin in the 1991 presidential election. He emphasizes that this result depicts the responsiveness of these leaders to regional public opinion. In other words, have voters become more or less reform oriented? Since such voter attitudes would shape the composition of the future parliament, they may have had some impact on the executive's electoral system preference.

According to Treisman, regional executives popularly elected in their region rather than appointed were also more likely to oppose Yeltsin publicly. However, as noted previously, Yeltsin proved willing to dismiss elected governors—but not presidents—who were disloyal to him during the 1993 constitutional crisis. And, since Treisman's analysis focuses primarily on opposition to Yeltsin prior to and during the this crisis, it is plausible that the distinction between appointed and elected executives proved less important.[11] Still, to the extent that the design of a regional parliamentary electoral system reflected the willingness of governors to oppose Yeltsin, Treisman's findings represent compelling arguments for incorporating both of these variables into the analysis.

To capture the changing popularity of Yeltsin in the regions and the responsiveness of regional politicians to voter preferences, I replicate Treisman's measure. Changes in public support for Yeltsin is measured as the regional difference between the percentage of the vote supporting Yeltsin in the 1991 election and the percentage of the vote supporting him in the April 1993 referendum.[12] Positive scores indicate increased support; negative scores indicate decreased support. To test for the likelihood that elected executives defied Yeltsin during the design of the regional electoral systems, a dummy variable is used in which one indicates those regions in which the chief executive was elected prior to the 1993 constitutional crisis but not removed by Yeltsin following the crisis.[13] The variable, Republic, again controls for differences between elected governors and the presidents of the republics.

Additional independent variables that may have influenced the design of the parliamentary electoral systems in Russia's regions are the level of competition among members of the old regime and the development of the party system. To capture intra-elite conflict in Russia's regions, the analysis employs the level of electoral competition that existed for two high-profiled positions: regional representatives to the upper chamber of Russia's national parliament.

At the same time as the 1993 Duma election, Russia's regions elected two representatives to the newly created Federation Council. These elections were unique because Russia's federal constitution did not specify how subsequent members would be selected, and direct Federation Council elections have not been repeated. However, three regions did not elect representatives to the Federation Council in December 1993. Chechnya and Tatarstan did not participate in the elections due to ongoing conflicts with the federal government over their sovereignty, while Cheliabinsk oblast did not have enough candidates competing to make the election valid.[14] Both Cheliabinsk oblast and Tatarstan eventually held elections to the Federation Council, on 15 May 1994 and 13 March 1994, respectively (McFaul and Petrov 1998 v1, 387–90).

Federation Council elections are important because they had the potential to become contests among rival patrons in the regions (see, for example, the republic of Buriatia discussed in the following chapter). Nevertheless, in 12 regions, only the minimum number of candidates necessary to validate the election actually competed. McFaul and Petrov (1998 v1, 179) describe the majority of such instances as "two bosses per district and a sparring partner" for the sake of appearing competitive. In 18 regions, there were only four candidates (two per seat), while 25 witnessed just five candidates competing for the two positions. The remaining regions had six or more candidates. Among the candidates competing, 40% were heads of the regional executives, 16% were heads of the regional legislatures, about 25% came from the economic or financial sectors (e.g., managers of large enterprises and commercial banks), 13% had been in the old Congress of People's Deputies, while between 8% and 11% were teachers, journalists, and other specialists (Sakwa 1995, 198).

One way to use the 1993 Federation Council elections to estimate the level of intra-elite competition in the regions would be to rely on the percentage of the vote the victors won. Although this measure has limits because it tends to reflect popular support more than elite division, another significant problem with it relates to an unusual aspect of the Federation Council's election law. During the 1993 Federation Council election, every voter had two votes, but not everyone used both votes. If a voter did not use his second vote, that vote was automatically allocated to the incumbent governor (McFaul and Petrov 1998 v1, 179). This system was designed to increase the electoral prospects of politicians loyal to Yeltsin in the majority of the regions; however, the frequency with which second votes were actually cast varies widely across the regions from 41.7% in Krasnodar krai to 99.4% in the republic of Ingushetia (McFaul and Petrov 1998 v1, 387–90). Due to the problems associated with interpreting the Federation Council's election results, this analysis relies on a more straightforward but equally relevant indicator of elite competition in the regions: the number of candidates competing per Federation Council mandate.[15] Intra-elite competition is considered to have been higher in those regions where more candidates competed for their region's Federation Council seats.

Measuring party development in Russia's regions during the early 1990s is a difficult proposition. As Golosov (2001, 2004) notes, official information on the regional parliamentary election results from December 1993 through 1994 is not available. Thus, there is not only substantial scholarly debate about whether political parties actually existed in Russia at this time (see the previous chapter); there is also little systematic information on party activities across Russia's regions during this period. Nevertheless, the 1993 federal elections to the Duma provide one source of information on party activity in Russia's regions.

Political parties were clearly emerging at the national level in 1993. In fact, the use of party-list PR to allocate half of the 450 seats to the Russian Duma was an explicit attempt on behalf of the federal executive to promote party development. While most political organizations that participated in the 1993 Duma election were hastily assembled and often revolved around one or a few political actors (McAuley 1997, 273), 35 associations sought to register for the party-list PR segment of the 1993 Duma election (Colton 1998, 16–17). Thirteen parties eventually ended up on the ballot with varying degrees of organization. Clearly, the most organized was the Communist Party of the Russian Federation (CPRF). Founded in February 1994, the CPRF picked up where the old Communist Party of the Soviet Union (CPSU) had left off. Other parties with relatively long histories were the Liberal Democratic Party of Russia (LDPR) and the Democratic Party of Russia (DPR), both of which emerged in 1990. However, 9 of the 13 parties were formed only in 1993 with 6 not existing until 21 September 1993 (Colton 1998, 20).

Since voting results can illustrate the popularity of a set of leaders or ideas more than party organization, the analysis employs a measure that more explicitly taps into the relevance of political parties to the electoral success of regional politicians. This indicator of regional party development is the percentage of SMD seats per region that party-nominated candidates, as opposed to candidates nominated by independent blocs of voters, actually won. In other words, to what degree were explicit ties to a national-level party relevant to the election of politicians in the regions where party affiliation was optional? In 19 regions, political parties nominated all of the deputies that won the 1993 SMD Duma seats within the regions' borders. Meanwhile, independent candidates won all of the 1993 SMD Duma seats in 38 regions.

The logic outlined in chapter 2 suggests that types of party organization are not necessarily the same when it comes to how they shape electoral system design. Regions where party development largely represents the activities of new political organizations should have been more likely to adopt an electoral system with greater proportionality. Meanwhile, regions where party development reflects the continued organization of old communist ties were more likely to adopt SMD electoral systems, all else being equal. Accordingly, the percentage of party-nominated, SMD deputies per region is separated into two variables: the percentage communist successor parties nominated (i.e., CPRF and the Agrarian Party of Russia) and the percentage all other parties nominated.[16]

The next explanatory variable included in the analysis measures ethnic heterogeneity in the regions. Since electoral systems play a critical role in the parliamentary representation of ethnic minorities, it stands to reason that the distribution of ethnic groups in the regions may have influenced electoral system choice. However, the relationship between electoral systems and ethnic minorities is a complicated one, because the consequences of electoral systems on ethnic representation are far from certain. For example, when an ethnic group enjoys majority or plurality status in certain territories, the group may prefer SMDs as a way to guarantee political representation in parliament. In the United States, for example, African American and Hispanic members of Congress are often elected from districts where their minority groups constitute a geographic majority (Grofman et al. 1992). Despite this apparent advantage, however, multimember systems may actually provide greater representation to ethnic minorities, because the larger magnitudes permit smaller parties a greater opportunity for survival, as well as the potential to influence policy as a minority party in a coalition government. By contrast, SMDs favor two-party systems, which work against smaller ethnic parties and favor broader, catchall parties often representing the ethnic majority. Under such systems, the major parties representing the ethnic majority will not require a coalition government to make policy, thus making irrelevant what would be small, but potentially pivotal parties under PR (Taagepera 1994, 237).

At the national level in Russia, ethnic representation has been proportional, and surprisingly, this proportionality has not varied dramatically between the PR and SMD halves of the election. Moser (2001) pinpoints two factors in explaining the legislative representation of ethnic minorities in Russia's Duma elections: the politicization of ethnic minorities in their ethnic homelands and the assimilation of certain non-Russian minorities (most notably Ukrainians). However, Moser also notes that different types of ethnic minorities perform better in the different segments of the election. Ethnic groups that were without a designated homeland and were more assimilated (Belorussians, Jews, and Ukrainians) fared better under the PR segment of the election. Meanwhile, more geographically concentrated minorities enjoyed greater representation in the SMD half of the election.

These findings suggest that the dynamic between Russia's national electoral system and the representation of minority groups could differ substantially from the dynamic between regional electoral systems and the representation of these same minority groups in the regional legislatures. Specifically, the federal structure of the Russian Federation itself intentionally recognizes the geographic concentrations of the more prominent minority groups in the country. As a result, some national minorities comprise either a majority (e.g., Chuvashia, Tuva) or a plurality (e.g., Kalmykia, Tatarstan) of the populations in their republics, which (not coincidentally) are named after these groups. In addition to the titular minorities in the republics, however, other ethnic minorities, as well as ethnic Russians, often make up sizable percentages of the populations living within the republics' borders. The republics of Bashkortostan and Dagestan serve as two striking examples of the ethnic heterogeneity in Russia's republics. In January 2001, approximately 22% of the population in Bashkortostan was Bashkir, 39% was Russian, and about 28% was Tatar (Goskomstat Rossii 2001, 296). The republic of Dagestan, meanwhile, consists of more than 30 recognized ethnic groups with populations ranging from 1,000 to 500,000 (see Ware and Kisriev 1999). The largest ethnicity in Dagestan is Avar, and its members comprise 27.5% of the population. Ethnic Russians, on the other hand, make up only 9% of the population there (Goskomstat Rossii 2001, 216).

While ethnic heterogeneity is generally perceived as a contextual difference between republics and other regions, it also varies significantly in other areas of Russia. Autonomous okrugs, in particular, are regions named after different non-Russian nationalities. The percentage of ethnic Russians in these regions ranges from 36% in Komi-Permiak to almost 68% in Evenk. Even the predominantly Russian oblasts vary in terms of their ethnic composition, ranging from 72% Russian in Orenburg to over 97% Russian in several other oblasts (Goskomstat 2001, v1). Accordingly, the number of ethnic groups in the regions and their relative sizes could influence the design of regional parliamentary electoral systems, since regions with many sizable ethnic groups are also less likely to have one group comprising a majority of the population. Such regions are likely to adopt more proportional electoral systems, all else being equal.

To measure the ethnic composition in the regions, I use the effective number of ethnic groups. This measure first weights the population percentage of each ethnic group against itself in order to emphasize larger groups and discount smaller groups. It then sums all of the weighted components: Σe_i^2, where e_i is the fractional share of the ith group. The result of this calculation is often called the Herfindahl-Hirschmann index. The effective number of ethnic groups is simply the inverse of the Herfindahl-Hirschmann index: $N_{eff} = 1 / \Sigma e_i^2$ (see Ordeshook and Shvetsova 1994, 108).[17]

While there are plenty of reasons to expect the preceding independent variables to influence electoral system choice in Russia's regions, the political environment in the regions also suggests that certain independent variables should matter in certain contexts and not in others. For example, where only the executive branch designed the electoral system, the pro-reform chief executives may have adopted SMDs as a way to show their support for Yeltsin, or because they interpreted Yeltsin's recommendation as a sign that SMD systems would favor reform-oriented politicians. As the months passed, however, chief executives probably designed their electoral systems with a greater understanding of which electoral features would benefit different types of politicians. Thus, the timing of the electoral system decision is more likely to prove significant where electoral system design was solely in the hands of the chief executive. Likewise, the composition of the regional legislatures should have mattered primarily in those cases where the parliament actually had a voice in the design of the electoral system.[18] Accordingly, the empirical analysis should examine whether electoral system choice in places where regional legislatures had been dissolved actually differ from those where the legislatures remained active.

Dichotomous variables are commonly included in regression analyses to assess whether certain explanatory variables have different effects in different contexts. For example, as indicated above, the inclusion of the dummy variable, Republics, permits one to determine the impact of executive political orientations while holding constant whether the particular chief executive headed a republic. However, an equally important contextual issue—the distribution of authority between the regional branches of government—happens to be highly collinear with region type.[19] In other words, the analysis must control for both the distribution of power among the regional branches of government and region type, but the distribution of power among the regional branches of government often reflects the type of region. The regional soviets in the republics were much less likely to have been dissolved following the 1993 constitutional crisis than other regional legislatures. In fact, these legislative bodies were operative in all but one republic, Sakha, during the period leading up to the new legislative elections. Meanwhile, although the other regions had independent regional executives when governmental reform was initiated in October 1993, this was not true of all republics.[20]

To assess the impact of the main theoretical variables on the bases of contextual differences, while avoiding the collinearity that results from including a dummy variable for region type alongside dummy variables for the distribution of authority between branches of government, the analysis divides the 86 regions into two samples. Cases where chief executives were the only regional institutions in power when the decisions were made are separated from cases where legislatures were active. The dichotomous variable, Republic, is then used to assess whether the increased liberty granted to these regions shaped their electoral system decisions while controlling for the effect of this contextual differences on other key theoretical variables.[21]

In addition to the dichotomous variable, Republic, the analysis employs a second dichotomous variable—called No Independent Executive—to distinguish those republics where active legislatures operated alone from those republics where active legislatures worked alongside an independent executive. In the latter instances, the combination of more outsider-oriented deputies in office and the threat of an executive veto were hypothesized (in chapter 2) as potentially bolstering the bargaining position of legislative outsiders. Thus, the variable, No Independent Executive, is used to indicate those cases where the legislatures not only remained active but also faced no threat of executive veto, which may have resulted in different electoral system decisions than would have been made had an independent executive existed. This variable also represents an important control variable for executive orientation because it distinguishes those regions where executives did not take a public position on Yeltsin's actions during the 1993 constitutional crisis from those where an independent executive simply did not exist.

EMPIRICAL RESULTS

Multivariate ordinary-least-squares regression analysis is used to determine the effect of each independent variable on the average district magnitude, weighted average district magnitude, and assembly size of the electoral systems that governed the first regional legislative elections. The results of the multivariate regression analyses are presented in tables 3.3 and 3.4.

Table 3.3 presents the findings for those regions where the governor was responsible for the design of the electoral system. Table 3.4 presents the findings for those regions where the regional soviet remained active during the design of the electoral system. The unstandardized coefficients listed in tables 3.3 and 3.4 estimate the size of the change in each dependent variable associated with a one-unit change in the given independent variable, holding constant all other independent variables in the equation. A positive coefficient indicates that an increase in the independent variable yields an increase in the proportionality of the electoral system. A negative coefficient suggests a negative relationship between the independent variable and the proportionality of the electoral system. The asterisks indicate whether the coefficient estimates meet standard levels of significance.[22] Tables 3.3 and 3.4 also report the standardized coefficients, or betas, of each independent variable. The betas indicate the number of standard deviations that the dependent variable shifts for each standard deviation change in the explanatory variable when the other independent variables are held constant. While interpreting betas is less intuitive than interpreting unstandardized coefficients, standardization assures comparability of the explanatory variables' impacts when the independent variables are measured differently.

TABLE 3.3 **INFLUENCES ON ELECTORAL SYSTEM DECISIONS MADE BY EXECUTIVES ONLY**

	Average DM	Beta	*WADM*	Beta	*Assembly Size*	Beta
	DEPENDENT VARIABLES					
Constant	1.01		1.00		11.42	
	(1.04)		(1.10)		(15.31)	
Political Openness, 1990	0.10	0.22	0.08	0.17	-0.40	-0.08
	(0.06)		(0.07)		(0.75)	
Executive's Position on Yelstin's Actions, 1993	-0.80	-0.30	-0.74	-0.29	8.20	0.30
	(0.40)		(0.43)		(4.89)	
Months since 1993 Duma Election	0.67***	0.87	0.62***	0.85	-0.00	-0.00
	(0.09)		(0.10)		(1.33)	
Level of Intra-elite Competition, 1993	-0.13	-0.13	-0.13	-0.13	-1.27	-0.12
	(0.13)		(0.14)		(1.68)	
New Party Development	-0.02	-0.01	0.12	0.04	-3.26	-0.10
	(0.40)		(0.43)		(4.84)	
Communist Party Prominence	0.39	0.09	0.25	0.06	4.32	0.10
	(0.54)		(0.58)		(6.74)	
Republic	3.50*	0.48	3.08*	0.43	24.90	0.33
	(1.29)		(1.37)		(15.21)	
Change in Public Support for Yeltsin	0.01	0.07	0.00	0.01	-0.15	-0.13
	(0.02)		(0.02)		(0.22)	
Independently Elected Executive	-0.86	-0.23	-0.86	-0.23	-1.05	-0.03
	(0.53)		(0.56)		(6.99)	
Ethnic Fractionalization Index	-1.06*	-0.40	-0.78	-0.30	6.33	0.23
	(0.51)		(0.54)		(6.35)	
Population Size (in tens of thousands)	—		—		0.01*	0.49
					(0.00)	
Adj. R²	0.57		0.48		0.45	
N	37		37		37	
SEE	0.79		0.84		9.26	

The first column for each equation provides the unstandardized coefficients with the standard errors in parentheses. The second column lists the standardized coefficients (or beta weights).

  * Indicates significance at the .05 level.

  ** Indicates significance at the .01 level.

*** Indicates significance at the .001 level. All tests are two-tailed.

TABLE 3.4   **INFLUENCES ON ELECTORAL SYSTEM DECISIONS WHERE REGIONAL SOVIETS REMAINED ACTIVE**

	Average DM		*WADM*		*Assembly Size*	
		Beta		*Beta*		*Beta*
Constant	0.60*		0.18		-25.07*	
	(0.24)		(0.33)		(12.86)	
Political Openness, 1990	0.07***	0.51	0.13***	0.61	-0.30	-0.03
	(0.02)		(0.02)		(0.89)	
Executive's Position on Yeltsin's Actions, 1993	0.17	0.21	0.18	0.14	-3.00	-0.05
	(0.11)		(0.15)		(5.83)	
Months since 1993 Duma Election	0.00	0.10	0.00	0.02	0.06	0.02
	(0.01)		(0.01)		(0.35)	
Level of Intra-elite Competition, 1993	-0.02	-0.05	-0.05	-0.09	3.28	0.10
	(0.06)		(0.08)		(2.91)	
New Party Development	-0.23	-0.19	-0.41	-0.22	23.70*	0.24
	(0.18)		(0.24)		(8.88)	
Communist Party Prominence	0.75**	0.44	1.02**	0.38	2.20	0.02
	(0.25)		(0.34)		(13.07)	
Republic	-0.16	-0.19	-0.27	-0.21	27.16*	0.40
	(0.23)		(0.31)		(11.55)	
Change in Public Support for Yeltsin	0.00	0.10	0.01*	0.27	-0.04	-0.02
	(0.00)		(0.00)		(0.13)	
Independently Elected Executive	0.22	0.25	0.65*	0.48	0.34	0.01
	(0.18)		(0.24)		(9.13)	
No Independent Executive	0.10	0.09	0.28	0.15	1.55	0.01
	(0.26)		(0.35)		(13.18)	
Ethnic Fraction-alization Index	0.06	0.14	0.16	0.24	13.33**	0.38
	(0.08)		(0.10)		(3.94)	
Population Size (in tens of thousands)	—		—		0.02***	0.57
					(0.00)	
Adj. R²	0.25		0.45		0.71	
N	49		49		49	
SEE	0.35		0.48		17.81	

DEPENDENT VARIABLES

The first column for each equation provides the unstandardized coefficients with the standard errors in parentheses. The second column lists the standardized coefficients (or beta weights).

  * Indicates significance at the .05 level.
 ** Indicates significance at the .01 level.
*** Indicates significance at the .001 level. All tests are two-tailed.

As the equations in tables 3.3 and 3.4 suggest, the range of variance in Russia's regional electoral system decisions explained by the theoretical model varies from a modest amount being explained (adjusted R^2 equals 0.25) to a large amount being explained (adjusted R^2 equals 0.71). More importantly, the equations provide support for the theory's main hypotheses.

First, where chief executives alone designed the electoral systems, the timing of the decisions had a substantial effect on electoral system proportionality, as measured by district magnitude: As more months passed, chief executives designed electoral systems with greater average district magnitudes. In fact, this variable had the strongest influence on the district sizes. Because the analysis controls for the political orientation of the chief executives, this result suggests that the adoption of more proportional systems did not necessarily reflect the desire of pro-Yeltsin politicians to design electoral systems that would elect reform-oriented politicians. While the negative coefficient for the variable, Executive's Political Orientation, indicates that this was a reasonable expectation, its effect is minimal. As a result, factors besides the election of reform-oriented politicians appear to have been more influential in shaping the electoral system decisions of regional executives.

One possible explanation for this result relates to the looming constitutional decisions in the regions. In many regions, the selection of a parliamentary electoral system was just the beginning of an institutional design process in which subsequent decisions focused on the allocation of powers between the executive and legislative branches of government. The prospects of negotiating a new constitution (in the republics) or a new charter (in the other regions) could have guided executive preferences over parliamentary electoral system design, if presidents and governors realized that electoral system choice could be used to attain greater leverage in subsequent constitutional debates. For example, presidents and governors could have promoted electoral systems that used both PR and SMDs as a way to win support from a greater number of political organizations. Likewise, mixing different electoral systems can be used to increase the likelihood of a fragmented parliament. The creation of a fragmented parliament may work to the advantage of the executive branch since elected deputies could find that their prospects for reelection depend on effective policy. From this perspective, the need to create a strong executive capable of ensuring consistent policy outcomes may counteract a tendency among legislative deputies to prefer limited executive power (Shugart 1997). The case study of electoral system choice in Saratov oblast in the next chapter provides an opportunity to test the validity of these explanations.

The second variable to influence the average district magnitude of the regional electoral systems designed by chief executives is the dichotomous variable, Republic. The regression analysis reveals that, based on the entire picture provided by the data (which includes 28 of the 37 cases being non-republic regions with district magnitudes equal to one), republican presidents were significantly more likely to adopt electoral systems with higher district magnitudes than were governors, all else being equal. This relationship is striking given the fact that there was only one republic, Sakha, among the 37 cases examined, and it adopted SMDs. In other words, the decision to adopt SMDs in Sakha was not the result of its "republicness" but the combination of political characteristics depicted by other independent variables in the model.[23] This result suggests that some unmeasured aspect of Sakha (i.e., something besides its ethnic diversity or the orientation of its governor) leads the model to predict that other republics with only presidents in office (had they existed) would have promoted electoral systems with higher district magnitudes.

One possible explanation of this finding draws on the idea that executives might design electoral systems that promote party fragmentation in order to gain greater leverage over the parliament (Shugart 1997). However, the ability to successfully implement this strategy probably varied between republics and other regions. While all independent executives, who were solely responsible for designing the electoral system, would probably use the decision to win support from future legislators or to produce a fragmented parliament (all else being equal), republican presidents were more likely to act in this manner than governors, because the former enjoyed greater liberty over institutional reform within their borders.[24]

The only other explanatory variable that seems to have substantially shaped the district magnitudes in those cases where only independent chief executives designed the electoral systems is ethnic heterogeneity. The ethnic fractionalization index is significantly and negatively correlated with average district magnitude, although its impact diminishes notably when the dependent variable is the weighted average district magnitude. Thus, to the extent chief executives considered the ethnic heterogeneity of their regions, those who governed regions with larger numbers of ethnic groups actually adopted electoral systems with lower district magnitudes.

The negligible influences of the other explanatory variables in the first two equations of table 3.3 are interesting, but not surprising. In fact, the theory presented in chapter 2 suggests that the political orientation of the regional parliaments was not likely to shape electoral system design where the regional parliament had no direct voice in the design process. It is more surprising, however, that neither the level of elite competition nor the degree of regional party development significantly influenced gubernatorial decisions, although there is no reason to assume that these issues would systematically factor into a chief executive's decision calculus.

It is perhaps most surprising that neither the presence of an elected executive (rather than an appointed one) nor the changing levels of public support for Yeltsin shaped the average district magnitudes of those electoral systems designed solely by chief executives. The explanation of this null result is presented in the analysis of the electoral formulas, which suggests that elected chief executives responsible for designing the parliamentary electoral systems used the electoral formula to increase proportionality rather than to make changes in the system's average district magnitude.

In general, the theoretical factors that were expected to influence the proportionality of the electoral systems failed to influence assembly size where regional executives alone made these decisions. Instead, executive decisions on assembly size appear to have simply reflected considerations about population size: Executives ruling more populated regions were significantly more likely to create legislatures with higher assembly sizes, all else being equal. The failure of the variable, Republic, to significantly shape assembly size is striking, however. The comparative case analysis presented in the following chapter examines this finding in greater detail, although a potential explanation of this null result is discussed below.

As expected, the equations in table 3.4 reveal that electoral system design where legislatures remained active in the regions was a dramatically different process than it was in places where the legislatures had been dissolved. While the timing of the decision was the most important explanatory variable when chief executives determined the district magnitudes, it failed to influence districting decisions where the regional soviets remained active. Instead, the estimate of outsider influence in the regional soviets emerges as the most powerful explanation of average district magnitude. The greater the estimated influence of political outsiders in the regional parliament (based on 1990 levels of electoral competition in the regions), the higher the average district magnitude of the new parliamentary electoral system. Notice that this result emerges despite the fact that the model controls for 1993 levels of intra-elite competition in the regions.

The only other variable to substantially affect both measures of district magnitude is the regional organization of the communist successor parties. The equations reveal that higher average district magnitudes were more likely in regions where candidates nominated by communist successor parties won a greater percentage of SMD seats in the 1993 Duma election. This result suggests that more proportional electoral systems were more likely where communist successor parties were most visible: where members of the old regime employed party labels. However, after the collapse of the Soviet Union, the old Soviet administrative and economic elite proved better at adapting to the challenges of electoral politics than many other groups in society. As a result, they regularly used their political experience and personal connections to maintain positions of power without joining political parties. The puzzle, then, is why were explicit ties to communist successor parties important to members of the old regime in some regions but not in others? Golosov and Shevchenko (1999, 130) provide a plausible explanation: "resourceful political actors choose to be affiliated with a party only in the conditions when this adds to their electoral chances." In other words, the decision to run as a member of a communist successor party rather than as an independent during the SMD half of the 1993 Duma election resulted from a belief that such an affiliation was necessary for electoral success. And a factor likely to convince such candidates that party affiliation would be necessary is stiff competition from rival candidates appearing to benefit from party affiliations of their own. Thus, the percentage of SMD deputies from a region who were nominated by a communist successor party is possibly an indicator of overall party development in the regions.[25]

Two other explanatory variables that influenced the average district magnitude of the electoral systems where the regional legislatures remained active are 1) the change in public support for Yeltsin over time and 2) whether the executive was elected rather than appointed. Both of these variables meet standard levels of significance for the weighted average district magnitude but not for the simple average. Where the regional legislature remained active, increased public support for Yeltsin created an environment favorable to the adoption of more proportional electoral systems. In other words, decreasing public support for Yeltsin did not necessarily lead institutional designers to defy him and adopt more proportional electoral systems. Rather, SMDs were liklier where public opinion was increasingly anti-Yeltsin and a more proportional electoral system was likely where public opinion was becoming reform-oriented, or pro-Yeltsin. Thus, where the regional legislatures shaped the design of the electoral system, changing political winds in the regions shaped the electoral system decisions. This finding suggests that institutional designers were somewhat responsive to public attitudes in those cases where regional legislatures remained active during the design process. Specifically, the leverage of political outsiders in the regional legislatures may have depended somewhat on public opinion in the region. At the same time, however, electoral systems with higher district magnitudes were more likely in regions where active legislatures operated alongside elected chief executives, all else being equal. Therefore, as Treisman (1999) would expect, regions with elected chief executives and active legislatures were more likely to defy President Yeltsin than regions with appointed governors.

While the dichotomous variable, Republic, affected the average district magnitude of the regional electoral systems where only executives designed the electoral systems, it fails to influence district magnitude where the legislatures remained active. This null result actually makes sense based on the theory presented earlier. Chapter 2 argues that where both an independent chief executive and the legislature were in office when the electoral system was designed, the final decision should reflect bargaining between the two branches. Specifically, the regional executive could only influence the electoral system through the threat of a veto, which means that executive influence depended on the size and orientation of the parliamentary majority. If the parliamentary majority had the same electoral system preference as the chief executive, the executive's influence should not be noticeable. If the parliamentary majority had an electoral system preference different from the chief executive, the executive's influence depended on the size of the parliamentary majority. Where the size of the parliamentary majority was greater, the possibility of a veto was an empty threat. In other words, executive influence over electoral system design was diluted in those places where the regional legislatures remained active. Accordingly, the ability of republican presidents to use electoral system design to their own advantage, as occurred when only executives designed the electoral system, becomes less noticeable where republican legislatures remained active.

The third equation in table 3.4 reports the factors that shaped assembly size in those regions where the regional legislatures had a voice in the institutional design process. As in table 3.3 and as the general literature on electoral systems would suggest, assembly size tends to reflect population size. However, the third equation in table 3.4 also suggests that, where the regional soviets remained active, republics were more likely to create larger assemblies than other regions. While this result fails to emerge when executives control electoral system design, the contextual difference is logical. As potential competitors for seats in the new parliaments, legislators are likely to prefer more electoral opportunities to fewer electoral opportunities. Meanwhile, executives are less likely to be concerned with the size of the parliament beyond the issue of whether it provides adequate representation given the region's population size. As a result, larger assemblies should be more likely where legislators have greater influence over the decision. And, since republican legislators felt less obliged to adhere to the 50-deputy cap that the federal executive outlined, larger assembly sizes should be most prevalent in republics where legislatures remained active.

Two additional factors shaped assembly size in those regions where the legislatures remained active: the development of new, noncommunist political parties and ethnic heterogeneity. That is, larger assemblies were more likely in regions where new, noncommunist parties nominated a larger percentage of winning SMD candidates in the 1993 Duma election and in regions with a higher number of effective ethnic groups. These results suggest a couple of important findings. First, electoral system design was more likely to reflect a region's political and societal heterogeneity if the regional legislature played a role in the decision than if the decision rested solely with the executive. Indeed, to the extent the executives considered social heterogeneity in their electoral system decisions, they designed electoral systems that were likely to underrepresent political and societal minorities. Second, even where legislatures remained active, political and societal heterogeneity significantly increased proportionality only through the assembly size, as opposed to the electoral system feature that has the greatest impact on electoral proportionality, the district magnitude. This suggests that regional legislators may have been more responsive to constituent interests than were executives, but only to the extent that it does not undermine their prospects for electoral success.

CHOOSING AN ELECTORAL FORMULA

Thus far, the analysis has focused on average district magnitude and as-sembly size as important electoral system decisions. Indeed, in terms of the proportionality of an electoral system, district magnitude is regularly con-sidered to be the most important element. However, the regional electoral systems in post-Soviet Russia also varied significantly in terms of their elec-toral formula, and the choice among different electoral formulas, or a com-bination of formulas, is an important issue to consider.

The preferred statistical method for examining this decision is multi-nomial logistic regression (or multinomial logit), which allows one to examine the influence of different independent variables on a depend-ent variable consisting of more than two, unordered categories. How-ever, this statistical technique also requires a significant number of cases to exist in each category of the dependent variable if the analyst plans to examine the effects of multiple explanatory variables. This degrees-of-freedom requirement limits the applicability of multinomial logit to the analysis of electoral system choice in Russia's regions. Specifically, due to collinearity issues, the 86 cases under investigation need to be separated in order to adequately assess the impact of the different explanatory variables. This division creates one population of 37 cases where only the executive was in power to design the electoral system and one of 49 cases where both branches of government remained in power while the electoral system was designed. In addition, the different electoral systems are divided into five distinct categories: 1) SMD-plurality, 2) SMD-majority, 3) only MMD-plurality, 4) MMD-plurality alongside SMD-plurality, and 5) SMD-plurality alongside party-list PR. The problem that emerges, therefore, is that most of these categories do not have a sufficient number of cases to perform multinomial logit. Collapsing the categories to three (SMD-plurality, SMD-majority, and "other") fails to overcome the problem.

Due to the constraint of comparing a relatively small number of cases, the effects of different theoretical variables on electoral system choice are investigated using partial correlation analysis rather than multinomial logit: Each independent variable is correlated on each type of electoral sys-tem while holding all other independent variables constant. The drawback to this approach is that it does not permit one to determine how well the theoretical model as a whole performs in terms of explaining variation in the dependent variable. However, the benefit of partial correlation analysis is that it provides some indication of which independent variables influ-enced the adoption of certain electoral formulas (or formula combinations) but not others.

Tables 3.5 and 3.6 present the partial correlation coefficients for the dif-ferent explanatory variables and the five different types of electoral systems de-scribed above. These results flesh out some distinctions among the adoption of

SMD-plurality systems, SMD-majority systems, and electoral systems that added greater levels of proportionality by using only MMD-plurality, mixing MMD-plurality with SMD-plurality, or mixing party-list PR with SMD-plurality. The results from the partial correlation analyses confirm a few previous findings. SMD-plurality systems, that is, those that Yeltsin recommended, were significantly less likely in regions where executives designed the electoral systems and where more time elapsed between the executives' decisions and the 1993 Duma election. Likewise, where the regional legislatures remained active, SMD-plurality systems were significantly less likely where the 1990 regional elections were more competitive, thus increasing the likely influence of political outsiders in the regional soviets.

What factors influenced the adoption of SMD-majority systems? According to the partial correlation coefficients, SMD-majority systems were more likely where the regional legislatures remained active and intra-elite competition was higher. The probability of their adoption increased even more if the legislature operated in the absence of an independent executive. Where the level of intra-elite competition was high, legislators preferred two rounds of balloting, so that many candidates could compete initially and electoral coalitions could be created if no single candidate enjoyed a majority of support. This electoral system, therefore, would allow rival insiders to compete initially but coalesce, if necessary, to keep political newcomers out of office. However, the process (or perhaps, the prospect) of negotiating with an independent executive appears to have constrained the adoption of such a system in many cases. Meanwhile, where executives alone were responsible for electoral system design, elected executives were significantly more likely to adopt SMD-majority systems than were appointed governors.

SMD-majority systems are generally more proportional than SMD-plurality systems because "the variety of parties having much in common does not adversely affect the total number of seats they gain since in this system they can always regroup for the second ballot" (Duverger 1954, 240). Accordingly, a larger number of parties tends to win parliamentary representation under SMD-majority, since it is unlikely that, among two similar parties, the same party's candidates will always compete and win in the second round (with the other party's candidates always failing to advance or win a seat). In some instances, the first party's candidate will win thanks to the support of voters for the second party's candidate, and in other instances, the second party's candidate will win thanks to the support of voters from the first party's candidate. What this means then is that, when provided with SMD-plurality as a default electoral system, the adoption of an SMD-majority electoral system is perhaps the simplest way of adding greater proportionality. And, in Russia's regions, the results of the partial correlation coefficients suggest that SMD-majority systems were most likely in those cases where political bargaining among branches or levels of government was unnecessary: where only the legislature made the decision or where only an elected executive made the

TABLE 3.5   **PARTIAL CORRELATION COEFFICIENTS OF INFLUENCES ON ELECTORAL SYSTEM TYPES WHERE ONLY THE EXECUTIVE WAS IN OFFICE**

	SMD-Plurality	SMD-Majority	MMD-Plurality	MMD-Plurality and SMD-Plurality	Party-list PR and SMD-Plurality
Political Openness, 1990	-0.30	-0.00	0.27	0.29	-0.20
Executive's Position on Yeltsin's Actions, 1993	0.17	0.17	-0.23	-0.17	0.10
Months since 1993 Election	-0.44*	-0.16	0.13	0.50**	0.11
Level of Intra-elite Competition, 1993	0.14	-0.26	0.12	-0.14	-0.06
New Party Development	-0.17	-0.06	-0.08	0.37	-0.07
Communist Party Prominence	-0.26	-0.28	0.20	0.39*	-0.17
Change in Public Support for Yeltsin	-0.08	0.11	-0.14	0.27	-0.16
Independently Elected Executive	-0.19	0.65***	-0.25	0.13	-0.01
Republic	-0.25	0.33	0.23	-0.01	0.02
Ethnic Fractionalization Index	0.13	0.09	-0.24	-0.03	0.12

N = 37

* Indicates significance at the .05 level.
** Indicates significance at the .01 level.
*** Indicates significance at the .001 level. All tests are two-tailed.

decision. These results lend support to the idea that the fewer the actors involved in the design of the electoral system, the less complicated the electoral system will be. Rather than adding party-list PR or mixing MMD-plurality with SMD-plurality to increase proportionality, designers simply shifted from SMD-plurality to SMD-majority.

None of the independent variables in either sample helps explain why regional politicians adopted only MMD-plurality systems as opposed

TABLE 3.6   **PARTIAL CORRELATION COEFFICIENTS OF INFLUENCES ON ELECTORAL SYSTEM TYPES WHERE THE LEGISLATURE REMAINED ACTIVE**

	SMD-Plurality	SMD-Majority	MMD-Plurality	MMD-Plurality and SMD-Plurality	Party-list PR and SMD-Plurality
Political Openness, 1990	-0.37*	0.00	0.12	0.44	-0.16
Executive's Position on Yeltsin's Actions, 1993	-0.18	0.05	0.18	0.08	-0.09
Months since 1993 Election	0.23	-0.27	-0.07	0.20	-0.33*
Level of Intra-elite Competition, 1993	-0.13	0.35*	-0.15	0.09	-0.19
New Party Development	0.26	-0.22	0.03	-0.13	-0.08
Communist Party Prominence	-0.16	-0.25	0.29	0.11	0.08
Change in Public Support for Yeltsin	-0.21	0.00	0.08	0.03	0.28
Independently Elected Executive	-0.46	0.14	-0.12	0.52**	0.03
No Independent Executive	-0.29	0.31*	0.04	0.13	-0.09
Republic	0.04	-0.06	0.14	-0.30	0.30
Ethnic Fractionalization Index	-0.27	0.23	-0.05	0.22	-0.05

N = 37

---

* Indicates significance at the .05 level.
** Indicates significance at the .001 level. All tests are two-tailed.

to some other alternative. However, if only executives designed the electoral system, MMD-plurality systems were often mixed with SMD-plurality when they took greater time making the decision or where political parties were more developed. Where regional legislatures remained active, MMD-plurality was more often mixed with SMD-plurality where the executive was elected rather than appointed. Thus, elected executives enjoyed more leverage over electoral system decisions than did appointed governors, where the regional legislatures remained active.

The partial correlation coefficients do not explain why an executive on his own would adopt a system that mixed SMD-plurality with party-list PR. Instead, the statistical analysis demonstrates that electoral systems combining SMD-plurality and party-list PR were significantly more likely in regions where legislatures remained active and decisions were made early. This finding confirms Golosov's (2004) speculation that the adoption of such systems resulted from the regional politicians mimicking the federal electoral system. The issue as to why chief executives might mix SMD-plurality with party-list PR is taken up in the next chapter, which relies on a comparative case analysis to highlight key nuances associated with the politics of electoral system choice.

CONCLUSION

The statistical analyses presented in this chapter highlight the intervening influence of the federal government, especially the federal executive, on the design of regional electoral systems. First, the 1993 crisis played a pivotal role in shaping regional electoral system design, when independent chief executives emerged as the only individuals commanding governmental authority in several regions, such as Saratov oblast and the republic of Sakha. However, the statistical analysis indicates that decreasing levels of uncertainty altered how executives designed their new legislative electoral systems. The multivariate results presented in table 3.3 and the partial correlation coefficients in table 3.5 suggest that, as time progressed, executives were more likely to adopt electoral systems with higher district magnitudes, and these systems most likely mixed MMD-plurality with SMD-plurality. The importance of timing holds regardless of whether the executive supported or opposed Yeltsin's actions in the 1993 constitutional crisis. It also holds despite the fact that the levels of intra-elite competition and party development in the regions failed to shape electoral design. Thus, while executives deviated from the adoption of SMD-plurality, they appear to have done so on the basis of personal assessments of politics in their regions, and only after they had either acquired more information on the likely consequences of the electoral systems or felt more confident that Yeltsin would not remove them from power for such deviation.

Another important finding is that, when the timing of the decision is controlled, some executives still strayed from Yeltsin's recommendation. Elected executives, in particular, were significantly likely to disobey Yeltsin's decree. Their waywardness, however, was generally limited to changing the electoral formula of the SMD system from plurality to majority. In addition, while electoral systems that combined MMD-plurality with SMD-plurality were more likely in cases in which executives made their decisions later, they were also significantly more likely where party systems were more developed.

The multivariate analysis in table 3.4 and the partial correlation coefficients in table 3.6 suggest that the degree of political competition in the regions in 1990 proved to be the most important factor determining electoral system design in those regions where the legislatures influenced the electoral system decision. The greater the political competition, the greater the likelihood that regional institutional designers adopted more proportional electoral systems: those with higher average district magnitudes or an electoral formula different from SMD-plurality. To the extent that greater competition in the 1990 elections can be correlated with more outsider-oriented politicians in office, these results support the assertion that, where a legislature designed the electoral system, its decision reflected the distribution of insiders and outsiders among its members.

Among the alternative electoral arrangements designed where regional legislatures remained active, SMD-majority systems were more likely in regions that experienced higher levels of intra-elite competition or where the regional legislatures made the decisions in the absence of an independent executive. Since most regional legislators were members of the old regime, the former finding emphasizes the strategic benefits that runoff elections provide to legislative candidates with similar orientations and backgrounds. The latter finding provides some circumstantial evidence for the assertion that electoral system decisions are less complex where fewer actors are involved in the process. Because the mixture of MMD-plurality and SMD-plurality was the preferred alternative to using only SMDs where the executive alone designed the electoral system, the fact that such systems were significantly more likely where elected executives existed alongside regional legislatures suggests that executive influence was higher where executives were elected. It also adds support to the notion that electoral system design becomes more complicated as the number of effective actors increases. Finally, the strongly negative relationship between the adoption of systems that combine party-list PR and SMD-plurality with the timing of the decision rather than other variables, like party development, indicates that these decisions are largely the product of legislators imitating the federal system.

Assembly size decisions in developing democracies are rarely examined in comparative politics. However, assembly size also determines the proportionality of new electoral systems. In Russia's regions, several factors influenced the size of the new legislatures. Where only the executive determined the assembly size, the region's population size proves to be the only significant explanatory variable, as Taagepera and Shugart (1989) would expect. Where the legislatures remained active during the design process, population size was still the most significant variable, but higher levels of ethnic fractionalization and party development also increased assembly size, as did the type of region, with republics adopting larger assemblies. The latter finding was expected due to the specific federal context in Russia at the time. The significant effects of ethnic heterogeneity and party development on assembly size where the legislatures remained active and the absence of these effects where the legislatures were dissolved suggest that legislatures were more responsive to societal needs than executives when designing electoral systems.

The next chapter relies on comparative case analysis to examine electoral system choice in the Russian Federation, so as to delve deeper into the politics of intra-elite and intergovernmental rivalries that large-N statistical analyses tend to gloss over. Specifically, chapter 4 relies on electoral information from regional newspapers as well as expert and scholarly accounts of the political developments to uncover nuances of the institutional design process. The four case studies provide an opportunity to investigate potential exceptions to the broad trends highlighted in this chapter. Chapter 5 considers whether the electoral systems governing the first parliamentary elections in Russia's regions produced the outcomes their institutional designers expected.

FOUR— DISCERNING TREES IN THE FOREST

The preceding chapter used a range of statistical analyses to assess the validity of the theoretical assertions about electoral system choice in Russia's regions presented earlier in chapter 2. However, its focus on the forest rather than the trees risks overlooking key subtleties of individual cases that also may advance our understanding of how regional electoral system decisions are made. Accordingly, this chapter examines the parliamentary electoral system decisions in four Russian regions: the oblasts of Novosibirsk and Saratov and the republics of Buriatia and Udmurtia. Specifically, the chapter discusses the results of the 1990 regional soviet elections in these four cases, develops a framework for comparing the compositions of their legislative bodies, and then investigates in each case the level of elite division and party development leading up to the 1993 constitutional crisis in order to determine whether these issues shaped the electoral preferences of the deputies. Where independent executives were in power when the institutional decisions were made, the comparative case studies consider the extent to which these actors influenced the choice of the parliamentary electoral system.

Like the majority of Russian regions, Novosibirsk oblast and the republic of Udmurtia adopted SMD-plurality systems to govern their first parliamentary elections. Saratov oblast, meanwhile, used a mixed electoral system in which 25 deputies were elected via SMD-plurality and 10 deputies were elected through party-list PR in a single oblast-wide district. The republic of Buriatia, on the other hand, relied on an SMD-majority system to elect its new legislative deputies. In addition, while the two oblasts both conformed to the 50-deputy limit outlined by the Russian president, both republics created parliaments exceeding this number.

Despite the differences in electoral system design, the four regions are similar to one another along an array of variables. The Russian president appointed governors in both Novosibirsk oblast and Saratov oblast well before the 1993 constitutional crisis. In comparison, neither republic had yet created an independent chief executive prior to the adoption of a new parliamentary electoral system. In addition, Novosibirsk resembles Saratov and Buriatia resembles Udmurtia in terms of how their publics voted in the 1993 federal Duma election (see Clem and Craumer 1995), as well as in the economic conditions prevailing in these regions at the time (e.g., percentage of the population below subsistence) (Centre of Regional Analysis and Forecasting 1998). In fact, following the 1995 federal Duma election, Russia's Central Election Commission classified each of the 89 regions in terms of its dominant political orientation based on the voting behavior of the populations in national elections. All four of the regions—Buriatia, Novosibirsk, Saratov and Udmurtia—were classified as predominantly communist (Central Election Commission 1996, 246–49).

Since republics differ from other regions in Russia on the basis of ethnic heterogeneity, the two republics selected were also chosen with their ethnic compositions in mind. The republic of Buriatia and the republic of Udmurtia resemble one another in terms of the size of their titular ethnic groups: In Buriatia, Buriats represent 24% of the population, while Udmurts represent approximately 31% of the population in Udmurtia (Karasik 1994).[1]

THE 1990 SOVIET ELECTIONS

The ascension of Mikhail Gorbachev to the post of general secretary of the Communist Party in March 1985 ushered in a new era for Soviet politics. Gorbachev began his tenure promoting a steady advancement of earlier Soviet policies and asserting that an acceleration of economic growth through economic restructuring, perestroika, could resolve the economic and social problems confronting the Soviet Union (for a discussion of the reforms, see Brown 1996; Miller 1993; Sakwa 1990; White 1994). Although Gorbachev only tentatively mentioned the need for changes to electoral procedures in the Soviet Union during the 26th Party Congress in 1986, by early 1987 Gorbachev's reforms began to take a more radical direction.

In January 1987, during an opening address to the Plenum of the Central Committee of the Communist Party of the Soviet Union (CPSU), Gorbachev indicated that the Soviet Union needed more democratic institutions if it was to overcome the "dogma" and "scholastic theorizing" that had inhibited the resolution of many social questions. Gorbachev then called for more open, competitive elections as a way to involve the population in governmental affairs and to weed out corrupt and incompetent officials. The 1987 Plenum adopted a resolution that supported the democratic ideas of Gorbachev and agreed to an electoral experiment. In June 1987, competitive elections were scheduled for about 5% of the deputies to district, town, and village soviets. These elections to local soviets in June 1987 validated the view among political reformers that competitive elections were possible in the Soviet Union (Urban 1990, 21–22).

As a political struggle between reformers and hard-liners ensued, Gorbachev reacted to harsh criticism from his conservative opponents by radically reforming the political system (see Eklof 1989; Hewett et al. 1991; Urban 1990).[2] Gorbachev used the 19th Party Conference in June 1988 to replace the old Soviet parliament with a 2,250-member Congress of People's Deputies. The election to the Congress of People's Deputies featured a radical innovation: a choice among candidates. Although the new Soviet electoral law (adopted 1 December 1988) maintained the Communist Party's political monopoly, it also allowed voter meetings of 500 or more to nominate candidates for the elections to the new Congress. As a result, the subsequent March 1989 elections gave Soviet voters the opportunity to choose from among 9,505 candidates (on the dynamics of these elections, see Aves 1992; Danilenko 1991; White et al. 1997).

In March 1990, the expansion of greater political choice continued, as regional and local elections were held in several Soviet republics, including the Russian SFSR and its administrative units (Colton 1991; White et al. 1997). However, in contrast to the transitional elections in Eastern Europe, opposition parties were officially absent in the March 1990 legislative elections. The only indication of partisan identification was whether a candidate was a member of the CPSU. A candidate who was not a CPSU member was identified as "non-party" *(bezpartiinyi)*. Nevertheless, some of the candidates in Russia were affiliated with political movements. The most prominent of these movements was the coalition of reformers under the banner of "Democratic Russia." Democratic Russia consisted of the Democratic Party of Russia, the Social Democratic Party of Russia, and the Democratic Platform. These three organizations formed a broad coalition of candidates who pushed for radical political and economic change. The coalition's goals included an end to the power and privilege of the Communist Party, a move toward a market economy, and the allocation of democratic freedoms and rights to Soviet citizens (Remington 1994, 70). Following the 1990 elections, however, steps taken by the coalition to consolidate into a single party were unsuccessful (Kelley 1991).

Besides opposition from the new democratic movements, the Communist Party establishment also encountered political competition during the March 1990 elections at the republic and local levels from political forces promoting an imperialistic and conservative brand of Russian nationalism. These movements included moderates who denounced the Communist

Party establishment, while openly identifying with anti-Gorbachev Communist Party leaders, as well as anti-Semitic radicals who sanctioned violence and admired the strong role the Communist Party played in integrating the nation (Moses 1991, 107). During the 1990 elections, the conservative, nationalist movements united under an umbrella group known as the Bloc of Public-Patriotic Movements of Russia. This electoral coalition enjoyed support from the General Staff of the Armed Forces of the Soviet Union, various prelates from the upper echelons of the Russian Orthodox Church, and the more conservative elements of the CPSU apparatus (Duncan 1992, 83). Following the 1990 elections, three major organizations on the Russian right—Pamiat' (Memory), Otechestvo (Fatherland), and the United Front of Working People (OFT by its Russian initials)—coalesced to form the Initiative Committee for the Creation of the Russian Communist Party. This organization eventually formed the Communist Party of Russia as a new faction of the CPSU (Orttung 1992).

Due to a lack of popular support, the 1990 elections were a disappointment for the Russian nationalists. The OFT, for example, won only 10 seats out of the 400-seat regional soviet in Leningrad (Orttung 1992, 456–57). Meanwhile, the elections yielded some notable democratic victories, including parliamentary majorities in the city soviets of Moscow, Leningrad, and Sverdlovsk (see Duncan 1992; Remington 1994). However, while democratic movements performed well in some city elections, conservatives performed well in the regions (Helf and Hahn 1992; 511–12). In the Novosibirsk oblast soviet, in particular, around 82% of the deputies elected in 1990 were affiliated with Communist Party of the Soviet Union. These were either members (or candidates for membership) of the CPSU, or members of the Communist Youth League (the Komsomol). In the soviets of Saratov oblast, the republic of Buriatia, and the republic of Udmurtia, the percentages of deputies affiliated with the CPSU were larger: 84%, 84%, and 89%, respectively.[3]

While the soviets elected in 1990 represent possible designers of the new parliamentary electoral systems, party affiliation represents a less-than-ideal measure for classifying regional legislators as political insiders or outsiders in the soviets under investigation. Specifically, in a comparison of the more conservative oblast soviets with the more democratic city soviets in Russia's regions, Fish (1995, 193–94) emphasizes that a deputy's declared party affiliation has limits for determining the precise distribution between democratic and conservative deputies:

> Some deputies elected on the basis of radical platforms turned out to be fair-weather democrats at best, conservatives at worst. Many were "waverers" who sided now with conservatives, now with progressive positions. Others started with no clear convictions and underwent radicalization after their elections. In every soviet, at least a few Communists sided with the "democrats." Some who entered the soviets as members of the CPSU quit after the elections but did not announce it publicly, so gauging even how many Communists sat in a given legislature is difficult.

These findings reinforce Badovskii and Shutov's (1997) caution against generalizing on the basis of party affiliations in the regions. As mentioned earlier, they argue that terms like "communist" and "democrat" tended to lose their meaning in the regions, since such terms rarely reflected a person's political or ideological views, but instead indicated affiliation with a group supporting a specific person among the national or regional leadership.

A lack of precision, however, does not preclude the possibility of making logical estimates about the distribution of interests among the members of the regional parliaments. One approach for distinguishing between political insiders and outsiders is to classify the soviet deputies based on their likely entrenchment within the party-state apparatus.

During the Soviet era, political recruitment and mobility varied on the basis of the societal and occupational backgrounds of party members. Following the death of Stalin, in particular, Soviet politics experienced a broadening of interests at the national and local levels. By the 1960s, the Communist Party apparatus witnessed an increase in the number of specialized cadres who tended to be co-opted into party work after having established strong professional ties outside the party apparatus (see Fleron 1970; Gehlen and McBride 1968; Skilling and Griffiths 1971). In an examination of the political and occupational backgrounds of first secretaries of committees at the oblast level, Clark (1989) finds that upward political mobility was most common for individuals who held varied and responsible positions in the party and state apparatus. Individuals holding industrial posts enjoyed the greatest mobility among those individuals in positions outside of the party or state apparatus. Meanwhile, individuals with careers in agriculture had an opportunity to enter and advance in the political realm, but their chances were less than those for individuals in industry. Other occupational segments in society did not enjoy a significant opportunity for political recruitment and mobility.

Drawing on data published in the mass media after the March 1990 soviet elections in the two oblasts and two republics, the elected deputies can be classified in terms of their ties to the old regime. The occupational positions of the elected deputies in the regions are divided into four categories: 1) positions in the Communist Party or state apparatus; 2) positions in industry/transportation; 3) positions in agriculture; and 4) other positions not encompassed in the preceding categories, such as doctors, directors of schools, students, newspaper editors, and so on. To differentiate among elected deputies within the preceding categories, the occupational positions are ranked high, medium, and low. For example, in the category of party/state positions, elected deputies whose previous positions were first or second secretaries at the oblast/republic, *raion* (region within the oblast), or *gorod* (city) level are classified as having high status. Deputies of the regional parliaments are classified as having medium status, if they were members of executive committees at the raion or gorod level, deputies or representatives of an oblast/republic-level committee, or members of an oblast/republic-, raion-, or gorod-level soviet. Finally, deputies in the party/state category have low status if their positions prior to election were as deputies or representatives of non-executive committees at the raion or gorod level. (For a more detailed depiction of the status classification process for all four occupational categories, see appendix C.)

Table 4.1 presents this information for the republic of Udmurtia to demonstrate the logic of this approach. Similar tables for the republic of Buriatia and the oblasts of Novosibirsk and Saratov have been published elsewhere (see Moraski 2003). The last column lists the distribution of newly elected deputies across the status categories for those deputies who were not members of the Communist Party (or Komsomol) during the 1990 regional elections.[4] While some occupational variation exists for nonparty members, it represented such a small fraction of the elected deputies in each region that collapsing them into one column permits the most worthwhile comparison. In addition to the raw number of deputies in each category, the tables also present these numbers as percentages of deputies in regional soviets as a whole. For example, 29 deputies in Udmurtia's soviet were members of the Communist Party and had held positions of high status within the party or state apparatus; this number represents around 15% of the soviet as a whole. Subtotals are also provided in the final row of each table to present the distribution of deputies in each of the four occupational categories regardless of status. For example, in the republic of Udmurtia, 52 deputies (about 26%) elected in 1990 were affiliated with the Communist Party and held positions in the party or state apparatus prior to the election.

Data such as those presented in table 4.1 can be used to estimate the minimum number of political insiders in each regional soviet. First, recognizing the dominant role of the Communist Party in Soviet society, the deputies elected in 1990 who were not listed as members of the Communist Party are categorized as outsiders. Then, drawing on the political mobility literature, occupational categories and status classifications are used to reflect the likelihood that the deputies affiliated with the Communist Party were political insiders. Since members of the party and state apparatus tended to be the most politically mobile during the Soviet period, likely insiders include deputies who were affiliated with the Communist Party and held such positions. While individuals affiliated with the Communist Party in industrial positions tended to have a good chance of political mobility in the Soviet era, their chances were not as good as those for members holding party or state positions. Therefore, only the deputies who were affiliated with the Communist Party and held high or medium positions in industry prior to their election in 1990 are considered political insiders. While deputies from the agriculture sector represent a third group of potential insiders, since heads of collective farms, like directors of enterprises, were directly accountable to the regional party committee (Hahn 1997a, 135), the chances of political mobility for these individuals during the

TABLE 4.1 **PARTY AND OCCUPATIONAL PORTRAIT OF THE 1990 SOVIET OF THE REPUBLIC OF UDMURTIA** (Likely Insiders in Bold)

	COMMUNIST PARTY MEMBERS BY OCCUPATIONAL SECTOR				UNAFFILIATED DEPUTIES
	Party/State Apparatus	Industry/ Transportation	Agriculture	Other	All Sectors
High status	**29 (15%)**	**28 (14%)**	**19 (10%)**	22[a] (11%)	4 (2%)
Medium status	**18 (9%)**	**22 (11%)**	6 (3%)	15[b] (8%)	14 (7%)
Low status	**5 (3%)**	6 (3%)	1 (1%)	3[a] (2%)	7 (4%)
Subtotal	52 (26%)	56 (28%)	26 (13%)	40 (20%)	25 (13%)

Likely insiders = 60.8%
N = 199

Percentages may not sum to 100 due to rounding.
[a] Includes one member of the Communist Youth League (Komsomol).
[b] Includes one candidate for membership in the Communist Party.

The Udmurtian Republic Electoral Commission published the 1990 Udmurtia republic soviet election results and occupational information for the deputies in *Udmurtskaia Pravda* (10 March 1990, 24 March 1990, 25 April 1990, 2 May 1990). These initial data were supplemented with additional information from Kirillov (2002, 46–53).

Soviet era were even less than those for individuals in industry. Accordingly, only the newly elected deputies who were affiliated with the Communist Party and who held high status positions in agriculture are classified as political insiders.

Summing up these categories, then, approximates the lower end of the range of political insiders elected in each regional soviet (in table 4.1, these numbers are in bold), while the percentage of deputies associated with the CPSU provides the upper end of the range. In Novosibirsk oblast, the proportion of potential insiders in the legislative branch spans 52% to 82%, and in Saratov oblast the percentage of potential insiders has a somewhat wider range: 49% to 84%. In the republics of Buriatia and Udmurtia, the ranges are 58% to 85% and 61% to 87%, respectively.[5]

These numbers provide some indication of the influence the old regime still had in the regional soviets that held power in these four regions following the collapse of the Soviet Union. Although the soviets represent potentially important actors in the design of the regional electoral systems, the level of their actual influence depended on the political dynamics among competing elites at the regional level and on regional reactions to the 1993 federal constitutional crisis. To examine the role of these regional soviets in the design of their new electoral systems, the comparative case analysis discusses the political events leading up to the new regional parliamentary elections within each region.

THE OBLASTS

As the data just presented suggest, the party nomenklatura enjoyed a clear majority in the Novosibirsk oblast soviet elected in 1990. The first chairman of the soviet was Vitalii Mukha, whose route to political power began in the factories of Novosibirsk. Mukha became the second secretary of the oblast committee of the Communist Party in 1987 and took the reigns of party power in the region with the 1989 retirement of the first secretary, A. Kazarezov. In November 1991, President Yeltsin appointed Vitalii Mukha head of the oblast administration in Novosibirsk, despite the fact that Moscow preferred Anatolii Manokhin, a laboratory manager at the Institute of Mathematics and a founding member of the local branches of Memorial and Democratic Russia. Manokhin, however, declined the appointment because he felt only an individual from the party nomenklatura (i.e., someone like Mukha) would be able to find a common language with the ranks of the executive apparatus and thus guarantee effective leadership. Manokhin instead accepted the position of presidential representative in the oblast (McFaul and Petrov 1998, 721–23). Following Mukha's appointment as head of the oblast administration, the chairman of the oblast soviet became Anatolii Sychev, a party insider who had worked his way up from the position of secretary of the party committee at Sibsel'mash.

Despite the prominence of former apparatchiks in the new regional legislature, nascent party organizations proved active in Novosibirsk during the 1990s. Almost immediately after the March 1990 oblast soviet election, 30 deputies—headed by an instructor of chemistry, Aleksandr Prosenko—formed the group Democratic Orientation (which later became Democratic Russia). However, the small number of democratic-oriented deputies meant that at this period the organization had no real influence.[6] For example, at the time of the August 1991 putsch, the oblast soviet unequivocally supported the coup leaders, but a month later attitudes had changed, and in an address of the Presidium of the Supreme Soviet of the RSFSR on 23 September 1991, the Novosibirsk oblast soviet was singled out for not being critical of the coup leaders (McFaul and Petrov 1998, 723).

The democratic movement also suffered from various internal divisions. Local organizations emerged including the Novosibirsk Democratic Front, the Party of Economic Freedom, and the Russian Movement for Democratic Reforms (Reitblat 1995, 277). The most dramatic rift within the regional reform movements occurred between Democratic Russia and Russia's Choice, when the regional head of Russia's Choice, Manokhin, accused Democratic Russia of being involved in a local budget scandal. Half of the gold extraction budget of the firm, Esbi, had disappeared. After the head of Democratic Russia, A. Manannikov, came out in support of the firm, the firm was exposed as a main contributor to Democratic Russia's advertising budget (McFaul and Petrov 1998 v2, 724–25).[7]

Party development in Novosibirsk was not limited to reform movements, however. Parties on the left—the Social Democratic Party of Russia, the Russian Social Democratic People's Party, and the Agrarian Party of Russia—also developed in Novosibirsk. Meanwhile, various small patriotic movements emerged in the oblast, such as Russian National Unity, the National Republican Party of Russia, and the National Salvation Front. In March 1993, the Liberal Democratic Party of Russia had even registered in the region (Reitblat 1995, 280–81). Thus, despite the apparent control of government institutions by members of the old regime in Novosibirsk, political parties were developing across the ideological spectrum. In fact, in the 1993 federal Duma election, candidates nominated by political parties won all four of the single-member-district seats allocated in Novosibirsk oblast: N. M. Kharitonov (Agrarian Party of Russia), I. C. Anichkin (Dignity and Charity), V. C. Lipitskii (Civic Union for the Sake of Stability, Well-being, and Progress), and I. V. Starikov (Russia's Choice). Meanwhile, two individuals elected in the party-list PR half of the 1993 Duma elections came from Novosibirsk: B. G. Saltykov (Russia's Choice) and V. A. Bokov (CPRF) (McFaul and Petrov 1998 v1, 558).

As political parties were developing in Novosibirsk during the first years of Russia's transition, the regional organs of power proved independent from the federal executive, even defiant. In November 1992, the Novosibirsk oblast soviet supported the Congress of People's Deputies and openly called for the abolition of the post of the Russian president. Novosibirsk later emerged as one of the main sources of regional opposition to President Yeltsin during the 1993 constitutional crisis. On 23 September 1993—two days after presidential decree #1400 dismissing the federal parliament—the Novosibirsk oblast soviet announced its support for the emergency session of Russia's Supreme Soviet and demanded that Yeltsin be removed from office. It also declared that Yeltsin's decrees lacked validity in the oblast and promoted eliminating the post of presidential representative to the region (Reitblat 1995, 266).

The constitutional crisis and standoff between the federal executive and federal parliament produced an extraordinary meeting of representatives from the legislatures of the Siberian republics, krais, and oblasts. On 29 September 1993, envoys from the republics of Buriatia and Tuva, the krais of Altai and Krasnoiarsk, as well as the oblasts of Amur, Chita, Gorno-Altai, Irkutsk, Kemerovo, Khakassia, Omsk, Tomsk, and Tiumen convened in Novosibirsk. During the session, the representative of the Novosibirsk oblast soviet, Anatolii Sychev, discussed the country's slip into serious political crisis and cited the unconstitutional presidential decrees issued on 21 September as the cause (Zharinov 1993).

Unlike most regions in the Russian Federation, opposition to Yeltsin was not limited to Novosibirsk's legislative branch. Despite his appointed status, the governor, Mukha, announced that he officially recognized Russia's vice president, Rutskoi, as the acting president. He also declared that those who supported Yeltsin's decrees should be considered criminals of the government. At the same time, Mukha urged the Siberian regions to take decisive action to guarantee the normal functions of their economies and suggested that the regional soviets should investigate ways to consolidate their budgets. On the same day, a message was sent to Moscow stating that the oblast administration and the oblast soviet believed Yeltsin should cease all actions associated with implementing his decrees and move to schedule simultaneous elections for the presidency and the Congress of People's Deputies (Reitblat 1995, 266–67). Yeltsin reacted as one might expect: Mukha was removed from his post on 5 October 1993.[8]

Having disposed of Mukha, Yeltsin named the mayor of Novosibirsk, Ivan Indinok, acting governor. At the time of the 1993 events in Moscow, Indinok had adopted a careful position and stated that, as mayor of Novosibirsk, he would concentrate his attention on deciding economic problems and maintaining order in the city.[9] The position of the Novosibirsk oblast soviet moderated with the removal of Mukha. The soviet reconsidered its earlier decisions about removing Yeltsin from power, the invalidity of his decrees, and the elimination of the presidential representative to Novosibirsk. Although the soviet decided to observe the presidential decrees, the deputies rejected the idea that regional soviets should dissolve themselves. The issue was not even voted upon (Reitblat 1995, 267–68).

In December 1993, the oblast soviet and the acting governor began devising a new organ of representative power and its election. However, it is not clear what influence the acting governor had over legislation intended to reform the parliament. For example, in the discussion of names for the new oblast parliament, Indinok proposed the "Legislative Council" and the "Legislative Assembly," but the deputies opposed these suggestions and adopted "the Oblast Council of Deputies" (Ivanov 1994). Likewise, while Indinok was officially appointed governor on 18 December 1993 ("Ivan Ivanovich Indinok . . ." 22 December 1993), the election law for the new Council of Deputies, which outlined the election of 48 representatives from 48 single-member districts, was adopted on 22 December 1993 ("Polozhenie o vyborakh . . ." 22 December 1993). In fact, at a press conference in January 1994, Sychev sought to dispel the belief that Yeltsin had dissolved the regional parliament by citing the law on the elections to the new oblast parliament as recent legislation passed by the soviet (Zharinov 1994). In January 1994, the regional soviet slightly altered the new electoral system: it increased the number of districts representing the city of Novosibirsk by one, and the number of deputies elected to the new oblast legislature grew to 49 (Ivanov 1994).

Given this account of politics in Novosibirsk oblast leading up to the design of the new parliamentary electoral system, several factors appear to have been crucial in determining the institutional decision. First, as the context surrounding Mukha's initial appointment as governor and the cooperation between Mukha and Sychev at the extraordinary meeting of representatives from the Siberian legislatures suggest, intra-elite competition in the upper echelons of power was limited. While political parties were developing in the region throughout the early 1990s, these parties had little influence over a political process that remained dominated by members from the old regime. Second, the majority of regional legislators were members of the old nomenklatura, whose electoral prospects were highest under SMD-plurality, and thanks to Yeltsin's removal of Mukha, these politicians played the primary role in the adoption of the electoral system. At the same time, the removal of Mukha seemed to encourage the regional elite to rally together, thus undermining potential divisions that would motivate members of the old nomenklatura themselves to promote a more proportional electoral system. Finally, given Indinok's initially temporary status, it is unlikely that the political environment in Novosibirsk following the 1993 constitutional crisis was one that enabled the acting governor to substantially affect the design of the new regional electoral system. Even if Indinok did seek to influence the type of electoral system, his tenuous position—and Yeltsin's demonstrated willingness to remove the oblast executive in Novosibirsk—is likely to have encouraged him to promote Yeltsin's recommendation, SMD-plurality, rather than some more proportional alternative.

As in Novosibirsk oblast, the political influence of the democratic movement in Saratov oblast was significantly limited. In the fall of 1989, various political clubs emerged in the region. These included a club from the factory district, Al'ternativa, and the Club-Seminar of Candidates for Deputies (KSK). In the oblast soviet, around 18 participants and activists close to the KSK won election while 4 of the 5 candidates nominated by Al'ternativa won election. Once in office, deputies from these two groups unified to form the foundation of the oblast branch of Democratic Russia (Ryzhenkov 1997, 110–16). However, the 1990 elections of the Saratov oblast soviet solidified the position of the Communist Party establishment. In particular, local party and state officials appealed to rural voters by claiming that the party's candidates would protect rural interests. They played on the fears of rural residents that an urban-dominated oblast soviet would discriminate against the countryside and agriculture in favor of the cities and heavy industry. Party candidates promised rural voters political payoffs, such as gas lines, water lines, and paved roads. In cities that had been primarily settled by Volga Germans prior to their deportation under Stalin, voters were encouraged to believe that thousands of these Germans would return and reclaim their property unless Communist Party candidates were elected (Moses 1994, 107).

Throughout 1990 and 1991, the polarization of post-Soviet society in Russia produced splits and rivalries in a presumably unified party and state establishment. In Saratov oblast, the person who symbolized this split within the establishment was Vladimir Golovachev. Golovachev was the secretary of the city committee of the Communist Party, but was elected chairman of the more pluralist city soviet in 1990.[10] Before the August 1991 coup attempt, politics in Saratov had escalated into conflict between Golovachev and the chairman of the oblast soviet, Konstantin Murenin.[11] Golovachev joined forces with the democratic caucus in the city soviet, while Murenin maintained his affiliation with the establishment in both assemblies. In early October 1990, Golovachev resigned his position as first secretary of the city committee *(gorkom)* of the Communist Party and began to pursue policies that diverged from those promoted by members of the old regime.[12]

The August 1991 coup attempt further split politicians in Saratov. By this time, first secretary Murenin had retired, and responsibility for directing the party was transferred to the second secretary in the oblast, K. P. Ponomarev. During the coup attempt, the oblast establishment instituted a media blackout as a way to cut off the public from Yeltsin's actions and appeals. Meanwhile, local democrats, led by Golovachev and members of the city soviet, opposed the coup (Moses 1994, 115). On 21 August, a meeting of 83 city soviet deputies condemned the actions of the coup leaders and supported Yeltsin. On 24 August, days after the coup attempt, Golovachev was named presidential representative to Saratov oblast (Ryzhenkov 1997, 119–20).

Despite Golovachev's actions during the coup attempt, his priorities as presidential representative raised doubts as to his dedication to democratic reform. During interviews with the media, Golovachev's main priority seemed to be the mobilization of support for the dissolution of the oblast soviet. Golovachev promoted this position on the basis that the 1990 elections had been rigged, but the democratic community in Saratov suspected that the ploy was an undemocratic attempt to place greater power in the hands of an unelected executive (Moses 1994, 117). Leaders of the democratic movement became further disillusioned with Golovachev after he supported the appointment of a party insider, Iurii Belykh, as governor.

A serious contender for the post of head of administration in Saratov oblast was the local chairman of Democratic Russia, Valerii Davydov. Heading a commercial real estate company, Davydov played an active role in the privatization of the city's property. However, Golovachev spoke out against Davydov's nomination on the basis that the appointment would compromise the economic interests of the oblast. When a scandal broke out connected with the privatization of the city's hotels, Davydov withdrew his candidacy (McFaul and Petrov 1998, 839). The final choice for governor came down to the two deputies from the oblast in Russia's Congress of People's Deputies: the leader of the oblast agricultural-industrial union, Iurii Kitov, and the director of the Dubkovskoi poultry plant, Iurii Belykh. Of the two agrarians, the Russian president appointed Belykh, presumably because he took more democratic positions in the Congress of Deputies (Ryzhenkov 1997, 114).

On 26 February 1992, it was officially announced from Moscow that Belykh would serve as the acting governor. Initially, the appointment was temporary because the oblast soviet did not support Belykh's nomination (Ryzhenkov 1997, 128). According to Moses (1994, 118), Belykh's appointment represented a compromise with the majority of the oblast soviet: "Although the oblast soviet could not legally block the individual selected as chief executive by Yeltsin, a majority of the soviet had essentially blackballed Yeltsin's first thirteen choices for the position by voting no confidence in them before finally approving Belykh." As a result, Belykh came to power without significant influence and lacking a united team that would have allowed him to develop a strong counterweight to the oblast soviet. Although the oblast soviet confirmed Belykh as the fully empowered head of the oblast administration on 15 May 1992, by September 1992 the two branches faced a level of gridlock that mirrored the paralysis of power at the center (Ryzhenkov 1997, 128–30).

The events of September and October 1993 granted the Belykh administration an opportunity to finally rid itself of the oblast soviet and end the political deadlock in the region. While top politicians in Novosibirsk oblast publicly denounced President Yeltsin's actions, in Saratov oblast politicians expressed regret for the tragic losses of life that occurred during the crisis, and they avoided open opposition. The constitutional crisis did produce, however, a special session of the Saratov oblast soviet on 12 October 1993. A crucial issue for the special session was whether the soviet should dissolve itself in accordance with the suggestion of President Yeltsin. A deputy chairman of the oblast soviet, Aleksandr Kharitonov, introduced self-dismissal as "the most acceptable route" for ending confrontations between the representative and executive organs of power during the upcoming process of institutional reform. When the session voted on the issue of self-dismissal, 139 of the 208 deputies present supported the proposal (54 voted against the proposal, 6 abstained, and 9 refused to enter even an abstention). However, despite having the support of a majority of the deputies present, the motion failed because self-dismissal required a qualified majority. After the vote, a large group of deputies left the special session, thereby ending quorum. Of the remaining deputies, 107 presented declarations about the difficulties involved with continuing the activities and functions of the oblast soviet ("Informatsionnoe soobshchenie . . ." 13 October 1993).

On 13 October 1993, Belykh responded to the extraordinary session of the oblast soviet by ordering the cessation of its activities in accordance with article 5 of presidential decree #1617, which stated that if a soviet failed to meet the necessary quorum to function, its authority was to be temporarily allocated to the executive branch. Belykh announced that the administration would not only take over the functions of the soviet but would also found a temporary oblast committee to investigate questions regarding the reform of the representative branch (Belykh 1993). Thus, while the issue of self-dismissal did not pass the Saratov oblast soviet, events associated with the vote provided the impetus for Saratov's appointed governor to assume its responsibilities. In contrast to Novosibirsk oblast, the events surrounding the 1993 federal constitutional crisis led to the dissolution of the legislative branch and placed electoral system choice in the hands of the governor.

By the time of the 1993 federal Duma elections, various party organizations existed in Saratov. Two people from Saratov were elected to the federal Duma in 1993 via national party lists: O. O. Mironov (CPRF) and V. N. Iuzhakov (Russia's Choice). Since many regions failed to have any local politicians win seats through national party lists, these results indicate a notable degree of party activity with the most active parties being the Communist Party of the Russian Federation and the Russian Communist Workers' Party on the left, Democratic Russia on the right, and various nationalist parties including the Liberal Democratic Party of Russia and the party called Great Power (Derzhava). At the same time, however, parties failed to control the SMD half of the 1993 federal Duma election in Saratov. Of the four representatives elected via SMDs in Saratov, only one, A. M. Dorovskikh, was nominated by a political party (the Liberal Democratic Party of Russia) (McFaul and Petrov 1998 v1, 559–60).[13]

In February 1994, the temporary executive committee examining the reform of the representative branch released its recommendations for the creation of a new oblast Duma: it proposed the creation of a 25-member parliament elected through majoritarian districts (Ryzhenkov 1997, 165). Almost immediately the recommendations were criticized by various political organizations. Democrats expressed dissatisfaction that the committee did not consider the use of party lists, emphasizing that the results of 1993 federal Duma elections revealed party-list elections created more electoral opportunities for a wider range of parties. Communists in the oblast, confident in their chances under a majoritarian system, opposed the introduction of party lists. Most political organizations, however, were unified in their opposition to the committee's suggestions largely because they were not consulted in the process (Maliakin 1995, 417).

On 2 March 1994, the oblast administration held an open forum on the conditions for elections to a new oblast Duma. Approximately 30 representatives from social and political organizations participated in the forum. These representatives expressed a variety of opinions related to the size of the new parliament, the ability of deputies to hold positions besides their posts in the new Duma, the use of a majoritarian system, and the designation of electoral districts (Ryzhenkov 1997, 165–66). In the end, the wave of dissatisfaction seemed enough to force a meaningful compromise from the oblast administration. On 16 March 1994, Belykh published an official decree announcing the date of the election and guidelines for it. The decree announced that the representative body in Saratov oblast would be elected on 29 May 1994 for a two-year period and would consist of 35 deputies, of whom 25 would be elected on the basis of SMD-plurality and 10 through party-list PR in a single oblast-wide electoral district. According to the decree, these decisions reflected the informed opinion of the temporary committee and the recommendations of President Yeltsin as presented in the fall 1993 presidential decrees (Belykh 1994).

In contrast to Novosibirsk, several factors appear to have favored the adoption of a more proportional electoral system in Saratov. First, while the majority of regional legislators were members of the old nomenklatura, whose electoral prospects were highest under an SMD format, the oblast soviet was dissolved following the 1993 federal constitutional crisis, and this regional branch of government was not responsible for designing the electoral system. Specifically, the dissolution of a potentially combative legislature granted Yeltsin's appointed governor, Belykh, some degree of freedom in designing the future parliamentary electoral system. Of course, Belykh also encountered contradictory information as to which type of electoral system should be implemented. On one hand, he was accountable to President Yeltsin, who recommended the creation of SMD-plurality. On the other hand, the 1993 Duma elections suggested that communists and other insiders might perform well in SMDs, while party-list PR would increase the opportunities available to newly formed reform parties.

A second factor that probably favored the adoption of a more proportional electoral system in Saratov oblast was the fact that reform-oriented politicians were represented in the regional elite, even if the effectiveness of this representation (through Davydov) or its sincerity (through Golovachev) could be called into question. A third and related factor shaping the design of Saratov's parliamentary electoral system was the surprisingly high level of communication between the regional administration and the nascent, but growing, political parties in society. Belykh responded to societal demands for greater input in the design of the new parliament, and his administration consulted various political organizations prior to decreeing the new electoral system. Since Belykh would have to work alongside the newly elected parliament in designing the future charter of the oblast, such consultation was an important opportunity for him to build bridges across different segments of the elite. Ultimately, various aspects of Saratov's political context—the existence of competing elite interests, a developing party system, the distribution of political power into the hands of a governor receiving mixed signals from the federal level—converged to produce an electoral system that combined SMD-plurality with party-list PR.

THE REPUBLICS

As in the oblasts, the constitutional crisis at the federal level influenced the design of the electoral systems in the republics by spurring institutional reform.[14] However, while the constitutional crisis may have created a greater impetus for reform in Buriatia and Udmurtia, the crisis did not directly shape the distribution of political power in these two regions. Although both republics had discussed the selection of a president prior to October 1993, neither had yet elected one. Moreover, during these early years of post-Soviet politics, Yeltsin granted the republics greater sovereignty and had not appointed executives in any of them. As a result, following the constitutional crisis at the federal level, and even some criticism by these republican parliaments, President Yeltsin did not attempt to remove specific politicians from power as he did in Novosibirsk oblast. In addition, neither republican soviet considered the issue of self-dismissal, as had occurred in the oblast soviet of Saratov. In both the republic of Buriatia and the republic of Udmurtia, the regional soviets designed the new electoral systems under more independent circumstances.

The formation of new political organizations began rather early in the republic of Buriatia. In November 1988, participants of an all-union group of socioecological experts on the Baikal developed an initiative group called the People's Front Assisting Perestroika (NFSP). Despite the election of one of its leaders—Sergei Shapkhaev, a senior lecturer at the Eastern-Siberian Technological Institute—to the USSR Congress of People's Deputies in 1989, the NFSP became divided between its moderate and radical wings. The radicals, especially Buriats, supported the liquidation of the Buriat autonomous republic and the creation of a union republic, which would unite the Buriat people into a single territory (Tiukov 1995, 42–43). By the summer of 1989, its activists dispersed as they formed new organizations, including the local branch of Memorial (McFaul and Petrov 1998, 103). Alongside democratic organizations, nationalist groups also emerged. For example, in 1988 the society GESER, which promoted the advancement of Buriat culture and language, was formed. Like the NFSP, GESER disintegrated by the middle of 1989 due to internal disagreements about the union of Buriat people into a single administrative unit, and some of its members founded the Buriat-Mongol People's Party (Tiukov 1995, 43–44).

Despite their activity, these early political organizations lacked genuine political power in Buriatia. Although 35 deputies with democratic views formed the parliamentary group Democratic Action, members of the nomenklatura dominated the republic's soviet after the March 1990 elections. In addition, the 1990 promotion of Anatolii Beliakov—the first secretary of the Communist Party in the republic from 1984 to 1990—to the Central Committee resulted in the return of two prominent politicians in the party-state apparatus (both of whom Beliakov had ousted earlier) to positions of power. These two individuals were Vladimir Saganov, a former chairman of the Council of Ministers in Buriatia, and Leonid Potapov, a former secretary in the regional party committee. Following the 1990 elections and the departure of Beliakov, Potapov became first secretary of the Buriat committee of the Communist Party when he defeated Saganov in a battle for the post. Two weeks later, Saganov was confirmed as chairman of the Council of Ministers (Tiukov 1995, 45). Over the next few years, two camps supporting these two leading representatives of the old Soviet elite dominated politics in the republic.

The August 1991 coup attempt only slightly altered the republic's power structure. The liquidation of the Communist Party of the Soviet Union initially undermined Potapov's position in the region. At the same time, the chairman of the republic's soviet, D. Budaev, was removed from his post for taking an "unprincipled position" during the coup attempt: He did not support Yeltsin or the coup leaders. Although Saganov emerged as the de facto leadership in the republic, his own position was tenuous because he had formed and headed a republican committee for the state of emergency on 21 August. Any question as to the continued influence of the old regime disappeared in October 1991, when Potapov again returned to power after being elected the chairman of the republican soviet (Tiukov 1995, 47–48).

Between August 1991 and September 1993, different political organizations rose and fell in the republic of Buriatia, but the general trend was a consistent decline in activities of the democratic organizations there and a strengthening of communist and nationalist organizations. For example, the Socialist Party of Workers (SPT) emerged in the republic alongside the Russian Party of Communists (RPK). In February 1992, the local branch of the CPRF united the majority of communist organizations in the republic with approximately four thousand people attending its founding assembly. By the fall of 1993, a strong communist movement had asserted itself with as many as ten thousand members, a large faction of soviet deputies, and substantial support in the localities. Meanwhile, the majority of democratic parties were in a state of disarray (McFaul and Petrov 1998, 103).

As previously alluded to, the 1993 federal constitutional crisis did not have as great an impact on the design of political institutions in Buriatia as it did in the oblasts of Novosibirsk and Saratov. However, Yeltsin's decrees did divide the political elite in the republic of Buriatia. Specifically, while the Supreme Soviet of the republic condemned presidential decree #1400, the Council of Ministers supported it. On 14 October 1993, at an extraordinary session of the Council of Ministers, the government proposed to remove Potapov (chairman of the soviet) and to terminate the soviet's activities (McFaul and Petrov 1998, 104). However, with the publication of President Yeltsin's decree #1617, "On the Reform of the Representative Organs of Power and the Organs of Power of Local Self-Government," the Supreme Soviet moderated and chose to initiate constitutional reform, including the reform of executive power and that of the legislative branch (Tiukov 1995, 49). It was the subsequent constitutional process that determined the design of the parliamentary electoral system in Buriatia.

Power politics between two rival groups of elites, Potapov's faction and Saganov's faction, shaped the process of constitutional reform in Buriatia. With relatively equal power, the two sides initially decided to cooperate in the reform process. They created a new presidium responsible for leading the republic through the adoption of a constitution. The presidium consisted of relatively equal numbers from both factions, including Potapov and Saganov themselves. However, the social structure and political background of presidium members reflected the main constituencies of Potapov and Saganov. In other words, the members represented the old nomenklatura, specifically the existing heads of enterprises and established political officials. By 24 November 1993, the new presidium introduced the idea of creating the post of a president (McFaul and Petrov 1998, 104–5).

With the prospect of national elections in December 1993, both sets of insiders moved to consolidate their positions by establishing separate political parties. Potapov and his supporters organized the bloc Social Justice. Social Justice took a left-oriented position regarding reform, which included promoting social programs and a guided-market economy. Its political base was the alliance of the CPRF, the Union of Manufacturers and Industrialists (SPP), and the Agrarians. Saganov and his closest supporters organized the Buriat branch of the Party of Russian Unity and Accord (BO PRES), which was headed by Saganov himself. Saganov promoted a liberal market and drew some support from the emerging class of entrepreneurs, bankers, and leaders of investment funds. However, Saganov's supporters were far from homogeneous, and their interests among the nomenklatura did not consistently coincide with newer business interests. The federal elections of 1993 provided a test of popular support for the two sides. Specifically, in a duel between the two leaders for election to the Federation Council, Potapov was elected with 42% of the vote (coming in first place), while Saganov acquired only 25% and finished fourth (McFaul and Petrov 1998 v2, 104–5). Meanwhile, national parties in the republic proved relatively undeveloped as the winner of Buriatia's sole single-member-district seat in the 1993 Duma election was an independent (N. Ia. Kondakov), and Buriatia failed to have a local politician win a seat via a national party list (McFaul and Petrov 1998 v1, 551).

By January 1994, Potapov and his supporters appeared victorious, while Saganov's influence was declining. The republican soviet returned to the process of adopting a new constitution. With the defeat of Saganov's party in the federal elections, Potapov's opponents within the establishment sought to find new ways to stymie Potapov's personal influence in the republic. To undermine Potapov's position, opponents proposed an upper age limit of 55 for candidates to the post of president (Potapov was already 59 years old at the time). They also proposed separating the posts of president and chairman of the government. Neither of these attempts to neutralize Potapov's potential power (even at the expense of Saganov, who was 58 at the time) passed the soviet. Then, with the defeat in the Federation Council election fresh in his mind, Saganov ceded to the popularity of Potapov and announced that he would not compete for the post of president in the republic (Tiukov 1995, 57).

As this discussion suggests, the creation and powers of a republican president dominated the constitutional debates in Buriatia. However, reforming the new parliament also was an important part of the constitutional process. Specifically, the soviet set the new assembly size at 65 deputies. As a constitutional article adopted by the soviet, the decision required a constitutional majority to pass—two-thirds of soviet deputies (Namsaraeva 1994). The constitutional process also provided that the procedure for governing parliamentary elections would be determined just as any other piece of legislation. As a result, although the Supreme Soviet only needed a simple majority to design the new electoral system, the previously adopted constitutional article setting the size of the new regional parliament restricted the options available. During the design of the electoral system, a debate emerged over the use of multimember districts as a means for guaranteeing the representation of the smaller nationalities in Buriatia (Subbotin 1994). To employ multimember districts, however, the soviet would have had to use either fewer and larger geographic districts to elect parliamentary deputies or change the constitutional article determining the size of the new parliament. Rather than divide the population into fewer districts or readdress an issue already adopted by a qualified majority, the Supreme Soviet created 65 single-member districts (Selivra 1994). On 22 February 1994, the constitution of the republic of Buriatia was adopted, stating that the new legislature would consist of 65 deputies (Burkova et al. 1996). The subsequent law on the elections of the assembly stated that these 65 deputies would be elected through SMD-majority elections ("O vyborakh deputatov . . ." 16 March 1994).

The choice of SMD-majority in the republic of Buriatia reflects the powerful position of the old nomenklatura in the soviet at the time. To the extent that a party system had developed in Buriatia, its two-party structure reflected the division among members of the old regime. Thus, while members of the former nomenklatura were divided over the election of a republican president (which involved the prospective success of one of two rival opponents), the choice of an electoral system emerged as less controversial. Specifically, the two camps of insiders seem to have agreed upon an electoral system that worked in favor of their common interest. The use of single-member districts included the prospect of preserving what was essentially a two-party system. Moreover, requiring winners to attain a majority of the vote would allow the deputies in the two rival camps to compete against one another in the first round of the elections, but to unite in the second round to maintain the position of the existing elite. While requiring candidates to win 50% of the vote probably worked against the representation of smaller nationalities in the republic, it would probably also encourage candidates competing in more plural districts to consider minority interests if they hoped to actually win the seat.

In the republic of Udmurtia, the 1990 soviet elections reaffirmed the position of members of the old regime while also permitting some change of personnel in the republican power structure. Specifically, in April 1990, a collective farm director and ethnic Udmurt, Valentin Tubylov, was elected chairman of the Supreme Soviet. The director of a ball-bearing factory, a Russian named Nikolai Mironov, was elected head of the government. Neither leader previously held such influential posts; rather, the high points of both men's careers were posts as first secretaries of raion committees (McFaul and Petrov 1998, 268). Despite these personnel changes, however, the influence of the nomenklatura remained dominant (Shukin 1995, 3). For example, in reaction to the August 1991 coup attempt, the republican first secretary of the CPSU, Nikolai Sapozhnikov, promoted the creation of republican and local structures supporting the coup leaders. At the same time, the presidium announced that it should assume all governmental authority in the region while the Council of Ministers operated in disarray and the political leadership of the Supreme Soviet fought amongst itself.[15]

Following the coup attempt, the regional soviet in Udmurtia initiated the process of reforming governmental power in the region. While the constitution of Udmurtia that was eventually adopted in December 1994 created a parliamentary form of government, politics prior to its passage (and for years afterwards) were characterized by continual attempts to establish the post of president. As in Buriatia, the debate over the presidency overshadowed legislative reform.

Udmurtia's republican soviet considered the adoption of a republican president as early as October 1991. However, during the discussion of the post, the deputies were unable to agree whether the person holding the position should know the Udmurt language. In January 1992, elections for the position of president were postponed for an undetermined period of time. The post of president became an object of debate between the Council of Ministers, who promoted its introduction, and the head of the leadership in the Supreme Soviet, Tubylov, who was against it. While deputies forming the bloc Democratic Udmurtia, as well as other Udmurt groups, supported the introduction of a presidency, they comprised less than half of the soviet and were not able to overcome Tubylov's opposition (McFaul and Petrov 1998, 268–69).

In the spring and summer of 1993, the issue of the presidency took on new vigor with the rise of Aleksandr Volkov to the chairman of the Council of Ministers. Volkov, a former deputy minister, became chairman of the Council of Ministers when an investigation into the use of extra-budgetary funds acquired from the sale of oil quotas forced the existing chair to resign on 11 June 1993. Volkov quickly made the creation of the presidency a top priority. Of the 21 months of Volkov's term as chairman of the Council of Ministers, eighteen months were a campaign for the creation of a presidency (Shukin 1995, 8–9).

Volkov's rising influence divided the Council of Ministers and the Supreme Soviet into rival camps, headed by their own leaders, Volkov and Tubylov, respectively (Egorov 1998, 79). The 1993 federal constitutional crisis only slightly affected institutional reform in Udmurtia by temporarily uniting these two emerging rivals. After presidential decree #1400, an extraordinary session of the Supreme Soviet on 22 September 1993 adopted a resolution declaring the actions of Yeltsin unconstitutional. The session promoted concurrent elections for the Russian presidency and the Congress of People's Deputies (Tubylov 1993a). The Council of Ministers also supported the position of the Russian Supreme Soviet, and both Volkov and

Tubylov worked together in their opposition to Yeltsin (McFaul and Petrov 1998, 269). However, as in most Russian regions, opposition to the presidential decrees moderated as Yeltsin emerged victorious. Following the shelling of the White House, the presidium in Udmurtia announced that the events resulted from an inability of the two sides to resolve political opposition through a method of mutual compromises ("Zaiavlenie Prezidium . . ." 5 October 1993). By 9 October 1993, Tubylov announced that the soviet would follow Yeltsin's lead and reform the organs of governmental power in the republic (Tubylov 1993b).

In the months of November and December 1993, the soviet began work on a law that would create the post of president in the republic and on laws governing the formation of the legislative branch. Largely in response to the Yeltsin administration's announcement that the Russian president would appoint presidential representatives to the republics, the soviet proposed to elect a republican president and a new bicameral parliament in September 1994. However, the creation of a republican presidency introduced the likelihood that one faction would dominate republican politics and leave the losing side with no meaningful influence in the region. Since both Volkov and Tubylov appeared to have relatively equal levels of political potential, the outcome of an electoral battle between the two sides was uncertain (Egorov 1998, 80). Thus, as the momentum from the constitutional crisis slowed, the soviet's deputies reconsidered this decision and postponed the elections until after the formal adoption of a constitution (McFaul and Petrov 1998 v2, 269).

During the 1993 Duma election, political parties appeared to be on the rise in Udmurtia. The Communist Party of the Russian Federation confronted an equally organized competitor on the left in the Russian Communist Workers' Party (McFaul and Petrov 1998 v2, 270–71). The Party of Russian Unity and Accord managed to win one of the two SMD seats elected in Udmurtia during the 1993 Duma election (the other seat went to an independent). In the party-list half of the election, two politicians from Udmurtia won seats to the Duma thanks to their placements on the lists of the Women of Russia and the Liberal Democratic Party of Russia (McFaul and Petrov 1998 v1, 552). However, the power struggle within the old regime's elite eventually captured nascent party politics in the republic. In September 1994, a regional party of power, called Udmurtia, was formed under the leadership of Volkov (McFaul and Petrov 1998 v2, 270). This new party was intended to aid Volkov in his quest for the republican presidency.

In several ways, then, the political situation in Udmurtia resembled the political situation in Buriatia. First, in both republics, the old regime—although divided into two rival camps—proved dominant. While national parties were developing in the republics (more so in Udmurtia than in Buriatia), these organizations were unable to supplant the existing elite divisions. Perhaps this aspect of elite politics in the two republics resulted from the high-stakes debate over the creation of an independently elected president: rival camps in both republics appeared confident that one of the members of the old regime could win a presidential election, even if the actual winner was uncertain. This belief suggests a second commonality across the two republics: the rival factions were confident in their ability as members of the old regime to win elections employing majoritarian principles.

A third similarity emerged between the two republics in November 1994, when Tubylov decided that he would not compete for the post of president (Shukin 1995, 9). However, while the withdrawal of one candidate in Buriatia (the chairman of the Council of Ministers, Saganov) spurred the adoption of the presidency there, the withdrawal of Tubylov (chairman of the republican soviet) in Udmurtia impeded the adoption of a presidency. Left with the ambitious Volkov as the presidential frontrunner, the majority in Udmurtia's soviet chose to create a parliamentary form government and to hold a referendum on the question of whether the republic should create an independently elected president. This alternative retained Tubylov as a candidate for the top executive position and forced Volkov to broaden his influence among the deputies if he wished to defeat Tubylov.[16]

The decision to create a parliamentary republic and hold a referendum on the question of creating a presidency had important repercussions for the entire process of institutional reform. Previously, the soviet in Udmurtia considered the use of multimember districts as a means for increasing the representation of the smaller nationalities in the republic (Petrov 1995, 25–34). The soviet also considered the creation of a bicameral parliament (Egorov 1996). However, with the decision to create a parliamentary republic, the soviet decided it should consolidate legislative power into a single chamber and rejected the idea of a bicameral parliament (Shukin 1995, 10). As a result, the constitution of the republic of Udmurtia created a unicameral legislature consisting of 100 deputies. The members of the soviet also decided that the next set of deputies should be elected using SMD-plurality ("Zakon Udmurtskoi Respubliki . . ." 27 December 1994; Konstitutsii Respublikh v sostave Rossiiskoi Federatsii, 238–64). At the same time as the elections to the new republican soviet took place, voters in Udmurtia also rejected the creation of a presidency (although less than one-third of eligible voters participated in the referendum) (McFaul and Petrov 1998 v2, 269).

CONCLUSION

The comparative analysis of four Russian regions emphasizes the importance of the political positions of the institutional designers (governors versus legislators) as well as their political orientations (insider versus outsider) to the design of the parliamentary electoral systems. In the republics of Buriatia and Udmurtia, legislators designed the new parliamentary electoral systems, and these legislatures adopted systems that political insiders, who dominated each legislature, preferred. The choice of single-member districts emerged as the final option in both republics despite the fact that the ruling nomenklatura in both regions were divided into rival, but relatively equally powerful, camps.

It is significant, however, that the intra-elite divisions in the republics primarily involved members of the old regime, that political parties were relatively inconsequential, and that the number of nomenklatura factions was essentially limited to two. In particular, although the rival camps in both republics were initially uncertain as to which camp would be able to control the post of president, should it be created, both sides believed that the new president would be a member of the old nomenklatura. Of course, presidential elections are truly winner-takes-all elections that would necessarily leave one rival faction in the region without executive power. Thus, in the end, Saganov's weakened camp (unsuccessfully) sought to undermine its opponent's prospects of presidential power in Buriatia, while the pro-Tubylov camp in Udmurtia's soviet promoted the adoption of a parliamentary form of government rather than risk the election of Volkov. Although SMD parliamentary elections are also winner-takes-all, the number of seats available are numerous, thus making it unlikely that a single party, or faction, will lack representation. Accordingly, while the division of the old regime into two rival camps bred conflict over the adoption of a presidency in the two republics, it was not enough to inhibit the adoption of SMDs in the republics, especially since the actual distribution of seats between the two factions was uncertain. Likewise, the weakness of party organizations in these two republics probably bolstered the rivals' confidence in the benefits that SMD systems would provide.

Two additional points are worth noting when comparing electoral system design in the republics. First, elite concerns about ethnic representation initiated some debate regarding the use of multimember districts. Such debates lend credence to Rokkan's (1970) contention that concern about minority unrest, due to a lack of adequate political representation, should yield more proportional electoral systems. Interestingly, while low magnitude, multimember-district electoral systems would increase the electoral opportunities available to geographically concentrated nationalities, such systems also preserve some of the electoral advantages that political insiders enjoy from better local organization and preexisting patron-client ties. In the end, however, neither republic adopted multimember districts. Instead, Buriatia adopted a majority electoral formula to allocate seats in its single-member districts, while Udmurtia created a relatively large legislative assembly.

Second, it is worth highlighting that the new assembly sizes in both republics exceeded the 50-deputy maximum recommended by President Yeltsin's decrees, while the sizes of the new regional legislatures in the oblasts were below the limit. This difference provides one indication that politicians in Buriatia and Udmurtia did not feel bound by recommendations from the center. Although assembly size has been strongly correlated with population size (Taagepera and Shugart 1989), this relationship does not necessarily hold in Russia's regions, thanks largely to the inconsistency with which Yeltsin's decrees on institutional reform were enforced across the regions.[17] As a result, the republics of Buriatia and Udmurtia with one million and 1.6 million residents in 1994, respectively, adopted relatively large assembly sizes: 65 and 100. By contrast, both oblasts of Novosibirsk and Saratov had populations of approximately 2.7 million residents (Goskomstat 1998, 99–100) but adopted much smaller assembly sizes with 35 and 49 deputies, respectively.

The selection of electoral systems in the oblasts of Novosibirsk and Saratov demonstrate how political instability and center-periphery relations can influence the design of subnational electoral institutions. The 1993 constitutional crisis had serious ramifications on the distribution of political power in both cases. In Novosibirsk, the removal of Mukha and the installation of Indinok increased the legitimacy and cohesiveness of the popularly elected oblast soviet. As a result, the soviet played the primary role in the design of the electoral system. Perhaps more interesting is the fact that Indinok was unlikely to feel any incentive to diverge from the adoption of SMD-plurality, which Yeltsin recommended and the oblast soviet preferred. Thus, while political parties appear to have been as developed in Novosibirsk as they were in Saratov, such development failed to significantly influence the electoral system decision.

The case of Saratov not only demonstrates how the interests of a governor can influence electoral system choice but also how political organizations in society can exert some influence on the decision-making process under the right circumstances. First, the 1993 federal constitutional crisis led a substantial portion of the Saratov oblast soviet to promote the soviet's dissolution. Yeltsin's decrees then gave Belykh the justification to disband the regional legislature. In the absence of a combative soviet, Belykh enjoyed some liberty over the design of the future parliament's electoral system.

Belykh, however, encountered contradictory information regarding the type of electoral system to adopt. On one hand, in October 1993, Yeltsin recommended that the regions adopt SMD-plurality systems to govern their new regional parliamentary elections. On the other hand, the December 1993 federal Duma election indicated the ability of communists and other insiders to perform well in such elections and the electoral opportunities that party-list PR provided to new organizations and parties. Given the history of gridlock between Belykh and the conservatives in the oblast soviet, the adoption of SMDs clearly would have worked against Belykh's ideological interests. In this context of uncertainty, the Belykh administration held consultations with various political organizations in Saratov before decreeing the new electoral system. These consultations permitted the administration to collect more information as to how different electoral systems might operate in the oblast. The consultations also provided Belykh with the opportunity to try to build support across the different parties that might win election to the new parliament, although the attempt ultimately failed (see Maliakin 1995, 431–38). This feature of the design process is especially significant since Belykh needed to work with the newly elected parliament in designing the future charter of the oblast. In the end, Belykh decreed a mixed electoral system where 25 seats were allocated through SMD-plurality and 10 through PR in a single, oblast-wide electoral district. In many ways, this electoral system reflects the various competing interests confronting Belykh and his willingness to seek consensus.

The results of the four-case comparison provide greater insight into how regional electoral systems were actually designed in Russia. For example, the cases of institutional design in Buriatia and Udmurtia highlight the relevance that intra-elite conflict can have on such design. Likewise, Saratov oblast demonstrates how a regional executive used the process of designing the regional parliamentary electoral system to increase his support with various regional political actors. Of course, this opportunity also reflects the timing of the decision and the freedom granted to the regional executive from Moscow. In Saratov oblast, the temporary executive committee on legislative reform recommended using SMDs as late as February 1994. This recommendation changed only after informed consultations with regional organizations based on their reactions to the 1993 Duma election. Although these consultations surely influenced Belykh's final decision, the ability of the administration to proceed with its electoral system "experiment" probably required Moscow's permission (Maliakin 1995, 418). In contrast, two other Russian regions adopted mixed electoral systems—the republics of Marii El and Tuva—but held their regional elections concurrently with the 1993 federal elections. Golosov (2004, 211) speculates that the design of these two mixed systems reflected a decision to imitate the national parliamentary electoral system. Ironically, given that both of these regions were republics, if Golosov's speculation is correct, then the freedom to imitate seems to have required the freedom to deviate.

When comparing the findings in this chapter with those in chapter 3, it becomes evident that mixing quantitative and qualitative methodologies permits greater insight into the politics of institutional choice than using either approach in isolation. One reason for this is that different methodologies have different shortcomings. For example, the statistical analyses of electoral system design in chapter 3 find a strong correlation between political competition levels in the regions and the proportionality of the regional parliamentary electoral systems, in which legislators participated in the design process. While one can certainly generalize about this finding across Russia's regions, the level of political competition in each region is a less-than-ideal measure of the distribution of insiders and outsiders in the regional soviets. The comparative case analysis, meanwhile, employs better data on the distribution of insiders and outsiders in the four regional soviets considered, but any finding on the basis of just four cases questions one's ability to generalize. Since the strengths and weaknesses of the qualitative and quantitative studies are mirror images of one another, combining them compensates for their respective shortcomings. For example, since both approaches find that the proportionality of the electoral system was negatively correlated with the estimated percentages of political insiders in parliament where regional soviets influenced electoral system design, one can be more confident that this finding is robust.

Mixing methodologies not only grants one greater confidence in the robustness of certain findings, it also highlights inconsistencies that can guide future research. For example, while the comparative case analysis confirms the preceding chapter's finding that intra-elite competition influences electoral formula decisions more than decisions about district magnitude, it also suggests that intra-elite competition can in some cases yield a higher assembly size. While the statistical analysis reveals that this outcome cannot be generalized across the regions in post-Soviet Russia, future research needs to be conducted to determine whether the relationship is theoretically relevant to other settings.

After having investigated the design of Russia's regional parliamentary electoral systems using two different methodologies, the next chapter examines the effects that these parliamentary electoral system decisions have had on party politics and political representation in the regions. Unfortunately, Russia's Central Election Commission has never officially published results for regional parliamentary elections held between December 1993 and December 1994. Thus, the availability of data constrains the analysis of the political consequences of the different electoral systems. Nevertheless, the combination of a few statistical analyses and a continuation of the four case studies in the context of other scholarly findings—that is, a continued reliance on a mixture of different methodologies—provide ample insight into how regional parliamentary electoral systems shaped Russian politics during the 1990s.

FIVE— MIDWIVES AND GRAVEDIGGERS

With the collapse of authoritarian regimes in Latin America and the transitions from communist rule in Eastern Europe, the interest in the impact that institutions have on the direction and success of democracy has been dramatically renewed. Democratic constitutional design has undergone substantial change as constitution writers choose more deliberately among a wide array of institutional options. In addition to choices among electoral rules, constitutional engineers must decide whether federalism and decentralization is appropriate. Likewise, the costs and benefits of presidential, parliamentary, and semi-presidential arrangements can vary substantially (see Bernhard et al. 2001; Cheibubb et al. 2004; Coppedge 1994; Frye 1997; Linz 1990; Mainwaring 1993; Power and Gasiorowski 1997; Saideman et al. 2003; Samuels 2004; Stepan and Skach 1993). However, when considering the effects of institutions on the development of democracy, especially in ethnically plural states, "the most important choice facing institutional designers is that of a legislative electoral system" (Lijphart 2004, 99).

The preceding chapters have examined the range of decisions that electoral system designers confront. They also have considered the factors that influence political actors holding different positions in government and different political orientations. It is crucial to emphasize, however, that while these new rules help structure politics within the new regime, the results of founding elections are also particularly difficult to predict. Voters usually have little experience with choosing among candidates, and not surprisingly, party identification tends to be weak. Meanwhile, candidate images are likely to be unclear, while popular trust in (and the quality of) opinion polling can be relatively low. These factors often combine to produce high percentages of "don't knows" and "undecideds" in surveys taken before founding elections, just when the excitement associated with the transition frequently yields substantial shifts in the public mood as events unfold (O'Donnell and Schmitter 1986, 61). Ultimately, then, electoral system design can be a high-stakes affair, because "momentary confrontations, expedient solutions, and contingent compromises are in effect defining rules which may have a lasting but largely unpredictable effect on how and by whom the 'normal' game of politics will be played in the future" (O'Donnell and Schmitter 1986, 66).

As outlined in chapter 1, the scholarly endeavor to better understand the political consequences of electoral systems has a long lineage with the most studied effects being how electoral systems influence party development. Elster, Offe, and Preuss (1998, 111), for example, label electoral systems "the midwives of political parties." Of course, electoral systems not only aid in the birth of political parties but also determine their survival or demise by influencing the thresholds of representation through such features as assembly size, district magnitude, the electoral formula, and legal thresholds. In this way, then, electoral systems are instrumental in the birth of some political parties and the death of others. Although the consequences of different electoral systems have been shown to be relatively stable and predictable in consolidated democracies (see, especially, Taagepera and Shugart 1989), the effects of electoral systems in emerging democracies are less predictable.

In the postcommunist setting, electoral system decisions have produced several surprises. For example, prior to the 1994 elections, Bulgaria's system produced fewer parties than did the electoral systems of Hungary, the Czech Republic, or Slovakia, despite being more proportional. At the same time, Hungary's electoral system, which is far less proportional, produced the greatest number of parties (Elster et al. 1998, 128). Likewise, in many cases in Eastern Europe institutional designers adopted legal thresholds to prevent party fragmentation in parliament and to provide themselves with an increased electoral advantage. To their surprise, legal thresholds often worked against them in the subsequent election as the public's preferences swung away from the parties in power (Moraski and Loewenberg 1999). Meanwhile, contrary to experiences in Western Europe and other developed democracies, the single-member-district half of Russian national elections has actually produced greater party proliferation than the proportional representation segment of the elections there (Moser 2001).

Such inconsistencies among the performances of electoral systems in Eastern Europe and those in established democracies probably stem from the unusual characteristics of these emerging party systems, such as their lack of programmatic structure, their weak organizational bases, and the volatility of voter alignments (Elster et al. 1998, 128). They also certainly reflect different experiences under state socialism, with different countries possessing different levels of development and division within the democratic opposition. These cases, therefore, contradict prior assertions that the effects of electoral systems can be adequately predicted and determined (Sartori 1994, 29).

Just as national institutions shape democratic politics by determining the level of consensus needed for key political decisions (see Lijphart 1999 and Powell 2000), institutional decisions at the subnational level also have important ramifications for democracy in the country as a whole (Friedrich 1968, 197). Moraski and Reisinger (2003), for example, demonstrate substantial variation in democratic indicators across the 89 administrative subjects of the Russian Federation. Such variation is notable because a country cannot be considered democratic if its constituent parts are undemocratic. Accordingly, this chapter examines the political consequences of the parliamentary electoral systems in Russia's regions. Did more proportional systems encourage party development? If so, how? Did less proportional systems in fact work to the electoral advantage of political insiders? Given the findings at the national level in the postcommunist context, it is not a foregone conclusion that parliamentary electoral systems in Russia's regions actually worked as federal and regional actors expected.

The first half of the chapter considers these questions across all of Russia's regions. The second half of the chapter compares the results of the first parliamentary elections in the oblasts of Novosibirsk and Saratov and the republics of Buriatia and Udmurtia. This discussion highlights the nature of the electoral campaigns, the level of public interest in the elections, and the distribution of parliamentary seats across politicians with different backgrounds and party affiliations.

REGIONAL ELECTIONS AND PARTY DEVELOPMENT

Political parties are a real and necessary part of politics in new democracies. The development and operation of a healthy party system plays a crucial role in regime transition and democratic consolidation, because party ties can bolster the legitimacy of the system in times of political uncertainty (Pridham and Lewis 1996, 5). However, a decade after the collapse of the Soviet Union, political parties remained largely undeveloped in Russia's regions: Of the 3,481 deputies elected in the regions by January 1998, only 635 (roughly 18%) were members of national political parties and 17 of Russia's regional parliaments had no representation of national parties at all. While the largest portion of these 635 deputies belonged to the Communist Party of the Russian Federation (CPRF), which won seats in 42 regions, the CPRF's total of 279 deputies still constituted only 8% of the total number of deputies (Ross 2002, 39).

To assess the impact of electoral systems on party politics in Russia's regions, Golosov (1999) analyzed regional parliamentary election results from 1995 to 1998. Specifically, he considers whether the weighted average district magnitudes of a parliamentary electoral system and the parliament's assembly size (measured as the average number of voters per seat) influenced levels of party competition and success.[1] While larger district magnitudes are expected to increase the electoral opportunities available to political parties, fewer and larger districts are hypothesized as possessing the potential to undermine the advantages that close personal connections provide to local bosses. As expected, Golosov finds that elections governed by higher average district magnitudes and more populated electoral districts produced greater levels of party representation. These features of the regional parliamentary electoral systems are significantly correlated with greater representation of legislative deputies nominated by political parties, regardless of their orientation. Higher district magnitudes also promoted the election of legislators nominated by certain national parties (i.e., Our Home is Russia and Lebed-oriented parties, like Honor and Motherland) but not others (the Agrarian Party, CPRF, the Liberal Democratic Party of Russia, the Russian Communist Workers' Party, and Yabloko). Meanwhile, more densely populated districts were correlated only with the success of the CPRF and Yabloko. These results suggest that only the CPRF and Yabloko were institutionalized sufficiently to translate their national electoral appeal into political clout at the regional level.

Different types of electoral systems have also shaped party development in Russia's regions. In a book on regional party development in Russia from 1993 to 2003, Golosov (2004) examines whether SMD-plurality systems, which prevailed in most of the regions, created higher barriers to party success than other types of electoral systems.[2] As expected, Golosov finds that the use of party-list PR and MMD-plurality increased party development in Russia's regions. When used, then, MMD-plurality systems are found to have lowered the threshold for party representation. Meanwhile, party-list PR naturally supports party development by excluding independents from competing for a specific number of seats. Golosov (2004, 226) also discovers that party-list PR has been associated with a substantial degree of political fragmentation in Russia's regions: "Some of the elections held by mixed electoral systems in the regions of Russia brought spectacular examples of political fragmentation. For instance, in the 1993 elections in Marii El, eight [party-list] PR seats were distributed among seven parties."

In comparison to MMD systems, Golosov expects SMD-majority systems to undermine party development, since parties need 50% of the vote to win representation. However, the empirical analysis reveals that, while SMD-majority suppressed strong, ideologically rigid parties (like the CPRF) in Russia's regions, it also encouraged the rise of more moderate and less disciplined parties. This finding reflects the fact that candidates from ideologically rigid parties have not performed well in runoff elections in which electoral success usually depends on an ability to build coalitions with other parties and candidates. This aspect of SMD-majority, therefore, produces greater electoral opportunities to smaller and more flexible parties. In sum, then, Golosov concludes that SMD-plurality has not only been the most common electoral system in Russia's regions but has also been the worst electoral system in terms of promoting party politics in Russia.

Regional parliamentary electoral systems have clearly influenced party politics in post-Soviet Russia. However, party development is just as much a reflection of societal divisions and elite competition as it is of electoral system design. Therefore, the absence of strong, institutionalized parties in Russia's regions also probably reflects the fact that state officials and economic elites represented the only actors with the organizational capacity and financial resources to compete effectively in regional elections. If this is true, then the design of certain electoral systems, like SMD-plurality, probably reinforced the clientele-oriented and corporatist nature of Russian politics, which has undermined Russian progress toward democratic consolidation.

REELECTING THE OLD GUARD?

To assess whether certain electoral systems bolstered existing patron-client ties by favoring insiders, I conduct a multivariate regression analysis that examines variations in the percentage of political insiders elected in the first round of legislative elections.[3] Slider (1996, 243–44) notes that the most striking result of the first post-Soviet parliamentary elections in Russia's regions was the electoral success of administrative and economic elites: "Overwhelmingly, the new assemblies consisted of political and economic leaders who already dominated most institutions in a particular region: chief administrators in the cities and rural districts, directors of major industrial enterprises, and chairmen of collective/state farms." To substantiate his point, he lists the number of administrative elites, heads of industrial enterprises, and directors of collective farms elected to the legislative assemblies in 85 of the 89 regions.[4] While these data complement the insider/outsider classification scheme employed in chapter 4, they do not distinguish among elites with different party affiliations, nor do they depict variations in the pool of candidates across the regions. From the latter perspective, employing these data therefore forces the effects of the electoral systems to clear a higher hurdle if they are to prove significant. That is, they must not only have encouraged greater diversity among the regional candidates, but this greater diversity had to actually shape the composition of the ensuing parliament.[5]

The main theoretical variables included in the analysis of insider success correspond to the different features of the first parliamentary electoral system in each region. As in chapter 4, the simple average district magnitude and the weighted average district magnitude (WADM) are used to measure the districting options employed. Average district magnitude should be negatively correlated with the percentage of insiders winning representation in the regional assemblies, since systems with lower magnitudes were expected to benefit local patrons, while those with larger magnitudes were expected to provide greater electoral opportunities to political newcomers.

Another aspect of the regional electoral systems that may have shaped the representation of regional insiders is the size of the assembly relative to the regions' voting populations. As Golosov (1999) argues, fewer voters per district should be more favorable to personalized politics (see also Carey and Shugart 1995). Therefore, regional insiders should enjoy greater electoral success where the size of the assembly is large relative to the population size (i.e., where there are fewer voters per legislative seat). Accordingly, the model includes the average number of voters per parliamentary seat, in order to control for the effect of voter density per electoral district on the representation of regional insiders in the first post-Soviet regional parliamentary elections.[6]

Besides average district magnitude and the voter density of the electoral districts, the analysis also examines whether the representation of political and economic insiders varied on the basis of the electoral formula. As in chapter 4, the electoral systems are separated into five categories in order to assess the influence of the different electoral formulas while controlling for potentially similar average district magnitudes. In other words, the model should distinguish between the use of SMD-plurality and SMD-majority as well as between electoral systems that increase proportionality by using only MMD-plurality or mixing SMD-plurality with different MMD electoral formulas. Accordingly, four dichotomous variables are included in the model: 1) SMD-majority, 2) MMD-plurality with SMD-plurality, 3) MMD-plurality only, and 4) party-list PR with SMD-plurality. Regions that used only SMD-plurality are captured as those instances in which all of the preceding dichotomous variables equal zero.

While the features of the parliamentary electoral systems are expected to affect the representation of administrative and economic elites, several additional factors also must be controlled for. Specifically, there must be some measure of the degree to which voters were likely to support political newcomers rather than the existing elite. In other words, besides the type of electoral system, the representation of insiders is likely to depend on the willingness of citizens to vote for politicians with new ideas and politicians from different backgrounds. Previous research on voting in Russia during this time period has demonstrated that urban voters and voters with higher education were more likely to prefer reform-oriented parties (see White, Wyman, and Kryshtanovskaya 1995 and White, Rose, and McAllister 1997). In elections since 1989, large cities in Russia have provided strong support for economic reform and democracy. Inhabitants of large cities in Russia have been more tolerant of diverse views, more willing to take risks, and more interested in the opportunities created by economic reform: "[Urban residents] considered the orientation toward security and egalitarianism in communism as primarily benefiting the least efficient and the least adventuresome. They

TABLE 5.1 **INFLUENCE OF THE REGIONAL PARLIAMENTARY ELECTORAL SYSTEMS ON THE REPRESENTATION OF POLITICAL INSIDERS**

	Equation 1	Beta	Equation 2	Beta
Constant	98.92***		99.00***	
	(11.62)		(11.86)	
Average District	-4.70*	-0.31	—	
Magnitude	(2.09)			
WADM	—		-4.84*	-0.34
			(2.44)	
SMD-Majority	-7.39	-0.14	-8.20	-0.15
	(6.33)		(6.36)	
MMD-Plurality and	4.64	0.11	7.03	0.17
SMD-Plurality	(5.33)		(6.43)	
MMD-Plurality, only	-0.46	-0.01	0.08	0.00
	(6.48)		(6.98)	
Party-list PR and	2.68	0.04	7.94	0.11
SMD-Plurality	(7.40)		(8.21)	
Average Number of Voters	0.06	0.06	0.06	0.14
per Parliamentary Seat	(0.06)		(0.06)	
Percentage of Urban	-0.25	-0.23	-0.27	-0.25
Residents	(0.15)		(0.16)	
Percentage of Residents	-2.13***	-0.46	-1.95**	-0.42
with Higher Education	(0.63)		(0.63)	
Percentage Registered	-1.69*	-0.23	-1.45	-0.20
as Unemployed, 1994	(0.80)		(0.82)	
Crimes per 10,000	0.04	0.21	0.04	0.20
Residents, 1994	(0.02)		(0.02)	
Republic	3.17	0.10	3.05	0.09
	(4.55)		(4.62)	
Level of Intra-elite	-2.09	-0.15	-2.10	-0.15
Competition, 1993	(1.47)		(1.49)	
New Party	4.49	0.11	3.79	0.09
Development	(4.64)		(4.74)	
Prominence of Communist	3.94	0.08	3.15	0.06
Successor Parties	(5.75)		(5.89)	

TABLE 5.1   **CONTINUED**

	Equation 1	Equation 2
Adj. R^2	0.33	0.31
N	74	74
SEE	11.35	11.45

The first column for each equation provides the unstandardized coefficients with the standard errors in parentheses. The second column lists the standardized coefficients (or beta weights).
* Indicates significance at the .05 level.
** Indicates significance at the .01 level.
*** Indicates significance at the .001 level. All tests are two-tailed.

believed they would benefit far more from the market and would be able to tolerate the insecurity it would bring" (Hough et al. 1996, 8). By contrast, rural areas have been primarily conservative. At the same time, the best-educated segments of the population represented individuals who most likely possessed the skills to adapt to political and economic reform. Accordingly, then, urban and more educated residents should have been more willing to vote for politicians other than the old elite, all else being equal.

Additional factors that likely shaped the electoral success of candidates with close ties to the old regime include the economic and social conditions in the regions. Across Russia's regions, political and economic insiders dominated the parliaments elected in March 1990. Accordingly, the fate of these regional insiders probably depended on the relative economic and social situations in their regions. In other words, regional voters may have attributed their socioeconomic fortunes to the policies of the dominant political orientation in parliament. If this is true, then voters in regions that were economically better off in relative terms probably rewarded insiders as the incumbents, while voters in the regions that experienced relatively more economic suffering probably punished insiders. To control for the economic and social conditions in the regions, the analysis includes the percentage of the population registered as unemployed in each region in 1993 and the number of crimes per 10,000 people in each region during 1993.[7]

The analysis also controls for whether a region is a republic. As emphasized throughout this book, the ethnic diversity of Russia's republics has yielded important asymmetries in the country's federal system. Stepan (2000), in particular, has argued that the increased liberty granted to republics also gave elites in these regions an edge in building undemocratic political machines. To capture these federal differences, a dummy variable is included in the analysis in which a region receives a one if it is a republic.

Finally, the regression analysis uses three independent variables from chapter 4 to control for pre-existing party development and levels of intra-elite competition. In the previous chapter, two measures were used to assess regional party development: the percentage of SMD deputies per region

TABLE 5.2 **INFLUENCE OF THE REGIONAL PARLIAMENTARY ELECTORAL SYSTEMS— WITH ASSEMBLY SIZE ADDED—ON THE REPRESENTATION OF POLITICAL INSIDERS**

	Equation 1	Beta	Equation 2	Beta
Constant	90.94***		91.05***	
	(11.41)		(11.84)	
Average District Magnitude	-5.27*	-0.35	—	
	(2.00)			
WADM	—		-4.92*	-0.34
			(2.34)	
SMD-Majority	-7.65	-0.14	-8.59	-0.16
	(6.01)		(6.11)	
MMD-Plurality and SMD-Plurality	4.63	0.11	6.42	0.15
	(5.06)		(6.18)	
MMD-Plurality, only	0.78	0.02	0.44	0.01
	(6.17)		(6.70)	
Party-list PR and SMD-Plurality	7.01	0.10	11.81	0.17
	(7.21)		(8.04)	
Assembly Size	0.18**	0.36	0.16	*0.33
	(0.07)		(0.07)	
Average Number of Voters Per Parliamentary Seat	0.08	0.20	0.07	0.18
	(0.05)		(0.06)	
Percentage of Urban Residents	-0.33*	-0.31	-0.34*	-0.32
	(0.15)		(0.15)	
Percentage of Residents with Higher Education	-2.04***	-0.44	-1.86**	-0.40
	(0.60)		(0.61)	
Percentage Registered as Unemployed, 1994	-1.20	-0.17	-1.00	-0.14
	(0.78)		(0.81)	
Crimes per 10,000 Residents, 1994	0.06**	0.30	0.05*	0.28
	(0.02)		(0.02)	
Republic	-5.33	-0.16	-4.54	-0.14
	(5.33)		(5.41)	
Level of Intra-elite Competition, 1993	-1.41	-0.10	-1.46	-0.10
	(1.42)		(1.45)	
New Party Development	3.01	0.08	2.54	0.06
	(4.44)		(4.58)	

TABLE 5.2   **CONTINUED**

	Equation 1		Equation 2	
		Beta		Beta
Prominence of Communist	2.98	0.06	2.42	0.05
Successor Parties	(5.47)		(5.66)	
Adj. R²	0.39		0.37	
N	74		74	
SEE	10.78		11.00	

The first column for each equation provides the unstandardized coefficients with the standard errors in parentheses. The second column lists the standardized coefficients (or beta weights).
* Indicates significance at the .05 level.
** Indicates significance at the .01 level.
*** Indicates significance at the .001 level. All tests are two-tailed.

during the 1993 Duma election nominated by communist successor parties and the percentage nominated by all other parties. Meanwhile, the number of candidates that competed per seat in the 1993 Federation Council election for each region provided an indication of intra-elite competition in the regions.

Table 5.1 presents the results of the multivariate analyses. The two equations in table 5.1 suggest that the models explain a nice amount of variance in the representation of insiders: the adjusted R^2s equal 0.33 for the equation using the simple average district magnitude and 0.31 for the equation using the weighted average. As expected, higher average district magnitudes are correlated with the electoral success of politicians having experience outside the traditional political and economic structure. While higher district magnitudes appear to have benefited political newcomers, the average number of voters per parliamentary seat fails to emerge as statistically significant. In fact, the positive sign of the coefficient suggests that, if anything, regional insiders performed better where the number of voters in the electoral districts were higher. This positive relationship probably reflects the circumstances under which larger assembly sizes were adopted: chapter 4 demonstrates that larger assembly sizes were more likely where legislators played a greater role in the design process. Since political insiders dominated the existing legislatures, larger assembly sizes probably emerged in those regions where a large number of insiders felt confident in their chances of electoral success and demanded legislatures large enough to accommodate them.

Table 5.2 provides some support for this interpretation. It replicates the regression analyses in table 5.1, but adds a variable indicating simply the size of the regional assemblies. The relationship between assembly size and insider success is strongly significant and positive. In other words, larger assembly sizes are clearly correlated with higher percentages of insider deputies, but there are no theoretical reasons to think that the existence of a larger assembly would have systematically provided regional insiders with an electoral advantage.

In none of the equations of tables 5.1 and 5.2 do the dummy variables measuring the different electoral formulas attain statistical significance. In other words, employing runoff elections rather than plurality elections in single-member districts did not substantially hurt the electoral prospects of political and economic insiders across Russia's regions. Likewise, the electoral opportunities available to political newcomers were not significantly increased by combining party-list PR with SMD-plurality, combining MMD-plurality with SMD-plurality, or relying solely on MMD-plurality. These variables fail to attain significance even when the district magnitude measures were removed from the model. Thus, the average district magnitude of the regional parliamentary electoral systems, not their electoral formula, determined the representation of insiders or outsiders in the new parliaments. These findings lend additional support to the contention that district magnitude is the most important feature of a parliamentary electoral system.

Of the other independent variables included in the analyses, the percentage of the population with higher education and the percentage of the population registered as unemployed prove significant. In other words, regions with more urban voters and regions that performed worse economically tended to elect legislative deputies from outside the pre-existing political and economic power structures. One surprising result is the positive coefficient of the number of crimes per 10,000 residents. While it fails to attain standard levels of significance in table 5.1 (although it is strongly significant in table 5.2), the coefficient suggests that proven elites—those with more experience and clout—tended to perform better in regions where restoring social order was likely to have been an important political issue.

The insignificance of the dichotomous variable indicating whether a region is a republic emerges as an interesting null result. In particular, it confirms previous empirical findings questioning Stepan's (2000) hypothesis that republics are less competitive and potentially less democratic than other Russian regions (see Moraski and Reisinger 2003a). It is also interesting that the levels of party development and elite competition failed to affect the representation of insiders in the new regional assemblies. The following case studies examine this result in greater detail and suggest that, although the lack of significance between party development and insider representation is important, it is not necessarily surprising. Likewise, the measure of intra-elite competition suggests that while such competition could have entailed the rise of new political interests in the region, it could just as easily indicate competition among different regional factions consisting of political and economic insiders.

ELECTION OUTCOMES IN FOUR REGIONS

The comparative case analysis of electoral system choice in Novosibirsk, Saratov, Buriatia, and Udmurtia demonstrated the role that various political actors holding different political positions and different political orientations can play in the design of parliamentary electoral systems. Electoral system design in the oblasts of Novosibirsk and Saratov highlighted the importance of center-periphery relations on institutional decisions at the subnational level. Specifically, the 1993 constitutional crisis influenced the distribution of power among the different branches of government in both cases. In Novosibirsk, the appointed governor, Mukha, was removed by President Yeltsin and replaced by a more loyal supporter. However, this intervention from the center seemed to increase the legitimacy of the regional legislature, which had been elected in the semi-competitive elections of March 1990. As a result, the oblast soviet played a prominent role in the design of the electoral system. By contrast, the constitutional crisis affected institutional design in Saratov by permitting an appointed governor, Belykh, to emerge as the only branch of power with the authority to design the new electoral system. That is, decrees from the federal executive provided Belykh the opportunity to dissolve the oblast soviet. However, due to an atmosphere of electoral uncertainty as well as competing incentives associated with federal and regional demands, the Belykh administration decreed a mixed electoral system in which 25 seats were allocated through SMD-plurality and 10 through party-list PR in a single, oblast-wide electoral district.

In the more autonomous regions, the republics of Buriatia and Udmurtia, legislators designed the parliamentary electoral systems free of executive oversight or federal intervention. In both republics, the regional legislators adopted systems that representatives with close ties to the old regime, who also dominated the legislatures, most preferred. However, while a significant amount of intra-elite conflict yielded the adoption of 65 SMD seats allocated on the basis of majority rule in Buriatia, the intra-elite competition in Udmurtia appeared to have only increased the assembly size, as the designers created a 100-seat legislature governed by SMD-plurality

Given the contextual differences that existed across Russia's regions, to what extent did the results of the first post-Soviet parliamentary elections in these cases differ? Can these differences be attributed to variations in their electoral systems?

In the first post-Soviet parliamentary elections in Novosibirsk oblast, which occurred on 26 March 1994, 202 candidates competed for the 49 single-member-district seats. Among these candidates were individuals affiliated with the local branches of the CPRF, Russia's Choice, the Liberal Democratic Party of Russia, Democratic Russia, the Party of Economic Freedom, and the electoral association Unity, which promoted the economic interests of farmers and peasants (McFaul and Petrov 1998, 727). However, the majority of candidates registered under a party label were only nominally affiliated with a party. An especially large number of candidates were heads of local administration and leaders of industry, who ran as independent candidates with no connection to any political party or movement (Reitblat 1995, 269–71).

Voter turnout for the parliamentary election in Novosibirsk oblast reflected a lackluster election campaign in which policy programs were largely absent. Only 33.6% of the voting population turned out to cast their ballots. In the more rural raions of the oblast, turnout was higher than the oblast average at 37%. In the oblast capital, turnout was only 25%, while the average turnout in other cities in the region was around 32% (Reitblat 1995, 270). The low level of voter turnout proved relatively important to the election results, since the oblast law on elections required voter turnout to surpass 25% of registered voters for a district mandate to be allocated. As a result, only 34 deputies were elected during the initial March 1994 elections. Of this total, 11 were former deputies of the soviet elected in March 1990. Due to low participation levels, repeat elections continued until December 1996 with one district still failing to elect a representative to the new parliament (McFaul and Petrov 1998 v2, 727–28).

The campaign and results of the parliamentary elections demonstrated the advantages that the political and economic elite in Novosibirsk oblast enjoyed. Almost two-thirds of the initially elected deputies were either municipal heads of the administration (12) or managers of industrial enterprises and collective farms (10). By comparison, one deputy came from the public health sector while four deputies had been employed in public education. Blue-collar workers, such as builders or employees at collective farms, were completely absent, as were representatives from the business and trade sectors (Reitblat 1995, 270).

The electoral success of local administrative heads reflected their unique positions of power and the appeal of their campaign promises. Specifically, the municipal heads promised to repair transportation services, to build more housing, to establish new employment opportunities with local firms, and to pay wage arrears. Practically no one from the previous oblast soviet proposed a specific political program and those who did lost their bids for reelection. In addition, only three candidates who had been affiliated with a political party were elected in the initial March 1994 elections: one deputy from the CPRF, another from the CPRF faction Fatherland, and one deputy from Russia's Choice. Even these deputies relied on campaign strategies that resembled those of the municipal heads as opposed to strategies that emphasized their positions as representatives of political parties (Reitblat 1995, 271). In the subsequent repeat elections, candidates with party affiliations (representing the Liberal Democratic Party of Russia, in particular) managed to pick up five seats (McFaul and Petrov 1998 v2, 728).

Elections to the Duma of Saratov oblast were held on 29 May 1994. Of the regional legislative elections held in the spring of 1994, Saratov's parliamentary election was the only one to use a proportional representation system. This fact piqued the interests of politicians in Moscow, and as a result, several high profile politicians visited Saratov during the election campaign, including Vladimir Zhirinovskii, Egor Gaidar, and Gennadii Ziuganov. This elite interest in the election did not necessarily inspire participation among the masses. Only 37.1% of registered voters participated in the election overall, while one of the 25 single-member-district seats was not allocated because voter turnout in that district did not meet the 25% required (McFaul and Petrov 1998 v2, 846–47).

Although 16 electoral groups initially sought to participate in the party-list segment of Saratov's parliamentary election, only 9 acquired enough signatures to register their lists. Registration required the collection of 20,000 signatures across no fewer than eight raions within the city of Saratov and/or across the oblast proper. Of the registered electoral blocs, only three could be considered truly national parties—the Democratic Party of Russia, the Agrarian Party of Russia, and the Party of Russian Unity and Accord. However, three additional organizations emerged with less direct links to nationally organized electoral blocs—the Yavlinskii bloc in Saratov oblast, For Democracy (which incorporated the regional branch of the CPRF), and Democratic Choice (which was the regional branch of Russia's Choice). The three remaining associations represented local societal and professional organizations: Union of Reserve Officers, Saratov Land Union, and Labor (Ryzhenkov 1997, 166–73).

Campaign money and the ability to capitalize on existing organizational structures played critical roles in Saratov's legislative election. The Democratic Party of Russia spent the most money on the campaign, one million rubles, and its support, as well as that for Democratic Choice and the Yavlinskii bloc, was roughly comparable to its support in the oblast during the 1993 Duma election. For Democracy, with its ties to the CPRF, and the Union of Reserve Officers enjoyed better administrative and party organizations, as the agricultural sector supported the Agrarian Party. Thus, the party-list PR results fulfilled the expectations of most political observers at the time with the main exception being the failure of Labor to win any seats (Ryzhenkov 1997, 174–75). Of the nine organizations that competed in the party-list segment of the election, only six surpassed the 5% legal threshold needed to attain seats in parliament. For Democracy and the Agrarians each won three seats with 27.9% and 22.6% of the vote, respectively. Democratic Choice (10.7%), the Democratic Party of Russia (10.1%), the Union of Reserve Officers (10.0%), and the Yavlinskii bloc (7.7%) received one seat each (McFaul and Petrov 1998 v2, 847).

In the SMD-plurality segment of the election, 135 candidates competed for 25 seats (Ryzhenkov 1997, 173). While candidates from several electoral groups won seats in these elections, the majority of victors in this segment of the election proved to be independents. The political organizations winning SMD seats were the Union of Reserve Officers, which won three districts, and the Yavlinskii bloc, which won two. For Democracy, Democratic

Choice, and Fatherland (which had failed to acquire enough signatures to register in the party-list half of the election) won one district each. The professional backgrounds of the remaining candidates included heads of municipalities (5), directors of industrial enterprises (4) and farms (3), doctors (2), gubernatorial deputies (2), and the chairman of the preceding oblast soviet (N. Makarevich) (McFaul and Petrov 1998 v2, 847).

Elections to the People's Assembly in the republic of Buriatia were held simultaneously with the election of the republic's first president on 16 June 1994. Although six candidates initially competed in the presidential elections, two eventually withdrew from the race—the minister of interior economics, V. Ivanov, and the head of the faculty at a local agricultural institute, V. Khameev. Accordingly, the official results listed only four candidates: the chairman of the Supreme Soviet, Leonid Potapov; deputy chairman of the soviet's minister for economics, Aleksandr Ivanov; the owner of a private investigation company and ex-KGB officer, Valerii Shapovalov; and the minister of education, Sergei Namsaraev. Namsaraev enjoyed support from the bloc Education and the Future, while Shapovalov's candidate was advanced by a local branch of Russia's Choice (Tiukov 1995, 59).

The main competitors in the race were Leonid Potapov and Aleksandr Ivanov. While Potapov relied on a traditional campaign, which included personal visits throughout the republic, Ivanov focused more heavily on the mass media. In addition to television campaign ads, a member of the initiative supporting Ivanov's candidacy hosted a television show called *June 16th,* which openly promoted Ivanov and attacked his main rivals. For example, the program suggested that poor health conditions would inhibit Namsaraev and Potapov from adequately performing the official responsibilities of the presidency (McFaul and Petrov 1998, 108). On 16 June, 54.1% of voters cast ballots in the first round of the presidential election. Potapov received 46.2% of the vote, Ivanov 25.7%, Namsaraev 7.9%, and Shapovalov 15.7%. The presidential runoff was held on 30 June. On the eve of the second round of voting, Shapovalov declared his support for Potapov, and Potapov went on to win the presidential election with 71.7% of the vote, compared to Ivanov's 24.9%. Turnout in this second round decreased slightly to 50.8% (Tiukov 1995, 60–61).

Elections to the People's Assembly in the republic of Buriatia relied on 65 single-member districts using a majority formula. In relative terms, political parties proved quite active in Buriatia's parliamentary election: 398 candidates competed for the 65 seats (an average of 6.1 candidates per seat) with 154 of these candidates being affiliated with voter associations. The central battle involved Social Justice and the movement For a Meaningful Life (McFaul and Petrov 1998, 108). Potapov and his supporters formed Social Justice leading into the 1993 federal elections (see chapter 4). After its victory in the federal elections, Social Justice expanded its base. A particularly pivotal union occurred on 16 March 1994 between Social Justice and the Buriat branch of the CPRF, which was later followed by a union with the Agrarians. Another important shift in regional politics was the change in the political orientation of the Union of Manufacturers and Industrialists (SPP) away from Russia's Choice toward Potapov leading up to the regional elections. During the parliamentary elections, Social Justice nominated candidates for all 65 seats. In addition, the pro-Potapov Union of Manufacturers and Industrialists ran 25 candidates (Tiukov 1995, 58–62).

The creation of For a Meaningful Life reflected the decision among democratic organizations to unify in order to be competitive in the elections. One of the key initiators of the union was the former chairman of the republic's Council of Ministers and an earlier rival of Potapov, Vladimir Saganov. For a Meaningful Life was formed in February 1994. By April, the movement included 17 organizations, such as the Buriat branch of the Party of Russian Unity and Accord (BO PRES), Unity and Progress, Young Buriatia, the Union for Multi-child Families, the Baikal Foundation, the Union of Composers, and the Center for German Culture (Tiukov 1995, 58). Thus, the regional parliamentary election represented an extension of the intra-elite struggle between the political factions of Saganov and Potapov to include mass mobilization, as both sides sought to legitimate their positions by winning seats in parliament (Gel'man and Golosov 1998, 43).

In the first round of the parliamentary elections, only ten deputies were elected, despite a republican wide turnout of 54%. Saganov was included among these first few deputies. The results of the second round of elections filled 54 more seats with 48.4% of voters participating. The success of three political groupings reflected the intra-elite conflict that dominated the republic from 1991–1994. For a Meaningful Life, the Union of Manufacturers and Industrialists, and Social Justice divided the parliamentary seats relatively equally amongst themselves (Tiukov 1995, 62). The success of these locally grown political organizations with links to nationally organized parties highlight the intricacies of party development in the Russian Federation, which could easily be overlooked if the study of party development were to focus solely on the national level or to avoid the use of case studies. However, as Gel'man and Golosov (1998) suggest, the value of relying on locally organized political factions for party development remains unclear. Since the growth of political organizations in Buriatia developed from intense competition between two members of the regional elite, these organizations also faded quickly as the victory of Potapov's faction appeared decisive.

Among the 64 new deputies, 35 were ethnically Russian, 28 were Buriat, and one was ethnically German. In addition, the professional backgrounds of the elected deputies were largely skewed in favor of the administrative and economic elites in the republics. Nineteen legislative deputies worked within the executive branch of government with ten of these deputies actually holding positions as heads of municipalities. Three deputies were former members of the Supreme Soviet. Thirteen deputies were directors of enterprises and nine were managers of collective farms. The remaining nine deputies worked within the educational, law enforcement, or medical fields (Tiukov 1995, 52–63; McFaul and Petrov v2, 108).

The first post-Soviet parliamentary elections in the republic of Udmurtia occurred later than in the other three regions. Deputies to the new legislature were elected on 26 March 1995 with a voter turnout of 46.8%. As in Buriatia, the parliamentary elections in Udmurtia demonstrated a relatively high level of competition with a substantial level of participation among political parties. At the time of the election, 699 candidates were officially registered across the 100 single-member districts. The number of candidates ranged from 2 to 16 with 11 different political organizations nominating 293 of the candidates. The most prominent of these organizations were Udmurtia; Udmurtskii Soviet; Liberty, Lawfulness, and Accord; the Russian Communist Workers' Party; the Social-Ecological bloc; the republican branch of the CPRF; Udmurt Representatives of the Confederation of Business Women of Russia; and the Republic Center for Supporting Self-Government (Central Election Commission 1998, 159–61). In addition to the parliamentary elections in the republic, a referendum was held at the same time as to whether the post of president should be added to the republic's governmental structure. Only 30% of the 47% participating in the election voted in favor of creating an independently elected president (McFaul and Petrov 1998 v2, 273).

All of the deputies to Udmurtia's regional parliament were elected in the first round of voting (Central Election Commission 1998, 161). Among the 100 new deputies, 76 were ethnically Russian, 16 were Udmurt, 5 were Tatar, 2 deputies were Belorussian, and one was ethnically Korean.[8] The new assembly also represented a wide range of professional groupings. Twenty-one of the deputies were members of the previous parliament, while one deputy had been a legislative representative at the municipal level. Eighteen deputies held positions in the executive organs of power with 11 of these individuals serving as heads of local government. Four of the elected deputies came from law enforcement, and one was the local leader of a political party. Twenty-six deputies represented the industrial sector, which included manufacturing, farming, and production. The remaining 29 deputies held positions in various occupational sectors such as finance, trade, energy, science, and education.

Political parties, meanwhile, also made their presence known in Udmurtia with affiliated candidates winning 37 seats. These included the bloc Udmurtia (20); the republican branch of the CPRF (8); Liberty, Lawfulness, and Accord (2); the Russian Communist Workers' Party (3); Udmurt Representatives of the Confederation of Business Women of Russia (1); and the Republican Center for Supporting Self-Government (3) (Central Election Commission 1998, 161–62).

Table 5.3 summarizes the election results across the four regions. It highlights the levels of voter turnout, the degree of competition for district seats, the distribution of professional backgrounds among the elected deputies, and the percentage of deputies affiliated with political associations. Voter turnout was clearly higher in the republics than in the oblasts. Thus, while the use of party-list PR to elect a portion of legislators in Saratov did not significantly bring more voters to the polls, the presence of concurrent elections did. In the republic of Buriatia, the parliamentary election was held simultaneously with the republican presidential election. In the republic of Udmurtia, the parliamentary election was held in conjunction with a referendum on the question of creating an independently elected president. The differences in the average number of candidates competing per single-member districts provide some indication that the parliamentary seats were more sought after in the republics than in the oblasts.

Like voter turnout, the distribution of deputies by professional background does not seem to vary significantly across the four regions, despite the use of party-list PR in Saratov and a majority formula in Buriatia. It is possible that the different electoral systems produced different pools of candidates in the regions, however. As Cox (1997) notes, less proportional electoral systems not only mechanically underrepresent candidates who receive smaller vote shares, but the likelihood of such underrepresentation can discourage candidates from entering the electoral arena in the first place. Nevertheless, the more stringent test of whether the electoral systems had a significant and lasting impact on legislative politics in the regions—in terms of agenda setting, policy making, or government formation—is the degree to which they actually determined the composition of the new parliament.

In contrast to the professional background of the elites, the case studies presented show some variation exists among the regions in terms of the percentage of deputies explicitly affiliated with political parties. While Gel'man and Golosov (1998) note that a high level of party competition can emerge from substantial intra-elite conflict, both Buriatia and Udmurtia experienced such conflict leading up to their regional legislative elections, yet deputies affiliated with political parties dominated the new assembly in Buriatia. Although these parties were locally organized around two key political patrons, Potapov and Saganov, why did political organizations prevail to a greater extent in Buriatia than in Udmurtia? The type of electoral system may provide the answer.

As mentioned previously, 293 of the 699 candidates in Udmurtia expressed a party affiliation in the first post-Soviet parliamentary election, while 154 of the 398 candidates in Buriatia indicated party affiliations. These numbers represent surprisingly similar proportions among the candidates competing for seats in the two republican parliaments: 42% and 39%, respectively. Therefore, since the impact of parties on the candidate pool was essentially equivalent across the cases, it appears likely that political parties were more critical to electoral success in the SMD-majority elections of Buriatia than in the SMD-plurality elections of Udmurtia. This finding makes theoretical sense. Under SMD-plurality with many candidates (say, four), a candidate only needs to win more votes than any of her competitors,

TABLE 5.3   **SUMMARY OF THE FIRST PARLIAMENTARY ELECTIONS IN FOUR REGIONS**

	Novosibirsk Oblast[a]	Saratov Oblast	Republic of Buriatia	Republic of Udmurtia
Voter Turnout[b]	34%	37%	54%	47%
Average Number of Candidates per SMD[c]	4.1	5.4	6.1	7.0
Percentage of Administrative Elites	35%	32%	34%	40%
Percentage of Economic/Agricultural Managers	29%	28%	34%	26%
Percentage with Party Affiliations	17%	37%	90+%[c]	37%

[a] Percentages reflect only the results from those seats filled on 27 March 1994 in Novosibirsk *oblast*.
[b] These figures are based on the first round of voting.
[c] Tiukov (1995) does not provide exact numbers for Buriatia's party distribution. However, locally organized political parties representing rival republican elites clearly dominated the election and subsequent legislative politics.

and while party organization may help, it is not necessary if the candidate has powerful ideas or strong local ties. However, under SMD-majority, the candidate who may have won a seat with 25% of the vote under a plurality formula would face a runoff election due to the 50% threshold. Accordingly, the more effectively a candidate can coordinate her activities with other candidates and those who voted for these candidates in the first round, the better her chances of electoral success. It is in this context that political parties become more valuable and should be more prominent. The comparison of Buriatia and Udmurtia confirms this expectation.

While the different electoral formulas may explain why party-affiliated deputies prevailed in Buriatia's first parliament at a greater rate than in Udmurtia's, the level of intra-elite competition in Udmurtia probably explains why its legislature and Saratov's legislature witnessed relatively similar levels of party representation. It seems reasonable that Saratov's legislature, which used party-list PR to allocate 10 of its 35 seats, would end up with a higher percentage of party-affiliated deputies than Novosibirsk's legislature, which only used SMD-plurality. But focusing solely on the features of the two electoral systems fails to adequately explain why the percentage of party deputies in Saratov did not exceed the percentage in Udmurtia— which, like Novosibirsk, used SMD-plurality. Moreover, while Udmurtia elected a larger assembly than Saratov, there is reason to doubt that the larger assembly size compensated for the use of SMD-plurality. According to Carey and Shugart (1995), larger district sizes (i.e., more voters per seat) make party labels more appealing as the ability of candidates to cultivate a personal vote decreases. Therefore, since Udmurtia's assembly size of 100 and population size of 1.6 million produces substantially fewer voters per seat than Saratov's assembly size of 35 spread across 2.7 million residents, parties should have been less prominent in Udmurtia than in Saratov, all else being equal. This suggests then that higher levels of intra-elite competition in Udmurtia made up for a less proportional electoral system, which confirms Golosov's (2004) contention that intra-elite competition is fundamental to understanding party development in Russia's regions.

Finally, comparing the electoral outcomes in the republics permits some insight into how the new regional electoral systems influenced ethnic representation. In Buriatia, Buriats represented about 24% of the population, but won almost 44% of the seats in parliament. Ethnic Russians, on the other hand, won less than 55% of the seats despite comprising 70% of the population. In Udmurtia, Udmurts won only 16% of the seats although constituting 31% of the population, while ethnic Russians comprised only 59% of the population but won 76% of the seats. While various factors shape the legislative representation of ethnic groups—including how electoral districts are drawn—these results suggest that electing a smaller assembly via SMD-majority may be more accommodating to ethnic interests than electing a somewhat larger assembly through SMD-plurality.

CONCLUSION

Russia's first post-Soviet regional parliaments were elected on the heels of the 1993 federal constitutional crisis and charged with the responsibility of constitutional reform within their borders. Certainly, the degree and direction of reform in the regions reflected the ideological orientations and backgrounds of those deputies elected to office. In this way, then, the initial parliamentary electoral systems are likely to have had important and lasting consequences on regional politics even where they have since been altered. Perhaps more importantly, Russia's regional parliamentary electoral systems shaped the nature of electoral competition in Russia during a critical juncture in this state's post-authoritarian transition. Golosov (1999, 2004), in particular, demonstrates that the adoption of SMD-plurality electoral systems to govern Russia's regional parliamentary elections played a substantial role in undermining party development across the country. Ross (2002, 50), meanwhile, argues that "there can be no consolidation of democracy in Russia without a nationwide consolidation of parties and the party system."

If scholars of political parties are right and the development of institutionalized, competitive political parties are the best chance a polity has to effectively loosen the grip of regional patrons and supplant "clan-based" politics, then the choice of regional parliamentary electoral systems was an important element of Russia's post-Soviet transition. In each region, this decision was an opportunity to either continue down the familiar path of patron-client politics or to change the direction of regional politics and turn the corner toward a more open and more competitive political system. Given the entrenchment of insiders in post-Soviet Russian politics, especially at the regional level, the selection of regional electoral systems that would preserve patronage politics is not surprising. At the same time, however, this chapter stresses the fact that understanding the politics of electoral system choice in the smaller number of cases that deviated from the SMD-plurality norm is crucial to understanding what factors create an environment favorable to democratic politics. With this in mind, then, the following and final chapter highlights the main lessons to be learned from electoral system choice in Russia's regions. It also considers the implications of electoral reforms emanating from the federal government and whether these reforms can alter the path of electoral politics in Russia's regions.

SIX— ERODING FEDERALISM

In January 1992, post-Soviet Russia emerged as the successor of a former global superpower. The development of the new Russian state attracted international attention, foreign investment, and democratic expectations. However, the totalitarian nature of the previous regime complicated the transition. In contrast to previous transitions from authoritarian rule, the transitions in postcommunist Europe were triple transitions. Russia, in particular, has experienced an economic transition from a centrally planned economy to a more market-oriented system, a political transition from a noncompetitive, single-party system to a fluid multiparty system in which regular (if not fair) elections delegate political power, and a social transition in which the dismantling of state control over the daily lives of its population has produced an increase in individual liberty and a simultaneous decline in social welfare. In addition, unlike other former communist countries in Eastern Europe, where communism can be depicted as something imposed by a foreign power, Russia cannot deny its communist legacy, and Russian national identity must somehow come to grips with its past while moving forward to the future.

Despite this unique setting, Russia's regions operate as a natural laboratory to examine phenomena important to the study of political transitions and democratization. The regions consist of a large number of polities— 89—with diverging levels of sovereignty and a variety of ethnic compositions. At the same time, these polities share a common political history defined by decades of Soviet rule and the sudden collapse of a patrimonial communist regime. Moreover, since the polities are all members of a larger federation, cross-regional comparisons provide more control over international influences than can be attained through cross-national comparisons. Of course, the presence of a federal government also constrains the degree to which findings from Russia's regions can be generalized at the national level, but the limits on such comparisons are not consistent across all regions or all questions of scholarly interest. As this book demonstrates, federal influence over institutional design in Russia's republics, in particular, was minimal, which means that some aspects of the transitions in these regions may be compared to similar aspects of national-level transitions in other contexts. Meanwhile, electoral system decisions in Russia's other regions—where the federal government recommended a certain option and constrained the freedom of choice—could resemble the process of institutional design in transitional states where an occupying power seeks to impose democratic institutions (e.g., the United States in Afghanistan and Iraq).

While the book is intended to grant insight into the politics of electoral system choice at all levels of government, electoral system choice at the subnational level in federal states is itself an important question. Over the past 25 years, the number of federal states has grown as different countries have sought to accommodate territorially based ethnonational minorities. Among advanced industrial societies, Belgium, Spain, and Italy have been added to the list of federal states, while Corsica and the United Kingdom are debating federalism. In developing countries, regional divisions can be especially salient, and federalism is being debated or has emerged in Afghanistan, Burma, Ethiopia, Indonesia, the Philippines, South Africa, and Uganda (Bermeo 2002, 96–97).

The relationship between socialist federalism and the tragic wars in the former Yugoslavia have produced some debate as to whether federalism is a suitable institutional arrangement for developing states, especially for those with ethnically divided societies. Bunce (1999), in particular, points out that national federal structures can provide the building blocks for nationalist movements and secession. They define territories in ethnic terms, recognize distinct languages, divide the intelligentsia along ethnic lines, and grant ethnic leaders regional institutions and resources that can be used for divisive purposes. Despite the horrors of Yugoslavia, however, many authors contend that federal institutions promote ethnic accommodation more often than they produce ethnic conflict (see Amoretti and Bermeo 2004). While this debate is likely to continue, the design of regional electoral systems—as institutions with direct implications for representation within a federal system—speaks to the concerns present in this debate.

Electoral systems and federalism are usually considered to be two distinct mechanisms for managing societal and territorial conflict (Weaver

2002). More proportional electoral systems convey a more consensual vision of politics by permitting a larger number of societal interests a greater voice in politics. Federalism, on the other hand, manages conflict by devolving decision-making power to geographic subunits. However, the decisions are then in turn managed through majoritarian or proportional mechanisms. Thus, while federalism may increase minority representation and undermine the influence of national majorities, this is not always the case. In some instances, as among Spanish speakers in Catalonia, francophones in Ontario and the Canadian prairie provinces, or Catholics in Northern Ireland, devolution may in fact leave regional minority groups less protected than if the central government were more actively involved (Weaver 2002, 111). In other words, the design of certain regional institutions—like regional parliamentary electoral systems—determines the effectiveness of federalism in mitigating ethnic conflict. These decisions not only influence the degree of political representation and efficacy that societal groups possess at a level of government that is more likely to affect their daily lives; they also can either counteract or reinforce institutional decisions at the national level. The politics of electoral system choice at the subnational level, therefore, can have significant ramifications on democratization, yet experts on constitutional design have no clear advice on this issue (see, for example, Lijphart 2004).

LESSONS FROM RUSSIA

Electoral system choice in Russia's regions highlights the degree to which the consequences of parliamentary electoral systems on ethnic representation, as well as on party development, are endogenously determined. Specifically, these cases illustrate different ways by which preexisting societal characteristics manifest themselves in electoral system decisions. While more proportional representation systems are widely recommended for ethnically divided societies (see for example, Lijphart 1985 and Diamond 1999), this book demonstrates how the politics of electoral system choice can circumvent this normative prescription.

First, the statistical analyses in chapter 3 suggest that republican presidents were more likely than the governors of the other 68 Russian regions to design electoral systems with higher average district magnitudes. This outcome, however, does not simply result from higher levels of ethnic heterogeneity in the republics, as might be presumed. When controlling for region type, the statistical model estimating the electoral system decisions of regional executives actually indicates that more ethnic heterogeneity, if anything, led regional executives to design electoral systems with lower average district magnitudes. Therefore, while presidents designed electoral systems with higher district magnitudes than did governors, this prediction probably reflects different levels of sovereignty between the republics and other regions in Russia. That is, presidents enjoyed more freedom over electoral system design than their gubernatorial counterparts, who were constrained by their accountability to the Russian president. These results do not mean that ethnic differences were not important, however. The levels of ethnic heterogeneity and nationalism among the republics indirectly influenced electoral system design: they produced an asymmetrical federal arrangement in which republics acquired greater leverage—especially with regard to institutional decisions—vis-à-vis the federal government.

After controlling for variations in regional sovereignty levels, why would higher levels of ethnic heterogeneity lead regional executives to design less proportional electoral systems—systems with lower average district magnitudes? Ideally, more plural societies would adopt more proportional systems. The answer to this question again relates to key aspects of Russia's federal system.

The presence of federal subunits differentiated from one another along ethnic lines probably led many regional executives to feel as though ethnic accommodation on their part was unnecessary. Supporting this assertion is the fact that, regardless of the type of region (republic or not), executives who designed parliamentary electoral systems based their decisions more on information about which systems would work to their ideological advantage and on how much freedom they had to act on this information than on the level of ethnic heterogeneity in their regions. However, this explanation only accounts for why ethnic heterogeneity would not produce more proportional parliamentary electoral systems. Why might a negative relationship exist between ethnic heterogeneity and district magnitude in the regions?

Once again, the answer probably reflects the construction of Russia's federal system. The existence of federal subunits designated as representing specific ethnic groups increases the probability that a certain ethnic group will enjoy plurality, if not majority, status in the region. In such cases, the popular election of an independent executive moves politics toward a zero-sum game (see Linz 1990; Linz and Valenzuela 1994). Only one individual—usually representing only one ethnic group—will control this top governmental post, and where ethnicity cleaves politics, this individual is likely to come from the most influential (if not largest) ethnic group. Thus, to the extent that these executives feel as though the federal framework is responsible for addressing ethnic accommodation and are interested in bolstering their own positions of power, these executives are likely to use the design of parliamentary electoral systems to fortify their majoritarian electoral advantage.

Findings from Russia's regions suggest that while ethnic heterogeneity may produce a federal system that grants ethnic regions the opportunity to design more proportional electoral systems, ethnic segmentation along regional lines can also encourage regional executives to design less proportional parliamentary electoral systems in their regions. In this way, the design of regional parliamentary electoral systems by regional chief executives can undermine the ability of federalism to actually attain the goal of ethnic accommodation.

In contrast to regions where executives designed the regional electoral systems, higher levels of ethnic heterogeneity in regions where the legislative branch remained active and influenced electoral system design produced more proportional electoral systems. This outcome, however, was not achieved by increasing average district magnitudes. The case studies of electoral system choice in the republics of Buriatia and Udmurtia demonstrate that ethnic considerations entered the dialogue on electoral system choice but failed to convince a majority in either of the soviets responsible for selecting their electoral systems to forego the option of SMDs. Instead, both soviets decided to create larger-than-average parliamentary assemblies. These decisions confirm results from the statistical analyses indicating that greater ethnic heterogeneity produces larger assembly sizes where regional legislatures influence electoral system design, regardless of the presence or type of regional executive. Meanwhile, the statistical analyses fail to discover a relationship between ethnic fractionalizaton and the type of electoral system. Likewise, while the republic of Buriatia employed SMD-majority to govern its first parliamentary election, its ethnic distribution strongly resembles the ethnic distribution of the republic of Udmurtia, which adopted SMD-plurality. Thus, where regional legislatures influenced electoral system choice, ethnic concerns influenced the proportionality of the new parliamentary electoral system but did so through one of the least effective features of the electoral system, the assembly size.

In sum, the effect of ethnic heterogeneity on electoral system design—with regard to which features are affected and in which direction—seems to depend on the actors responsible for designing the new electoral system. Regional executives are more likely to alter the average district magnitude of an electoral system than some other electoral feature. However, regional executives are also more likely to adopt electoral systems with lower average district magnitudes, which are believed to work against ethnic accommodation. Regional legislatures, on the other hand, are more likely to increase assembly sizes when confronted with a more ethnically heterogeneous society. However, as the electoral outcomes in the republics of Buriatia and Udmurtia suggest, increasing assembly size is not necessarily the most effective means of accommodating ethnic demands. Since many factors influence ethnic representation—like the level of assimilation, the politicization of ethnic issues, and the territorial concentration of minorities—future research should continue to examine ways by which regional parliamentary electoral systems promote or impede the ability of federal systems to accommodate ethnic interests.

Russia's regions not only illustrate different ways by which ethnic heterogeneity shapes electoral system choice but also demonstrate the level of endogeneity that exists between party development and electoral system choice. Although most studies of institutional choice emphasize political bargaining between parties, this investigation examines electoral system design in an environment in which political parties were largely undeveloped. Even by the late 1990s, most national parties failed to meet LaPalombara and Weiner's (1966) classic definition of a political party. In fact, the party that is often accepted as meeting the criteria—the CPRF—had won parliamentary seats in only 42 regions as of January 1998 with its members constituting just 8% of regional legislators (Ross 2002, 39). Perhaps more importantly, party labels in the regions have been poor indicators of elite preferences, and party discipline is rare in the regional assemblies. Therefore, while party development is examined as a possible explanation of electoral system design, neither the political actors nor their preferences in Russia's regions were clearly defined on the basis of their party affiliations.

Soviet-era legacies of patronage and the absence of an independent civil society combined with rational assessments of the electoral environment to guide the institutional preferences of regional politicians. The collapse of the Soviet Union failed to dislodge members of the Soviet nomenklatura from many positions of power. Additionally, these political insiders actually dominated key governmental institutions in the regions and emerged as important political actors—often constituting a majority of deputies in the regional soviets—with a deep-seated interest in the design of the new regional parliamentary electoral systems. Since insider-oriented legislators already knew they could count on preexisting patron-client ties to improve their electoral prospects, they preferred electoral systems that rewarded such relationships. As a result, where insiders dominated the regional soviets and these soviets actually influenced the design of the regional parliamentary electoral systems, the new systems were significantly more likely to be those that preserved patron-client ties. That is, they were more likely to be SMD systems. Even higher levels of intra-elite competition in the regions failed to systematically increase the average district magnitudes of these parliamentary electoral systems. Instead, such competition merely encouraged the adoption of SMD-majority.

However, Russia's political context in the early 1990s, which included the presidential appointment of governors and the 1993 constitutional crisis, also determined whether regional legislators enjoyed any direct leverage over electoral system decisions. In many cases, regional soviets were dissolved, and in all but one of these instances, President Yeltsin appointed the regional executive who would design the new parliamentary electoral system. Since Yeltsin appointed most of these executives, the design of parliamentary electoral systems by these regional heads represented an opportune time to loosen the grip of the old nomenklatura in these regions. The executives could have designed electoral systems, like party-list PR, that would have defined politics in party terms and granted political newcomers greater access to the regional parliament. For the most part, however, they did not.

Party-list PR emerged in only three Russian regions—the republics of Marii El and Tuva and Saratov oblast—and in all three cases it was mixed with SMD-plurality. Of these three cases, only in Saratov oblast did an appointed governor alone design the new regional parliamentary electoral system. The case study of Saratov oblast suggests that governors who designed their electoral systems and took their time when making the decision could deviate from President Yeltsin's decree ordering the adoption of SMD-plurality and allocate some seats through party-list PR. However, the statistical analyses find that a combination of SMD-plurality with MMD-plurality was significantly more probable in regions where appointed governors defied Yeltsin. In other words, while appointed governors did prefer more proportional electoral systems to improve the electoral prospects of political newcomers, these demands were most often met through the use of MMD-plurality.

Although one might also suspect that party development would encourage governors to adopt party-list PR, the statistical analyses find that party development was more closely linked to MMD-plurality where appointed governors designed the electoral system. A plausible explanation for these results is that appointed governors who dedicated more time and energy to electoral system design may have decided against party-list PR because it would grant nationally organized institutions greater access to politics within their borders. Thus, while they preferred more proportional electoral systems to improve the electoral prospects of political newcomers, their preference could be met by employing MMD-plurality—a system that did not define the competitive arena solely in terms of political parties. This logic conforms to Luong's (2002) argument that electoral system choice could reflect power politics between a country's regions and its center. It also validates the belief expressed by one of the Duma's deputies, Boris Nadezhdin, who sponsored the 2001 bill to reform the regional electoral systems. He contended that any hope of the regions themselves initiating a reform that would permit "alien" federal parties to claim power in their territories should be discarded as naïve (Golosov 2004, 263).

In this context, then, the factors influencing the adoption of regional parliamentary electoral systems that mix SMD-plurality and party-list PR deserve special attention. According to the statistical analyses, these mixed electoral systems were significantly more likely to occur in regions where the legislature remained active and the decision was made early than in regions—like Saratov—where governors made the decision and took their time. This finding suggests that the adoption of electoral systems employing party-list PR probably resulted from regional actors imitating the federal government. For example, while the republic of Marii El mixed party-list PR with SMD-plurality, a relatively obedient regional legislature designed the electoral system. Not only did the republican soviet adopt an electoral system that resembled the federal Duma's electoral system; it also dissolved itself in accordance with Yeltsin's decrees. This outcome, however, also depended on the liberty that Marii El enjoyed as a republic to disregard the president's decree on electoral system design, so close to the 1993 constitutional crisis.

Of course, the use of party-list PR to govern regional parliamentary electoral systems would have been significantly more likely in Russia's regions if President Yeltsin had used his 1993 decrees to recommend this type of electoral system. Instead, however, Yeltsin ordered the adoption of SMD-plurality systems, which ultimately preserved patronage ties and maintained the political power of representatives from the old regime. Why did President Yeltsin order the adoption of SMD-plurality electoral systems?

First, it is plausible that the Russian president and his associates believed the disproportionality of SMD-plurality systems would benefit the pro-Kremlin party Russia's Choice. This explanation is supported by the fact that, in the fall of 1993, some members of Yeltsin's entourage promoted SMD-plurality for Russia's national parliamentary elections because they believed it would favor Russia's Choice. Although this view did not fully prevail at the national level, the administration did decide to use SMD-plurality to elect half of the seats to the federal Duma.

A second reason the Yeltsin administration ordered the adoption of SMD-plurality in the regions is that they may have believed this electoral system would spur the rise of a national two-party system, as Duverger's law suggests, and limit the dangers of party fragmentation, which did occur in the republic of Marii El. In fact, Duverger (1954, 228) suggests that SMD-plurality systems are capable of producing bipartism in countries where it has never existed if such countries already show a fairly clear tendency toward two parties, or a substantial amount of time is allowed to pass. From this perspective, the Yeltsin administration may have decreed SMD-plurality because they believed the roots of a two-party system already existed in Russia, with Russia's Choice representing one extreme and the CPRF representing the other, or they may have believed that these systems would simply produce a national two-party system over time.

The expectation that SMD-plurality could replace patron politics at the regional level with party competition is not unreasonable. Patron-client ties are common in developing states and are more likely to exist at the local level. In fact, patron-client ties and party development can coincide with one another as has occurred in many advanced democracies, including the United States. The problem, however, is that patronage networks and clientele-oriented politics preceded the introduction of competitive elections in Russia. While regional patronage could evolve into party politics, something was needed to motivate this transformation. To the extent that the transformation should occur sooner rather than later, electoral system choice provides the most immediate incentive. Even if party fragmentation was a major concern of the Yeltsin administration, more proportional electoral systems—party-list PR with a high legal threshold or MMD-plurality systems—were preferable for democratization. Instead, electoral system choice in most of Russia's regions merely bolstered the position of regional insiders and fortified the importance of patronage, when it could have redefined electoral competition along party lines.

These institutional decisions have been critical to the direction of Russia's transition not just because regional insiders have continued to benefit from Soviet-style patronage in the electoral arena, but also because these insiders have opposed the rise of a strong federal state in Russia:

> Post-communist Russian regionalism expressed specific bureaucratic and social interests that became increasingly deeply entrenched, deploying political resources against the centre and other federal subjects to ensure freedom of action to attract investment (above all foreign) and to exploit regional resources, and to ensure relative autonomy from popular accountability. . . . Although the regional institutions of the USSR created powerful patronage and political networks, their persistence was determined by specific regional coalitions able to exploit the new political and economic conditions. (Sakwa 2002, 5)

Thus, Russia's president failed to realize the vulnerability of a transitional state to the short-term political consequences of key institutional decisions. While SMD-plurality could eventually produce a national two-party system in Russia over time, this outcome assumes that regional patrons have accepted the democratic rules of the game. In a post-authoritarian context with little or no history of democratic practices, this is a dangerous assumption.

In sum, while political parties were extremely weak in Russia's regions, an endogenous relationship still existed between electoral system choice and party development, although it is not one that is frequently discussed. In Russia, electoral system design reflected the *lack* of party development in most regions. That is, the prevalence of patron politics over party politics more often than not produced electoral systems that preserved the status quo.

OVERCOMING INERTIA

Hahn (1997a, 130) contends that the democratization of national political institutions without corresponding changes at the local level is a prescription for disaster. The preceding discussion indicates how the adoption of majoritarian parliamentary electoral systems can contribute to this prescription for disaster: 1) They can undermine the goals of ethnic accommodation associated with federal systems, and 2) they can preserve preexisting patron-client ties where patrons are more interested in preserving the power they enjoyed during the previous regime than they are in the ideals of democracy. In Russia, the federal government recognized the consequences that regional parliamentary electoral systems have had on national politics and proposed a specific reform program. In 2002, it passed a law requiring that half of the deputies in the regional parliaments be elected via party-list PR and half via SMD-plurality. This reform should, theoretically, spur party development. However, there are reasons to believe that the reform of Russia's regional parliamentary electoral systems has as much to do with Putin's desire to consolidate power as with the advancement of democratic institutions.

Explicit attempts by the Putin administration to consolidate state power in Russia have drawn significant attention from the western media. They have ranged from a crackdown on the independence of the Russian media with state controlled interests taking over privately owned televisions stations (NTV and TV-6) to charges of corruption being brought against high-profile oligarchs (like Boris Berezovskii, Vladimir Gusinskii, and Aleksandr Khodorkovskii). While these tactics may signal the growing power of the Russian president and a return of authoritarian ways, close observers of the Kremlin emphasize that centralized power in Putin's Russia is a façade (Reddaway 2002). Shevtsova (2003, 229), in particular, argues that Russia's outward stability in 2002 "was deceptive, hiding underneath incompatible trends and permanent conflicts." Center-periphery relations in Russia exemplify these "incompatible trends and permanent conflicts," and as noted in the first chapter, reining in Russia's regions has been a prominent aspect of President Putin's administrative agenda.

By the time Putin became Russia's president, it had become clear that politics outside of Moscow had evolved into regional authoritarianism and corruption: "There were no alternatives to the regional clans—during the Yeltsin years, after a brief period of power struggle, power in most of the regions had been seized by clans dominated by Soviet *nomenklatura* with criminal ties" (Shevtsova 2003, 126). Many in Russia, including Yeltsin's successor, attribute this situation to Yeltsin's attempt to build a federation from the ground up. As the Soviet Union crumbled, Yeltsin won support across Russia's constituent regions by urging them to take as much autonomy as they could swallow. This approach, however, substantially weakened the central state, perhaps dangerously so. For example, although tax collection was federally controlled (via customs controls, a federal treasury system, and a tax police), regional leaders regularly found ways of retaining part of the revenues that should have been remitted to the federal government. Regions with the greatest political clout negotiated special tax breaks often solidified in bilateral treaties with the federal government. Weaker regions, meanwhile, capitalized on the fact that the federal budget only accepted money, and they made widespread use of barter and other surrogates to withhold funds and bail out local enterprises. These tactics produced almost unlimited opportunities for corruption and cronyism (Teague 2002, 207–9).

The election of Putin signaled a new direction in federal-regional relations: rather than erring on the side of allowing clientelism to erode federalism from the bottom up, Putin has decided to err on the side of dismantling federalism from the top down. First, the Putin administration moved to curtail the power of regional presidents and governors through the addition of a new layer of federal bureaucracy. In a 13 May 2000 decree, Putin divided Russia's 89 regions into 7 federal districts. These new "super-regions" corresponded closely to existing military districts, and five of the first presidential representatives were from the military or security services. Although

Putin justified this new layer of bureaucracy as necessary for promoting economic development in regions that regularly looked to the center for support rather than coordinating activities with their neighbors, many of the powers that regional executives acquired under Yeltsin were transferred to the new presidential representatives. The responsibilities of these representatives included overseeing the economic, political, security, and social situations in their regions, making policy recommendations, monitoring regional departments of key federal ministries and agencies, and approving personnel appointments to the regional departments of federal organs of government (Teague 2002, 210). Ultimately, the creation of the seven federal districts was intended to reverse the degree to which the federal government had become dependent on governors and presidents to guarantee law and order in the regions.

Next, Putin asserted greater control over the regions by reorganizing the composition of Russia's upper chamber of parliament, the Federation Council. Although members of the Federation Council were elected in 1993, from 1995 onward the two representatives from each region were the heads of the executive and legislative branches of government. On 17 May 2000, Putin proposed a bill replacing these "senators" with representatives nominated by the regional chief executives and parliamentary speakers and confirmed by the regional parliaments. Again the reform was promoted as being in the best interests of the regions: if regional executives and parliamentary speakers are to effectively govern their regions, they should be in their regions not in Moscow serving in the Federation Council. At the same time, Putin also proposed a bill granting the Russian president the power to remove regional executives from office and to dissolve regional legislatures.

Naturally, regional executives used their positions in the Federation Council to resist these reforms. In anticipation of such resistance, the Putin administration used various carrots and sticks to win their support. For example, Putin proposed the establishment of the State Council of the Russian Federation, an advisory body that would continue to give regional executives regular access to the Russian president after they relinquished their seats in the Federation Council. In addition, Putin sought support for his reforms by proposing a bill that would grant republican presidents and governors the right to dismiss municipal leaders (mayors) in their regions who adopted policies that violated federal or regional laws as determined by the courts. This proposal was particularly attractive because presidents and governors regularly came into conflict with the mayors of their regional capitals, and regional executives enjoy inordinate amounts of leverage over regional courts (see Solomon and Foglesong 2000).

Although many of Putin's proposals were watered down by the time they became laws, the power of the Russian president over the regions was substantially increased. Putin acquired the right to remove governors and republican presidents in instances where they failed to bring regional legislation into line with federal law or where they faced serious criminal charges and supporting evidence as presented by the prosecutor general. Likewise, the Russian president—not the regional executives—received the right to dismiss mayors who violated federal policies (Slider 2004, 163). Subsequent events suggest that this strengthening of the vertical hierarchy of executive power will continue. Following a wave of terrorist attacks in August–September 2004, Putin proposed replacing executive elections in Russia's regions with presidential appointees. The "reform" took effect in December 2004.

The decision to mandate uniform electoral systems across Russia's regions probably reflects Putin's desire to consolidate his power across the Russian Federation as much as a desire to promote party development, although the two interests could coincide. Requiring regional parliamentary elections to employ an element of party-list PR forces political competition to conform to party politics. This process will likely strengthen the hand of Putin's party—United Russia—in the regions, as regional legislators choose to align with the party of power. At the same time, the reform will not only require a majority of regional legislators to adopt a party affiliation; it will also undermine regionally based parties as they are forced to compete with candidates representing nationally organized parties. From this perspective, then, even electoral system design emanating from the federal government in Russia appears to conform to North's (1990) assertion that institutions are usually created to serve the interests of those with the power to devise them.

The installation of mixed electoral systems in Russia's regions continues a trend from the 1990s in which more than 20 countries selected a mixed system to elect the members of their parliaments (see Herron and Nishikawa 2001; Kostadinova 2002; Shugart and Wattenberg 2001). Although the consequences of mixed electoral systems still require further investigation, the decision to mandate them for Russia's regional parliaments certainly reflects the degree to which SMD-plurality elections have impeded the ability of parties to emerge, as well as the continuing legacy of patron politics in Russia. Time will tell whether changing the regional electoral systems from above can actually create a well-developed national party system. In the short run, however, institutional inertia in Russia's regions persisted. While the regional parliaments were to establish mixed electoral systems by 14 July 2003, many regions resisted the change. In May 2003, presidential envoy to the Central Federal District, Georgii Poltavchenko, noted that only 3 of the 18 regions in his district (Belgorod, Tver, and Vladimir oblasts) had complied with the federal legislation. The rate of compliance was even worse in the other federal districts (Radio Free Europe/Radio Liberty 15 May 2003). Such resistance to federal legislation has plagued center-periphery politics in Russia since the collapse of the Soviet Union (see Kahn 2002). Although mixed systems eventually were implemented across the regions, existing patronage networks will certainly be more difficult to dismantle now than they would have been in the early 1990s—before regional actors had acquired experience manipulating electoral outcomes or had established their own regional parties of power.

CONCLUSION

As outlined in the preface, this book uses electoral system choice in Russia's regions to develop a greater understanding of how institutional decisions are made and how these decisions can shape transitions from authoritarian rule. The emphasis on the design of subnational institutions, in particular, grants greater insight into how the interests of multiple actors determine institutional choice. These actors include members of parliament, heads of the executive branch, and even those outside the actual borders of the polity in question. Specifically, the book finds that regional executives and the federal executive played instrumental roles in the design of regional parliamentary electoral systems in Russia. These findings are important because the majority of work on electoral system choice neglects the preferences of political actors beyond those most likely to compete for seats under the new rules, yet the political leverage that such actors enjoy can shape institutional decisions in significant ways. The ability of an executive to veto a legislature's institutional decision may be enough to force legislators with a narrow majority to provide some concessions to legislators in the minority. Meanwhile, the ability of a federal executive—or some other political leviathan, such as an occupying power—to issue authoritative recommendations can constrain the range of institutional options under consideration.

Just as the book focuses on a wider range of potential institutional designers than commonly considered, it also avoids the assumption that these political players are organized along party lines. Certainly party politics matters in many cases. However, based on this study, institutional choice can have as much to do with the absence of political parties as with their presence. In Russia's regions, in particular, the legacies of Soviet-era patronage supplanted the needs of many regional politicians for political parties, and the leverage that these politicians possessed over the design of regional institutions allowed them to fortify their political positions and preserve patron-client ties. Thus, unless some external force intervenes, political institutions appear to reflect the nature of elite politics of the polity in which they were designed. Accordingly, party-list electoral systems are unlikely in transitional states where patronage permeates politics, unless the patrons themselves are already organized along party lines. The presence of patronage networks, however, does not preordain the adoption of SMD-plurality. Politics can be multipatron just as easily as multiparty. Thus, higher levels of intra-elite competition are likely to breed more proportional electoral systems in the form of either larger assembly sizes (creating more districts for more patrons to oversee) or SMD-majority.

Finally, as the bulk of this chapter emphasizes, the politics of institutional choice, even at the regional level, can substantially influence the viability of new democratic institutions. While democracy may appear most vulnerable to the authoritarian actions of national actors, I argue that authoritarian revivals can occur precisely because politicians at the national level become frustrated with the institutional and behavioral legacies of the old regime at lower levels of government. For example, where corrupt or incompetent politicians win office and use their resources to maintain power despite the presence of regular and otherwise fair elections, national-level politicians and many voters may decide that democratic elections are simply ineffective and too costly. More cross-national work needs to be done to better understand the degree to which frustration with regional and local politics drives national actors to roll back democratic reforms. But, ultimately, democratization is a multilayered phenomenon and it is reasonable to expect that the consequences of political institutions at lower levels of government greatly influence whether democratic politics can grow in previously uncultivated soil.

APPENDIX A

CHRONOLOGY OF KEY POLITICAL EVENTS

4 March 1990	Elections to the Congress of People's Deputies of the Russian Soviet Federated Socialist Republic (RSFSR) and the regional soviets within the RSFSR
12 June 1991	Election of Boris Yeltsin as president of the RSFSR
19 August 1991	Coup attempt against the president of the USSR, Mikhail Gorbachev
25 December 1991	Gorbachev resigns as president of the USSR
21 September 1993	President Yeltsin dissolves the Russian Congress of People's Deputies
13 October 1993	Initiation of governmental reform throughout Russia
12 December 1993	Ratification of the constitution of the Russian Federation and election of Russia's first federal assembly (Federation Council and State Duma)
17 December 1995	Second Duma election
16 June, 3 July 1996	Two rounds of Russia's first post-Soviet presidential election
19 December 1999	Third Duma election
31 December 1999	Boris Yeltsin resigns as president of the Russian Federation
26 March 2000	Former prime minister and acting president Vladimir Putin is elected president of the Russian Federation

APPENDIX B

INTRODUCTION TO FOUR REGIONS

NOVOSIBIRSK OBLAST

Novosibirsk oblast is located in the southeast of the West Siberian plain, at the union of the Ob' and Irtysh rivers. Its southwestern border forms an international border with Kazakhstan. To the south is Altai krai, while Tomsk oblast lies to the north. On its western border is Omsk oblast; Kemerovo oblast lies on the eastern border. The oblast is 178.2 thousand square kilometers, with a population of over 2.7 million people as of January 2001. Based on the January 1989 census, its ethnic composition is predominantly Russian (92%). Around 2.2% of the population is of German heritage. The oblast capital is 3,191 kilometers southeast of Moscow (Goskomstat Rossii 2001 v1, 519).

The capital city of the oblast—Novosibirsk—was known as Novonikolaievsk until 1925, having been founded in 1893 during the construction of the Trans-Siberian Railway. The city's initial prosperity stemmed from its close proximity to the Kuznetsk coal basin. After its official formation as an oblast on 28 September 1937, the region became heavily industrialized and was a major center of industrial production during World War II (*The Territories of the Russian Federation* 2001, 195). Since World War II, the oblast has continued to house a high proportion of the Soviet defense industry. The oblast currently has a fairly large amount of mineral resources, such as copper, gold and nickel, as well as limestone, marble, oil, and peat. The major industry in the region is the processing of metal, followed by the food industry and the energy complex. Novosibirsk also has a large concentration of scientific research facilities and has been able to attract and retain many foreign investors. According to a 1998 *Ekspert* magazine survey, the republic ranked nineteenth among Russia's regions in investment potential (Orttung et al. 2000, 390).

The last years of glasnost brought some turnover in personnel, but little alteration in ideas to the oblast government. Specifically, the first secretary of the Communist Party in the oblast, A. Kazarezov, retired in 1989 and was replaced by another member of the nomenklatura, Vitalii Mukha, in 1989. The 1990 elections of the oblast soviet introduced little change, although some informal oppositional organizations were already active within the limits of the elections. Democrats, in particular, formed the group, Democratic Orientation, and were somewhat successful in the elections to the city soviet in Novosibirsk (Reitblat 1995, 723).

SARATOV OBLAST

Saratov oblast is located in the southeast of Russia's Eastern European plain. As part of the lower Volga River valley, Volgograd oblast lies to its southwest and Kazakhstan lies to its south and east. Along its western border lie the oblasts of Voronezh and Tambov. The oblasts of Penza, Ul'ianovsk, and Samara compose its northern border. Saratov oblast is 100.2 thousand square kilometers, with a population of almost 2.7 million people as of January 2001. Based on the January 1989 census, its ethnic composition is predominantly Russian (85.6%) with around 3.8% being Ukrainian and 2.7% Kazakh. The oblast center is 858 kilometers south of Moscow (Goskomstat Rossii 2001 v1, 387).

The capital of the oblast—also called Saratov—was founded in 1590 as a fortress city along the Volga trade route. Like Novosibirsk, the city of Saratov is strategically located along the Trans-Siberian Railway. The oblast was formed in 1936 after earlier being part of Saratov krai. Prior to World War II, Saratov oblast became heavily industrialized and remained an important military center into the 1990s (*The Territories of the Russian Federation* 2001, 226). Its wealth of mineral resources, oil and gas as well as various building materials, makes Saratov oblast a major industrial area of the Volga region. Today, the most developed sectors are machine building, the chemical and petrochemical industries, energy, and food processing. According to a 1998 *Ekspert* magazine survey, the oblast ranked twenty-first among Russia's regions in investment potential (Orttung et al. 2000, 496).

At the end of the 1980s, the Communist Party enjoyed a firm and solid position in the oblast. Political changes in 1989 led the first secretary of the oblast party committee, Aleksandr Khomiakov, to leave Saratov for a position as a first deputy chairman of Gosplan in Moscow. In August 1989, Konstantin Murenin—an established member of the regional nomenklatura—became the last party leader of the oblast. The 1990 oblast elections also made Murenin the chairman of the oblast soviet. In the fall of 1989, several different oppositional organizations emerged from various voter groups, including the club Al'ternativa and the Club-Seminar of Candidates for Deputies (KSK). However, democratic candidates were not successful in winning seats to the regional soviet in March 1990, although the loosely organized bloc, Democratic Russia, performed fairly well in the elections to the city soviet (McFaul and Petrov 1998, 389).

THE REPUBLIC OF BURIATIA

The republic of Buriatia is located in the eastern Saian Mountains of southern Siberia. It lies mainly in the Transbaikal region to the east of Lake Baikal, which partially separates it from Irkutsk oblast to the north and west. Its southern border is the international boundary line between the Russian Federation and Mongolia. To its south and east lies a long border with Chita oblast while to the west is a relatively short border with the republic of Tuva. The republic is 351.3 thousand square kilometers, with a population of just over one million people as of January 2001. Based on the January 1989 census, its ethnic composition is predominantly Russian (70%) with around 24% being Buriat and 2.2% Ukrainian. The republic's center is 5,532 kilometers south and east of Moscow (Goskomstat Rossii 2001 v1, 387).

The capital city of the republic of Buriatia is Ulan-Ude. Historically, Buriatia was considered strategically important to the Russian state because it was located on the Mongol border. In the seventeenth century, the Transbaikal region was formally incorporated into the Russian Empire, and many ethnic Russians settled in the region. In 1905, a prominent nationalist, Jamtsarano, led a movement recognizing the affinity of Buriat culture with Mongolian culture. On 23 May 1923, a Buriat-Mongolian ASSR (Autonomous Soviet Socialist Republic) was established, but during Stalin's collectivization program many Buriats fled or were executed for treason. In 1937, the territory of the republic was reduced, when land was transferred to Chita oblast and Irkutsk oblast. In addition, the Mongolian script of the Buriat language was replaced with Cyrillic. In 1958, the Buriat-Mongol ASSR was renamed the Buriat ASSR. As the Soviet Union disintegrated, the region declared its sovereignty on 10 October 1990 (*The Territories of the Russian Federation* 2001, 52).

The republic of Buriatia is rich in mineral resources. It has gold deposits, coal, various nonferrous metals, and other minerals. It is one of the largest energy producers in the area and exports energy to the neighboring Chita oblast and Mongolia. Although over 13% of the republic's territory is dedicated to agriculture and almost half of its population works in agricultural, Buriatia must import agricultural products and is considered to be one of the poorest parts of Russia. According to a 1998 *Ekspert* magazine survey, the republic ranked fifty-seventh among Russia's regions in investment potential (Orttung et al. 2000, 63).

The first informal organizations emerged in Buriatia in 1988. In November 1988, socioecological experts on the Baikal developed an initiative group called the People's Front Assisting Perestroika (or the NFSP). Its participants were concerned with the cultural impact of perestroika and were active in the electoral campaign of 1989. However, the political face of the NFSP became divided between moderates and radicals. The radicals, especially the Buriats, promoted the liquidation of the Buriat autonomous republic and the creation of a union republic, which would include Buriats from the Ust-Ordynskoe Buriat okrug in Irkutsk oblast, the Aginskoe-Buriat okrug in Chita oblast, and the Ol'khovskii region of Irkutsk. As these divisions surfaced, the NFSP dissolved. By the middle of 1990, politics in the region became a battle between two factions centered around leading representatives of the soviet party elite who were never ousted from the republic (Tiukov 1995, 43).

THE REPUBLIC OF UDMURTIA

The republic of Udmurtia is located west of the Ural Mountains with the republics of Tatarstan and Bashkortostan to the south, Perm oblast to the east, and Kirov oblast to the west and north. The republic is 42.1 thousand square kilometers, with a population of over 1.6 million people as of January 2001. Based on the January 1989 census, its ethnic composition is predominantly Russian (58.9%) with around 31% being Udmurt and 6.9% Tatar. The republic's center is 1,129 kilometers south and east of Moscow (Goskomstat Rossii 2001 v1, 324).

The capital city of the republic of Udmurtia is Izhevsk. Historically, Udmurts (or Votiaks) first appeared as a distinct ethnic group in the sixth century. However, their territory has been occupied by different conquerors since the eighth century. In the thirteenth century, the Mongol Tatars occupied the region. By 1558, however, the Votiaks fell under the Russian rule. A Votiak autonomous oblast emerged on 4 November 1920. The oblast was renamed the Udmurt autonomous oblast on 1 January 1932 and became an ASSR on 28 December 1934. Like the republic of Buriatia, the republic of Udmurtia also declared its sovereignty in 1990 (*The Territories of the Russian Federation* 2001, 110–11).

The republic of Udmurtia is rich in oil, peat, and clays, and traditionally has been a leading weapons producer of imperial Russia and Soviet Russia. In the early 1990s, the military-industrial complex produced about 80% of the republic's GDP. However, with the decline of the Russian defense industry, the republic's economy faces significant problems. Other industries in the region include oil extraction and processing, automobile construction, and chemicals. According to a 1998 *Ekspert* magazine survey, the republic ranked thirty-seventh among Russia's regions in investment potential (Orttung et al. 2000, 586)

Nationality movements have played a relatively small role in the republic, since the initial creation of the Society of Udmurt Cultures (DEMEN) in December 1989 met hardened opposition from the first secretary of the republic, Petr Grishchenko. The 1990 elections in the republic introduced some moderate change in the republican leadership as an Udmurt— Valentin Tubylov—became chairman of the Supreme Soviet and a Russian— Nikolai Mironov—was elected head of the government (McFaul and Petrov 1998, 268). As in Buriatia, however, competition between two rival factions from the old elite quickly characterized regional politics.

APPENDIX C

CLASSIFYING LEGISLATIVE INSIDERS AND OUTSIDERS

CATEGORY 1: COMMUNIST PARTY/STATE POSITIONS

High Status
  First Secretaries at the oblast/republic, raion, or gorod level
  Second Secretaries at the oblast/republic, raion, or gorod level
  Heads of the Secretariat of republic-level soviets

Medium Status
  Deputies, secretaries of executive committees at the raion or gorod level
  Deputies, representatives, secretaries of an oblast- or republic-level committee
  Deputies or representatives of oblast/republic-, raion-, or gorod- level soviets
  Attorneys General at the oblast/republic level

Low Status
  Deputies or representatives of non-executive committees at the raion or
    gorod level
  Attorneys General at the raion or gorod level

CATEGORY 2: INDUSTRY/TRANSPORT POSITIONS

High Status
  General Directors of factories, enterprises, etc.
  Deputy Directors of factories, enterprises, etc.
  Heads/Chiefs of factories, enterprises, etc.

Medium Status
  Heads and managers of factory departments/sectors, engineers
  Representatives of industrial-sector committees

Low Status
  General Workers: machinists, bus drivers, lathe operators, electricians, etc.

CATEGORY 3: AGRICULTURE

High Status
  Directors and board chairmen of collective farms or state farms

Medium Status
   Managers of farm sectors
   Agronomists

Low Status
   Workers: zoo technicians, milkers, etc.

CATEGORY 4: OTHER PROFESSIONALS

High Status
   Head doctors of oblast/republic-, raion-, or gorod-level hospitals or clinics
   Heads/directors of schools, institutes, technical schools, etc.
   Directors of youth centers
   Heads of banks

Medium Status
   General Educators: professors, college instructors, lectures, teachers, etc.
   Members of the media: journalists, editors, and correspondents
   Bank managers
   Doctors

Low Status
   Veterans
   Students
   Pensioners

NOTES

1—THE RULES OF THE GAME

1. The regional parliamentary electoral systems are likely to be changed once more since President Putin signed a July 2005 law eliminating the SMD-plurality half of the Duma's electoral system.

2. See Colton (1998, 6–11) for a discussion of the main events leading up to the 1993 elections.

3. For an extensive discussion of the conquest of various nationalities and the creation of Soviet borders, see Pipes (1997).

4. There have been numerous proposals to reduce the number of Russian regions, and different regions have taken steps toward possible mergers. In December 2003, for example, voters in Komi-Permiak okrug and Perm oblast expressed overwhelming support for referendums that proposed the unification of these two regions (see Radio Free Europe/Radio Liberty, *Russian Political Weekly*, 16 January 2004).

5. The republic of Udmurtia reversed this decision via referendum in March 2000.

6. In addition to appointing governors, President Yeltsin also sought to develop widespread support for reform by appointing presidential representatives to these regions. The presidential representatives were to report whether local authorities were carrying out the will of the federal government, which was more or less conceptualized as the will of the president. While presidential representatives were not supposed to interfere directly in local politics, in practice there was a noticeable tendency for them to intervene in the work of the regional and local administrations (Barabashev 1994, 188). However, when the presidential representatives came into conflict with governors, Yeltsin increasingly took the governors' side, and the institution eventually atrophied (Kirkow 1998, 55).

7. The regions were Amur, Briansk, Cheliabinsk, Krasnoiarsk, Lipetsk, Orel, Penza, and Smolensk (McFaul and Petrov 1998 v1, 602–5).

8. Republics without presidents at the time include Altai, Buriatia, Chuvashia, Dagestan, Karelia, Khakassia, Komi, North Ossetia, and Udmurtia.

9. Yeltsin established the electoral systems in Moscow and Moscow oblast by special decree (Golosov 2004, 210). Accordingly, these two cases are not included in the subsequent analyses.

10. The oblast soviet in Penza dissolved itself after adopting the new law on elections to its regional parliament. Therefore, I do not include it in my analysis as an instance where the regional soviet was dissolved (McFaul and Petrov 1998 v2, 769). Likewise, I do not consider the soviet in Rostov oblast as having been dissolved because it was not dissolved until January 1994, and the new elections were held that March (McFaul and Petrov 1998 v2, 800).

11. In Yaroslavl' oblast, the soviet supported Yeltsin during the crisis and dissolved itself peacefully in accordance with Yeltsin's recommendation (McFaul and Petrov 1998 v2, 996).

12. The law was adopted on 10 November 1993, and the new elections were held in December 1993, along with the federal Duma election (McFaul and Petrov 1998 v2, 196).

13. One region, Koriak okrug, created an assembly below the prescribed range; the assembly consisted of only 8 deputies (McFaul and Petrov 1998 v1, 600–602; Slider 1996, 255–57).

14. Electoral regulations in two regions, Moscow city and Moscow oblast, were introduced by a special decree of the federal executive (Golosov 2004, 210); therefore, these two cases are not examined. Due to the 1994–1996 war, the republic of Chechnya is also excluded from the analysis.

2—BEYOND SELF-INTEREST

1. While the phrase "beyond self-interest" may connote explanations contrary to those that emphasize self-interest (Mansbridge 1990), this discussion should make evident that the title of this chapter means something quite different. It focuses on developing a more thorough, context-based understanding of self-interest.

2. Geddes also suggests that institutional designers in Eastern Europe enjoyed an institutional "blank slate" after the collapse of communism. Not everyone agrees that institutional design in Eastern Europe occurred on a blank slate, however. Elster et al. (1998) describe institutional choice as "rebuilding the ship at sea": a process clearly influenced by the existing system, the actors present, and the contextual fluctuations at the time. Both McAuley (1997) and Kitschelt (1995) support this alternative perspective.

3. Despite the ban on extra-state political activity, some independent organizations managed to exist. One such organization was the People's Labor Union (NTS)—a network of underground dissidents with links to émigré groups abroad (Fish 1995, 31).

3—THE POWER TO CHOOSE

1. The data used to calculate the weighted average district magnitude for the Russian regions come from a variety of sources. McFaul and Petrov (1998 v1, 590–602) provide in their table P.37 a detailed description of the initial electoral systems in the provinces. Descriptions of the republics' electoral systems are found in their corresponding chapters (1998, v2). Additional descriptions of the regional parliamentary electoral systems can be found in publications by the Central Election Commission of the Russian Federation (1998); Golosov (1999, 2001, 2004); Petrov (1995); and Slider (1996).

2. $WADM = (1 \times 100^2 + 100 \times 1^2)/200 = 50.5$

3. $WADM = (1 \times 8^2 + 7 \times 6^2)/50 = 6.32$

4. In addition, the dependent variable, WADM, has a mean of 1.37 and a variance of 0.80.

5. Lijphart's (1994) effective threshold is the midpoint between the minimum vote percentage that can earn a party a seat under the most favorable conditions and the maximum vote percentage that may be insufficient for a party to win a seat under the most unfavorable conditions. While several problems with this measure exist, the most fundamental for the issue at hand is that the calculation is largely dependent on district magnitude, which means that it also fails to distinguish between

SMD-plurality and SMD-majority systems. Since both systems have average district magnitudes equal to one, they both end up with identical effective thresholds (50%). To correct this, Lijphart assumes a relatively small number of candidates for SMD-plurality elections (4 to 5), which would indicate a lower threshold of 20% to 25%. The subsequent effective threshold is then taken to be the midpoint between 20% and 50%, that is 35%. However, this new threshold is not only arbitrary but is also contingent on assumptions about party competition that are questionable for settings where neither politicians nor voters have experience with electoral politics, and the dynamics of strategic voting and strategic party entry present in established democracies are less likely to occur. Moreover, this new estimated threshold fails to sufficiently distinguish between substantively different electoral system decisions in Russia's regions. It produces essentially the same scores for Saratov oblast—which adopted a mixed electoral system with 25 SMDs and one 10-member district (T_{eff} = 34%)—and other regions that adopted SMD-plurality systems (T_{eff} = 35%).

6. The congress was comprised of 1,068 seats of which 900 represented territorial districts and 168 represented national-territorial districts. I rely on the larger seat total, the 900 territorial districts.

7. The data for this measure come from McFaul and Petrov (1998 v1, 369–72).

8. The following analysis was conducted using the percentage of rural residents instead of, and in addition to, the average number of candidates. It failed to attain significance in either instance. In the latter case, the inclusion of percent rural also added substantial collinearity.

9. The scores reflect the accounts of individual case studies assembled in the *Political Almanac of Russia, 1989–1997* (McFaul and Petrov 1998, v2).

10. This timing variable was calculated from the dates provided in McFaul and Petrov (1998 v1, 602–5).

11. Treisman also confirms the argument presented earlier that republics enjoyed a higher level of independence from the center than the provinces did. He shows that republican governors were more likely to publicly oppose Yeltsin than provincial governors.

12. The data for this variable come from McFaul and Petrov (1998 v1, 379–84).

13. The information for this variable comes from McFaul and Petrov (1998, v2).

14. Three candidates were required to compete in the election for it to be considered valid (McFaul and Petrov 1998 v1, 179).

15. Most of this data come from McFaul and Petrov (1998 v1, 387–90). The exception is the data on Tatarstan. However, McAuley (1997, 105) provides a detailed account of the Federation Council election in Tatarstan, including some discussion of the three candidates competing for the two seats (republican president Shaimiev, speaker of the regional parliament Mukhametshin, and deputy speaker Grachev).

16. Data on party nominations of SMD deputies by region come from McFaul and Petrov (1998 v1, 550–67).

17. Data for this variable come from Goskomstat (2001 v1, passim).

18. Although as the case of Saratov oblast in the following chapter demonstrates, one cannot be certain that governors did not consider parliamentary interests, even in those cases where the regional soviet was dissolved.

19. This problem emerged in prior, unreported empirical analyses and prohibits an accurate interpretation of the regression coefficients.

20. It is important to note that all of the regions besides the republics are treated as though an independent executive held office, since President Yeltsin appointed temporary executives to replace disloyal governors whom he dismissed during the constitutional crisis.

21. This division of the population under analysis is preferable to one that separates the regions on the basis of region type, because the effects of the main explanatory variables for electoral system choice under different distributions of governmental power are more able to be generalized to contexts beyond Russia's regions.

22. Notice, however, that the analysis is not sampling cases from a larger universe but is looking at all the cases in the population. Therefore, the analysis does not need to rely on statistical significance in the way one does when working with samples; nonetheless, the significance levels of the unstandardized coefficients are reported as a way to assess each variable's impact.

23. Sakha did stray from Yeltsin's recommendation, however, by employing an SMD-majority system, which emphasizes the need to examine electoral formula decisions.

24. To test for multi-collinearity, each independent variable was regressed on the other independent variables in the model to determine whether the resulting adjusted R^2s were substantially higher than the adjusted R^2 for the original model. The models do not suffer from multi-collinearity. However, to test the robustness of the significance for Republic, the ethnic fractionalization index was removed from the analysis. The coefficient for Republic remained significant and positive. Finally, the regression analysis was conducted with the one republic (Sakha) removed as an additional check to determine whether the dummy variable was performing correctly. The coefficients of the remaining variables were exactly the same.

25. The analysis was also conducted using the percentage of SMD deputies elected in a region nominated by all parties (communist and non-communist). This variable was consistently insignificant.

4—DISCERNING TREES IN THE FOREST

1. Appendix B provides a brief historical and geographic introduction to each of the four regions.

2. At the 1987 Plenum, Gorbachev also proposed holding a conference of the CPSU to deal with major questions of policy, especially the issue of democratization. During the period leading up to what would be the party's 19th conference, the struggle between reformers and hard-liners intensified dramatically. Supporters of democratic reform depicted the administrative apparatus of the Communist Party as a usurper of the people's right to self-government. Meanwhile, in March 1988, while Gorbachev was on a trip in Yugoslavia, conservatives within the party responded to his reforms and the anti-establishment rhetoric with a letter supposedly written by a Leningrad chemistry teacher. The "Andreeva letter," published in *Sovetskaia Rossiia*, was laced with Stalinist rhetoric condemning Gorbachev's policy of perestroika and depicting it as an enemy ploy to undermine socialism and the nation as a whole (Eklof 1989, 29). It took three weeks for Gorbachev's response, but when it came it included several media addresses and a rebuke to Gorbachev's main rival, Egor Ligachev, from the Politburo.

3. These percentages were calculated from the election results as presented in the newspapers of the regions. For Novosibirsk oblast, see *Sovetskaia Sibir'* (9 March 1990,

21 March 1990, 10 April 1990, 24 April 1990, 15 June 1990). For Saratov oblast, see *Kommunist* (8 March 1990, 21 March 1990, 24 April 1990, 12 May 1990, 27 June 1990, 1 July 1990). For the republic of Buriatia, see *Pravda Buriatii* (10 March 1990, 12 March 1990, 23 March 1990, 11 April 1990, 8 May 1990, 16 May 1990). For the republic of Udmurtia, see *Udmurtskaia Pravda* (10 March 1990, 24 March 1990, 25 April 1990, 2 May 1990) and Kirillov (2002, 46–53).

4. Of all the deputies elected in the 4 soviets, 2 were candidates for membership in the CPSU, while 9 were members of the Communist Youth League (Komsomol), as indicated in the tables.

5. Notice that the numbers for Udmurtia are slightly different from those presented in Moraski (2003). The difference stems from the acquisition of information from Kirillov (2002). However, since the change increased the lower estimate of likely insiders from 56% to 61%, it actually lends greater support to the contention that political insiders dominated the regional soviet there.

6. An interesting metamorphosis that emphasizes the fluctuation of party affiliations in the regions occurred in 1993 when the former leadership of Democratic Orientation, Prosenko, became the head of the local branch of the nationalist front Salvation (Reitblat 1995, 265).

7. Neither Yabloko nor the Party of Russian Unity and Accord were active in the region (Reitblat 1995, 278).

8. It later became known from documents discovered in a White House office that Rutskoi had considered Mukha a candidate for prime minister in his government (McFaul and Petrov 1998, 723–24).

9. Moscow considered two additional candidates for the post of oblast head of administration. They included first deputy of the head of the oblast administration, Vasilii Kiselev, and presidential representative in the oblast, Anatolii Manokhin (Reitblat 1995, 272–73).

10. Those individuals competing on the side of Democratic Russia during the 1990 city soviet election managed to win almost 40% of the seats (McFaul and Petrov, 1998, 839).

11. In August 1989, Murenin became the last first secretary of the oblast committee of the Communist Party of the Soviet Union, and in 1990 he headed the oblast establishment.

12. Golovachev supported the removal of Saratov's "closed" status and openly sought to attract firms from France and Germany. He also supported the adoption of a new federal constitution drafted by the Yeltsin administration. Attempts by the establishment to undermine Golovachev merely enhanced his democratic image (Moses 1994, 114–15).

13. Independent voter blocs nominated the other three victors: A. N. Sergeenkov, A. N. Gordeev, and N. N. Lysenko (Moses 1994, 114–15).

14. It is important to emphasize, however, that the soviets in both the republic of Buriatia and the republic of Udmurtia already had begun formal discussions regarding the design of new constitutions.

15. In the end, however, the attempt to create local organizations supporting the coup leaders failed as did the coup itself (Moses 1994, 36).

16. Following the new legislative elections, Volkov indeed was able to broaden his influence and defeat Tubylov to become chairman of the parliament (Shukin 1995, 11).

17. According to Taagepera and Shugart (1989, 179–83), assembly sizes that are the cube root of the active population (defined as not just the voting population,

but the literate population) provide the optimal balance for communicating with both constituents and other representatives. Enlarging the assembly size above this level decreases the number of channels with constituents but increases the number of channels between legislators.

5—MIDWIVES AND GRAVEDIGGERS

1. Some values of the weighted average district magnitudes in Golosov's (1999) analysis differ from those in chapter 4. The discrepancies emerge because this book examines the first round of regional parliamentary elections, while Golosov focuses on elections between 1995 and 1998. For some regions, the election held between 1995 and 1998 was the first regional parliamentary election. For other regions, the election held during this period was actually the second regional parliamentary election and was governed by a different electoral law that included potential changes to the electoral system's districting and assembly size.

2. The Central Election Commission has not officially published data on the 1993–1994 regional elections. As a result, most of Golosov's data for these years come from sources similar to those used in the four case studies presented in this book, regional newspapers. However, while regional newspapers listed candidates by electoral district, they did not regularly provide details on party memberships. Also, while some regional election returns provided district-level information, others provided only a list of candidates. The inconsistency of these data forced Golosov to research specific articles across the 89 regions in the months prior to their elections.

3. While Russia's Central Election Commission has accumulated data on the 1993–1994 regional parliamentary elections, it has released them only on rare occasions and usually to influential organizations, such as Russia's presidential administration. Fortunately, Slider (1996) gained access to some of these data and published aggregated descriptions of the occupational backgrounds of the legislators elected in Russia's first post-Soviet regional elections.

4. For the republic of Karachaevo-Cherkesia, Slider does not provide a percentage but merely notes that executive officials and enterprise/farm managers held a majority of seats. He does not provide data for the republics of Adygeia, Chechnya, Khakassia, or North Ossetia.

5. Moscow and Moscow oblast are included in the analysis, because the question under investigation concerns the effects of the electoral systems, rather than how they were designed. Missing information for the republics of Adygeia, Karachaevo-Cherkesia, Khakassia, and North Ossetia are supplemented with data published by the Russian Federation's Central Election Commission (1998), thus raising the total number of regions to 88. Of the 88 cases, the lowest percentage of insiders was 13%, the highest 94%.

6. The data on registered voters are in thousands and come from McFaul and Petrov (1998 v2, 387–90).

7. The data come from Goskomstat (2001, 101–2; 270–1). Unfortunately, data for these variables are not available for several regions including the republic of Ingushetia and many of the autonomous okrugs, thus lowering the number of cases.

8. This information was acquired from the Central Election Commission of the Republic of Udmurtia on 20 May 1999.

BIBLIOGRAPHY

Aldrich, John H. 1995. *Why Parties? The Origin and Transformation of Political Parties in America*. Chicago: University of Chicago Press.

Amoretti, Ugo M., and Nancy Bermeo, eds. 2004. *Federalism and Territorial Cleavages*. Baltimore: Johns Hopkins University Press.

Aves, Jonathan. 1992. "The Evolution of Independent Political Movements after 1988." In *The Road to Post-Communism: Independent Political Movements in the Soviet Union, 1985–1991*, ed. Geoffrey A. Hosking, Jonathan Aves, and Peter J. S. Duncan. New York: Pinter Publishers.

Badovskii, D. V., and A. Iu. Shutov. 1997. "Regional Elites in Post-Soviet Russia: Aspects of Political Involvement." *Russian Social Science Review* 38(3): 32–55.

Barabashev, Georgii V. 1994. "Main Currents in the Development of Russian Local Self-Government: The First Post-Soviet Year." In *Local Power and Post-Soviet Politics*, ed. Theodore H. Friedgut and Jeffrey Hahn. Armonk, NY: M. E. Sharpe, pp. 187–91.

Barghoorn, Frederick C., and Thomas Remington. 1986. *Politics in the USSR*. 3rd ed. Boston: Little, Brown.

Barkan, Joel D. 1995. "Elections in Agrarian Societies." *Journal of Democracy* 6: 106–16.

Bawn, Kathleen. 1993. "The Logic of Institutional Preferences: German Electoral Law as a Social Choice Outcome." *American Journal of Political Science* 37(4): 965–89.

Beissinger, Mark R. 2002. *Nationalist Mobilization and the Collapse of the Soviet State*. New York: Cambridge University Press.

Belykh, Iurii. 13 October 1993. "Ob obrazovanii vremennogo oblastnogo komiteta po voprosam reformy organov predstavitel'noi vlasti i organizatsii mestnogo samoupravleniia." *Saratovskie Vesti*.

———. 16 March 1994. "29 maia—vybory v oblastnuiu dumu: o vyborakh v predstavitel'nyi organ gosudarstvennoi vlasti saratovskoi oblasti." *Saratovskie vesti*.

Benoit, Kenneth. 2002. "The Endogeneity Problem in Electoral Studies: A Critical Reexamination of Duverger's Mechanical Effect." *Electoral Studies* 21: 35–46.

———. 2004. "Models of Electoral System Change." *Electoral Studies* 23(3): 363–84.

Benoit, Kenneth, and Jacqueline Hayden. 2004. "Institutional Change and Persistence: The Evolution of Poland's Electoral System, 1989–2001." *Journal of Politics* 66(2): 396–427.

Benoit, Kenneth, and John W. Schiemann. 2001. "Institutional Choice in New Democracies: Bargaining over Hungary's 1989 Electoral Law." *Journal of Theoretical Politics* 13(2): 153–82.

Bermeo, Nancy. 2002. "A New Look at Federalism: The Import of Institutions." *Journal of Democracy* 13(2): 96–110.

Bernhard, Michael, Timothy Nordstrom, and Christopher Reenock. 2001. "Economic Performance, Institutional Intermediation, and Democratic Survival." *Journal of Politics* 63(3): 775–804.

Birch, Sarah. 2003. *Electoral Systems and Political Transformation in Post-Communist Europe.* Basingstoke, NY: Palgrave Macmillan.

Birch, Sarah, Frances Millard, Marina Popescu, and Kieran Williams. 2002. *Embodying Democracy: Electoral System Design in Post-Communist Europe.* Basingstoke, NY: Palgrave Macmillan.

Bogdanor, Vernon. 1984. *What is Proportional Representation? A Guide to the Issue.* Oxford: Martin Robertson.

Boix, Carles. 1999. "Setting the Rules of the Game: The Choice of Electoral Systems in Advanced Democracies." *American Political Science Review* 93(3): 609–24.

Brady, David, and Jongryn Mo. 1990. "Strategy and Choice in the 1988 National Assembly Election of Korea." *Comparative Political Studies* 24: 405–29.

Brown, Archie. 1996. *The Gorbachev Factor.* Oxford: Oxford University Press.

Brown, Ruth. 1998. "Party Development in the Regions: When Did Parties Start to Play a Part in Politics." In *Party Politics in Post-Communist Russia,* ed. John Löewenhardt. Portland, OR: Frank Cass, pp. 9–30.

Bunce, Valerie. 1999. *Subversive Institutions: The Design and Destruction of Socialism and the State.* New York: Cambridge University Press.

Buriatia Republic Electoral Commission. 10 March 1990. "Spisok narodnykh deputatov Buriatskoi ASSR, izbrannykh 4 marta 1990 goda." *Pravda Buriatii,* p. 2.

———. 23 March 1990. "Spisok narodnykh deputatov Buriatskoi ASSR, izbrannykh pri povtornom golosovanii 18 marta 1990 goda." *Pravda Buriatii,* p. 2.

———. 11 April 1990. "V Tsentral'noi izbiratel'noi komissii po vyboram narodnykh deputatov Buriatskoi ASSR." *Pravda Buriatii.*

———. 8 May 1990. "Soobshchenie Tsentral'noi izbiratel'noi komissii ob itogakh povtornykh vyborov narodnykh deputatov Buriatskoi ASSR po otdel'nym izbiratel'nym okrugam sostoiavshikhsym 5 maia 1990 goda." *Pravda Buriatii.*

———. 8 May 1990. "Soobshchenie Tsentral'noi izbiratel'noi komissii o rezul'tatakh vyborov narodnykh deputatov Buriatskoi ASSR pri povtornom golosovanii sostoiavsheemsia 12 maia 1990 goda." *Pravda Buriatii.*

Burkova, O. N., et al. 1996. *Kommentarii k Konstitutsii Respubliki Buriatiia,* Ulan-Ude: Buriatskoe knizhnoe izdatel'stvo.

Carey, John M., and Matthew S. Shugart. 1995. "Incentives to Cultivate a Personal Vote: A Rank Ordering of Electoral Formulas." *Electoral Studies* 14(4): 417–39.

Central Election Commission of the Russian Federation. 1996. *Vybory deputatov Gosudarstvennoi Dumy, 1995.* Moscow: Ves' Mir.

———. 1998. *Vybory v zakonodatel'nye (predstavitel'nye) organy gosudarstvennoi vlasti sub"ektov Rossiiskoi Federatsii, 1995–1997.* Moscow: Ves' Mir.

Centre of Regional Analysis and Forecasting of the Russian Academy of State Administration under the President of Russia. 1998. *Russia's Regions: Statistical Report of Socio-Economic Development, 1992–95.* http://www.region.rags.ru/maineng.htm.

Cheibubb, José Antonion, Adam Przeworski, and Sebastian Saiegh. 2004. "Government Coalitions and Legislative Success under Presidentialism and Parliamentarianism." *British Journal of Political Science* 34(4): 565–88.

Clark, William A. 1989. *Soviet Regional Elite Mobility after Khrushchev.* New York: Praeger Publishers.

Clem, Ralph S., and Peter R. Craumer. 1993. "The Geography of the April 25 (1993) Russian Referendum." *Post-Soviet Geography* 34(8): 481–96.

———. 1995. "The Politics of Russia's Regions: A Geographical Analysis of the Russian Election and Constitutional Plebiscite of December 1993." *Post-Soviet Geography* 36(2): 67–86.

Collins, Kathleen. 2002. "Clans, Pacts, and Politics in Central Asia." *Journal of Democracy* 13(3): 137–52.

Colomer, Josep M. 2005. "It's Parties that Choose Electoral Systems (or, Duverger's Laws Upside Down)." *Political Studies* 53(1): 1–21.

Colton, Timothy J. 1991. "The Moscow Election of 1990." In *Milestones in Glasnost and Perestroika: Politics and People,* ed. Ed A. Hewett and Victor H. Winston. Washington D.C.: The Brookings Institution, pp. 326–84.

———. 1998. "Introduction: The 1993 Election and the New Russian Politics." In *Growing Pains: Russian Democracy and the Election of 1993,* ed. Timothy J. Colton and Jerry F. Hough. Washington, D.C.: The Brookings Institution Press, pp. 1–36.

Coppedge, Michael. 1994. *Strong Parties and Lame Ducks: Presidential Partyarchy and Factionalism in Venezuela.* Stanford: Stanford University Press.

———. 1997. "District Magnitude, Economic Performance, and Party-System Fragmentation in Five Latin American Countries." *Comparative Political Studies* 30(2): 156–85.

Cox, Gary W. 1997. *Making Votes Count: Strategic Coordination in the World's Electoral Systems.* New York: Cambridge University Press.

Crawford, Beverly, and Arend Lijphart. 1995. "Explaining Political and Economic Change in Post-Communist Eastern Europe: Old Legacies, New Institutions, Hegemonic Norms, and International Pressures." *Comparative Political Studies* 28(2): 171–99.

Danilenko, Viktor. 1991. "Electoral Reform." In *Perestroika-Era Politics: The New Soviet Legislature and Gorbachev's Political Reforms,* ed. Robert T. Huber and Donald R. Kelley. Armonk, NY: M. E. Sharpe.

Debardeleben, Joan. 1997. *Russian Politics in Transition.* Boston: Houghton Mifflin Co.

Diamond, Larry. 1999. *Developing Democracy: Toward Consolidation.* Baltimore: Johns Hopkins University Press.

Duncan, Peter J. S. 1992. "The Rebirth of Politics in Russia." In *The Road to Post-Communism: Independent Political Movements in the Soviet Union, 1985–1991,* ed. Geoffrey A. Hosking, Jonathan Aves, and Peter J. S. Duncan. New York: Pinter Publishers.

Duverger, Maurice. 1954. *Political Parties: Their Organization and Activity in the Modern State.* New York: John Wiley and Sons.

Egorov, I. V. 1996. "Obshee i osobennoe v stanovlenii i funktsionirovanii system vlasti v respublikakh v sostave Rossiiskoi Federatsii (na materialakh Tatarstana i Udmurtskoi Respubliki)." In *Kuda idet Rossiia?* ed. T. Zaslavskaia. Moscow: Aspect-Press, pp. 158–60.

Egorov, Igor'. 1998. "Udmurtskaia Respublika." In *Organy gosudarstvennoi vlasti sub"ektov Rossiiskoi Federatsii,* ed. Vladimir Gel'man et al. Moscow: Mezhdunarodnyi Institut Gumanitarno-Politicheskikh Issledovanii, pp. 79–82.

Eklof, Ben. 1989. *Soviet Briefing: Gorbachev and the Reform Period.* Boulder, CO: Westview Press.

Elster, Jon, Claus Offe, and Ulrich K. Preuss. 1998. *Institutional Design in Post-communist Societies: Rebuilding the Ship at Sea.* New York: Cambridge University Press.

Fish, M. Steven. 1995. *Democracy from Scratch: Opposition and Regime in the New Russian Revolution.* Princeton, NJ: Princeton University Press.

———. 2003. "The Impact of the 1999–2000 Parliamentary and Presidential Elections on Political Party Development." In *The 1999–2000 Elections in Russia: Their Impact and Legacy,* ed. Vicki L. Hesli and William M. Reisinger. New York: Cambridge University Press, pp. 186–212.

Fleron, Frederic. 1970. "Representation of Career Types in the Soviet Political Leadership." In *Political Leadership in Eastern Europe and the Soviet Union*, ed. R. Barry Farrell. Chicago: Aldine Publishing Co., pp. 108–39.

Friedrich, Carl J. 1968. *Constitutional Government and Democracy*. Waltham, MA: Blaisdell Publishing Co.

Frye, Timothy. 1997. "A Politics of Institutional Choice: Post-Communist Presidencies". *Comparative Political Studies* 30(5): 523–52.

Gabel, Matthew J. 1995. "The Political Consequences of Electoral Laws in the 1990 Hungarian Elections." *Comparative Politics* 27(2): 205–14.

Garrett, Geoffrey. 1992. "International Cooperation and Institutional Choice: The European Community Internal Market." *International Organization* 45:533–60.

Geddes, Barbara. 1995. "A Comparative Perspective on the Leninist Legacy in Eastern Europe." *Comparative Political Studies* 28(2): 239–74.

———. 1996. "Initiation of New Democratic Institutions in Eastern Europe and Latin America." In *Institutional Design in New Democracies: Eastern Europe and Latin America*, ed. Arend Lijphart and Carlos H. Waisman. Boulder, CO: Westview Press, pp. 15–41.

Gehlen, Michael P., and Michael McBride. 1968. "The Soviet Central Committee: An Elite Analysis." *American Political Science Review* 62: 1232–41.

Gel'man, Vladimir. 2000a. "Izuchenie vyborov v Rossii: Issledovatel'skie napravleniia i metody analiza." In *Vybory i partii v regionakh Rossii*, ed. G. Liukhterkhandt-Mikhaleva and S. Ryzhenkov. Moscow: Letnii sad, pp. 12–43.

———. 2000b. "Subnational Institutions in Contemporary Russia." In *Institutions and Political Change in Russia*, ed. Neil Robinson. New York: St. Martin's Press, pp. 85–105.

———. 2004. "Federal Policies toward Local Government in Russia: The Process of Institution Building." In *The Politics of Local Government in Russia*, ed. Alfred B. Evans and Vladimir Gel'man. New York: Rowman and Littlefield, pp. 85–103.

Gel'man, Vladimir, and Grigorii V. Golosov. 1998. "Regional Party System Formation in Russia: The Deviant Case of Sverdlovsk Oblast'" In *Party Politics in Post-Communist Russia*, ed. John Löewenhardt. Portland, OR: Frank Cass, pp. 32–53.

Golder, Matt. 2003. "Electoral Institutions, Unemployment, and Extreme Right-Wing Parties: A Correction." *British Journal of Political Science* 33(3): 525–35.

Golosov, Grigorii V. 1999. "From Adygeya to Yaroslavl: Factors of Party Development in the Regions of Russia, 1995–1998." *Europe-Asia Studies* 51(8): 1333–65.

———. 2001. "Political Parties, Electoral Systems, and Women's Representation in the Regional Legislative Assemblies of Russia, 1995–1998." *Party Politics* 7(1): 45–68.

———. 2004. *Democracy Unclaimed: Political Parties in the Regions of Russia*. Boulder, CO: Lynne Rienner.

Golosov, Grigorii V., and Iulia Shevchenko. 1999. "Political Parties and Independent Candidates in Single-Member Constituencies." In *Elections in Russia, 1993–1996: Analyses, Documents, and Data*, ed. Vladimir Gel'man and Grigorii V. Golosov. Berlin: Ed. Sigma, pp. 127–49.

Goskomstat Rossii. 1998. *Rossiiskii statisticheskii ezhegodnik, 1998*. Moscow: State Statistics Committee of the Russian Federation.

———. 2001. *Regiony Rossii*. Moscow: State Statistics Committee of the Russian Federation.

Grofman, Bernard, Lisa Handley, and Richard G. Niemi. 1992. *Minority Representation and the Quest for Equality*. New York: Cambridge University Press.

Grumm, J. G. 1958. "Theories of Electoral Systems." *Midwest Journal of Political Science* 2: 357–76.

Hahn, Jeffrey W. 1994. "Reforming Post-Soviet Russia: The Attitudes of Local Politicians." In *Local Power and Post-Soviet Politics*, ed. Theodore H. Friedgut and Jeffrey Hahn. Armonk, NY: M. E. Sharpe, pp. 208–38.

———. 1997a. "Democratization and Political Participation in Russia's Regions" In *Democratic Changes and Authoritarian Reactions in Russia, Ukraine, Belarus, and Moldova*, ed. Karen Dawisha and Bruce Parrott. New York: Cambridge University Press, pp. 130–74.

———. 1997b. "Regional Elections and Political Stability in Russia." *Post-Soviet Geography and Economics* 38(5): 251–63.

Hain, Peter. 1986. *Proportional Misrepresentation: The Case against PR in Britain*. Aldershot, Hants (England): Ashgate.

Hallet, George H., Jr. 1937. *Proportional Representation: The Key to Democracy*. Washington, D.C.: National Home Library Foundation.

Harasymiw, Bohdan. 1969. "Nomenklatura: the Soviet Communist Party's Leadership Recruitment System." *Canadian Journal of Political Science* 2: 493–512.

Helf, Gavin, and Jeffrey W. Hahn. 1992. "Old Dogs and New Tricks: Party Elites in the Russian Regional Elections of 1990." *Slavic Review* 51(3): 511–30.

Hendley, Kathryn. 1997. "Legal Development in Post-Soviet Russia." *Post-Soviet Affairs* 13(3): 228–51.

Hermens, F. A. 1941. *Democracy or Anarchy? A Study of Proportional Representation*. South Bend, IN: University of Notre Dame Press.

Herron, Erik S., and Misa Nishikawa. 2001. "Contamination Effects and the Number of Parties in Mixed-superposition Electoral Systems." *Electoral Studies* 20: 63–86.

Hewett, Ed A., with Thane Gustafson and Victor H. Winston. 1991. "The Nineteenth Party Conference." In *Milestones in Glasnost and Perestroyka: Politics and People*, ed. Ed A. Hewett and Victor H. Winston. Washington, D.C.: The Brookings Institution Press, pp. 112–31.

Hoag, C. G., and G. H. Hallet. 1926. *Proportional Representation*. New York: Macmillan.

Horowitz, Donald L. 1985. *Ethnic Groups in Conflict*. Berkeley: University of California Press.

———. 1991. *A Democratic South Africa: Constitutional Engineering in a Divided Society*. Berkeley, CA: University of California Press.

Horwill, George. 1925. *Proportional Representation: Its Dangers and Defects*. London: Allen and Unwin.

Hough, Jerry F. 1998. "The Failure of Party Formation and the Future of Russian Democracy." In *Growing Pains: Russian Democracy and the Election of 1993*, ed. Timothy J. Colton and Jerry F. Hough. Washington, D.C.: The Brookings Institution Press, pp. 669–711.

Hough, Jerry F., Evelyn Davidheiser, and Susan Goodrich Lehmann. 1996. *The 1996 Russian Presidential Election*. Washington, D.C.: The Brookings Institution Press.

Huntington, Samuel P. 1991. *The Third Wave: Democratization in the Late Twentieth Century*. Norman, OK: Oklahoma University Press.

Independent Institute of Elections (Nezavisimyi Institut Vyborov). http://vibory.ru/elects/lead_r.html. 7 April 2004.

"Informatsionnoe soobshchenie o vneocherednoi sessii oblastnogo soveta narodnykh deputatov." 13 October 1993. *Saratovskie vesti*.

Ishiyama, John T. 1993. "Founding Elections and the Development of Transitional Parties: The Cases of Estonia and Latvia, 1990–1992." *Communist and Post-Communist Studies* 26(3): 277–99.

"Ivan Ivanovich Indinok—glava administratsii Novosibirskoi oblasti," 22 December 1993. *Sovetskaia Sibir'*.

Ivanov, G. 27 January 1994. "Vnosiatsia izmeneniia." *Sovetskaia Sibir'*.

Jasiewicz, Krzystof. 1993. "Structures of Representation" In *Developments in East European Politics*, ed. Stephen White, Judy Batt, and Paul G. Lewis. Basingstoke, NY: Macmillan Press, pp. 253–79.

———. 1998. "Elections and Voting Behaviour" In *Developments in Central and East European Politics*, ed. Stephen White, Judy Batt, and Paul G. Lewis. Durham, NC: Duke University Press, pp. 166–87.

Kahn, Jeffrey. 2002. *Federalism, Democratization, and the Rule of Law in Russia*. New York: Oxford University Press.

Kaminski, Marek M. 1999. "How Communism Could Have Been Saved: Formal Analysis of Electoral Bargaining in Poland in 1989." *Public Choice* 98: 83–109.

———. 2002. "Do Parties Benefit from Electoral Manipulation? Electoral Laws and Heresthetics in Poland, 1989–93." *Journal of Theoretical Politics* 14(3): 325–58.

Karasik, Theodore W. 1994. *Russia and Eurasia Facts and Figures Annual*. Gulf Breeze, FL: Academic International Press.

Katz, Richard S. 1980. *A Theory of Parties and Electoral Systems*. Baltimore: Johns Hopkins University Press.

Kelley, Donald R. 1991. "Gorbachev's Reforms and the Factionalization of Soviet Politics: Can the New System Cope with Pluralism?" In *Perestroika-Era Politics: The New Soviet Legislature and Gorbachev's Political Reforms*, ed. Robert T. Huber and Donald R. Kelley. Armonk, NY: M. E. Sharpe.

Kempton, Daniel R., and Terry D. Clark. 2002. "An Introduction to Center-Periphery Relations" In *Center-Periphery Relations in the Former Soviet Union*, ed. Daniel R. Kempton and Terry D. Clark. Westport, CT: Praeger, pp. 1–10.

Kim, Jae-On, and Mahn-Geum Ohn. 1992. "A Theory of Minor-Party Persistence: Election Rules, Social Cleavage, and the Number of Political Parties." *Social Forces* 70(3): 575–99.

Kirillov, A. D., ed. 2002. *Udmurtiia v gody reform*. Izhevsk: Ministerstvo Narodnogo Obrazovaniia Udmurtskoi Respubliki.

Kirkow, Peter. 1998. *Russia's Provinces: Authoritarian Transformation versus Local Autonomy?* New York: St. Martin's Press.

Kisriev, Enver, and Robert Bruce Ware. 2001. "Dagestan's People's Assembly Election, 1999." *Electoral Studies* 20: 463–501.

Kitschelt, Herbert. 1995. "Formation of Party Cleavages in Post-Communist Democracies." *Party Politics* 1(4): 447–72.

Kitschelt, Herbert, Adenka Mansfeldova, Radoslaw Markowski, and Gabor Toka. 1999. *Post-Communist Party Systems: Competition, Representation, and Inter-Party Competition*. Cambridge: Cambridge University Press.

"Konstitutsiia Udmurtskoi Respubliki" [adopted 4 December 1994]. 1995. *Konstitutsii Respublikh v sostave Rossiiskoi Federatsii*. Vol. 1:238–64. Moscow: Izvestiia.

Konstitutsiia Udmurtskoi Respubliki: Sbornik dokumentov i materialov. Chast' 2. 1995. Izhevsk: Izdatel'stvo Udmurtskogo IUU.

Kostadinova, Tatiana. 2002. "Do Mixed Electoral Systems Matter? A Cross-national Analysis of their Effects in Eastern Europe." *Electoral Studies* 21: 23–34.

Lakeman, E. 1974. *How Democracies Vote: A Study of Electoral Systems*. London: Faber and Faber.

LaPalombara, Joseph, and Myron Weiner. 1966. "The Origin and Development of Political Parties." In *Political Parties and Political Development*, ed. Joseph LaPalombara and Myron Weiner. Princeton: Princeton University Press, pp. 3–42.

Lapidus, Gail W. "Asymmetrical Federalism and State Breakdown in Russia." *Post-Soviet Affairs* 15(1): 74–82.

Lijphart, Arend. 1985. *Power-Sharing in South Africa*. Berkeley, CA: Institute of International Studies, University of California.

———. 1986. "Proportionality by Non-PR Methods: Ethnic Representation in Belgium, Cyprus, Lebanon, New Zealand, West Germany, and Zimbabwe." In *Electoral Laws and their Political Consequences*, ed. Bernard Grofman and Arend Lijphart. New York: Agathon Press, pp. 113–23.

———. 1992. "Democratization and Constitutional Choices in Czechoslovakia, Hungary, and Poland, 1989–1991." *Journal of Theoretical Politics* 4(2): 207–23.

———. 1994. *Electoral Systems and Party Systems: A Study of Twenty-Seven Democracies, 1945–1990*. New York: Oxford University Press.

———. 1999. *Patterns of Democracy: Government Forms and Performance in Thirty-Six Countries*. New Haven: Yale University Press.

———. 2004. "Constitutional Design in Divided Societies." *Journal of Democracy* 15(2): 96–109.

Linz, Juan J. 1990. "The Perils of Presidentialism." *Journal of Democracy* 1(1): 51–69.

Linz, Juan J., and Arturo Valenzuela, eds. 1994. *The Failure of Presidential Democracy*. Baltimore: Johns Hopkins University Press.

Lipset, Seymour Martin, and Stein Rokkan, eds. 1967. *Party Systems and Voter Alignments: Cross-National Perspectives*. New York: The Free Press.

Lukin, Alexander. 1999a. "Electoral Democracy or Electoral Clanism? Russian Democratization and Theories of Transition." *Demokratizatsiya* 71(1): 93–110.

———. 1999b. "Forcing the Pace of Democratization." *Journal of Democracy* 10(2): 35–40.

Luong, Pauline Jones. 2002. *Institutional Change and Political Continuity in Post-Soviet Central Asia: Power, Perceptions, and Pacts*. New York: Cambridge University Press.

Mainwaring, Scott. 1993. "Presidentialism, Multipartism, and Democracy: The Difficult Combination." *Comparative Political Studies* 26(2): 198–228.

Maliakin, I. 1995. "Saratovskaia oblast'." In *Rossiiskii sbornik*, ed. Ekaterina Mikhailovskaia. Moscow: Panorama, pp. 397–461.

Mansbridge, Jane J., ed. 1990. *Beyond Self-Interest*. Chicago: Chicago University Press.

Matland, Richard E., and Donley T. Studlar. 1996. "The Contagion of Women Candidates in Single-member District and Proportional Representation Electoral Systems: Canada and Norway." *Journal of Politics* 58(3): 707–34.

Mayhew, David R. 1974. *Congress: The Electoral Connection*. New Haven: Yale University Press.

McAuley, Mary. 1997. *Russia's Politics of Uncertainty*. New York: Cambridge University Press.

McFaul, Michael, and Nikolai Petrov, eds. 1998. *Political Almanac of Russia 1989–1997*. Vols. 1–2. Washington, D.C.: Carnegie Endowment for International Peace.

"Metodika opredeleniia deputatskikh mandatov mezhdu obshcheoblastymi spiskami kandidatov." 19 March 1994. *Saratovskie vesti*, p. 6.

Miller, Arthur H., Gwyn Erb, William M. Reisinger, and Vicki L. Hesli. 2000. "Emerging Party Systems in Post-Soviet Societies: Fact or Fiction?" *Journal of Politics* 62(2): 455–90.

Miller, John. 1993. *Mikhail Gorbachev and the End of Soviet Power.* London: Macmillan.

Miller, John H. 1989. "Putting Clients in Place: The Role of Patronage in Cooption into the Soviet Leadership." In *Political Leadership in the Soviet Union,* ed. Archie Brown. Oxford: MacMillan, pp. 54–95.

Mitchell, Paul. 1995. "Party Competition in an Ethnic Dual Party System." *Ethnic and Racial Studies* 18(4): 773–96.

Monroe, Burt L., and Amanda G. Rose. 2002. "Electoral Systems and Unimagined Consequences: Partisan Effects of Districted Proportional Representation." *American Journal of Political Science* 46(1): 67–89.

Moraski, Bryon J. 2003. "Electoral System Design in Russian *Oblasti* and Republics: A Four-Case Comparison." *Europe-Asia Studies* 55(3): 437–68.

Moraski, Bryon, and Gerhard Loewenberg. 1999. "The Effect of Legal Thresholds on the Revival of Former Communist Parties in East-Central Europe." *Journal of Politics* 61(1): 151–70.

Moraski, Bryon J., and William M. Reisinger. 2003. "Explaining Electoral Competition across Russia's Regions." *Slavic Review* 62(2): 278–301.

———. 2006. "Eroding Democracy: Federal Intervention in Russia's Gubernatorial Elections." *Democratization* (forthcoming).

Moser, Robert G. 1995. "The Impact of the Electoral System on Post-Communist Party Development: The Case of the 1993 Russian Parliamentary Elections." *Electoral Studies* 14(4): 377–98.

———. 1997. "The Impact of Parliamentary Electoral Systems in Russia." *Post-Soviet Affairs* 13: 284–302.

———. 2001. *Unexpected Outcomes: Electoral Systems, Political Parties, and Representation in Russia.* Pittsburgh: Pittsburgh University Press.

Moses, Joel C. 1991. "The Challenge to Soviet Democracy from the Political Right." In *Perestroika-Era Politics: The New Soviet Legislature and Gorbachev's Political Reforms,* ed. Robert T. Huber and Donald R. Kelley. Armonk, NY: M. E. Sharpe.

———. 1994. "Saratov and Volgograd, 1990–1992: A Tale of Two Russian Provinces." In *Local Power and Post-Soviet Politics,* ed. Theodore H. Friedgut and Jeffrey W. Hahn. Armonk, NY: M.E. Sharpe, pp. 96–137.

———. 2002. "Political-Economic Elites and Russian Regional Elections, 1999–2000: Democratic Tendencies in Kaliningrad, Perm, and Volgograd." *Europe-Asia Studies* 54: 905–31.

Mozaffar, S., and R. Vengroff. 2002. "A 'Whole System' Approach to the Choice of Electoral Rules in Democratizing Countries: Senegal in Comparative Perspective." *Electoral Studies* 21: 601–16.

Namsaraeva, E. 23 February 1994. "Deputatov budet 65." *Buriatiia.*

North, Douglass C. 1990. *Institutions, Institutional Changes, and Economic Performance.* Cambridge: Cambridge University Press.

Novosibirsk Oblast Electoral Commission (Novosibirskaia oblastnaia izbiratel'naia Komissiia). 9 March 1990. "Deputaty novosibirskogo oblastnogo soveta narodnykh deputatov, izbrannye 4 marta 1990 g." *Sovetskaia Sibir'.*

———. 21 March 1990. "Deputaty novosibirskogo oblastnogo soveta narodnykh deputatov, izbrannye 17 marta 1990 g." *Sovetskaia Sibir'.*

———. 10 April 1990. "Deputaty novosibirskogo oblastnogo soveta narodnykh deputatov, izbrannye 7 aprelia 1990 g." Sovetskaia Sibir'.

———. 24 April 1990. "Deputaty novosibirskogo oblastnogo soveta narodnykh deputatov, izbrannye 14, 19, 20, 21 aprelia 1990 g." *Sovetskaia Sibir'.*

———. 15 June 1990. "Informatsionnye soobshchenie oblastnoi izbiratel'noi komissii po vyboram v novosibirskoi oblastnoi sovet narodnykh deputatov." *Sovetskaia Sibir'*.

"O vyborakh deputatov Narodnogo Khurala Respubliki Buriatiia." 16 March 1994. *Pravda Buriatii*.

O'Donnell, Guillermo, and Phillipe C. Schmitter. 1986. *Transitions from Authoritarian Rule: Tentative Conclusions about Uncertain Democracies*. Baltimore: Johns Hopkins University Press.

Ordeshook, Peter C., and Olga V. Shvetsova. 1994. "Ethnic Heterogeneity, District Magnitude, and the Number of Parties." *American Journal of Political Science* 38(1): 100–123.

Orttung, Robert W. 1992. "The Russian Right and the Dilemmas of Party Organization." *Soviet Studies* 44(3): 445–78.

Orttung, Robert W., with Danielle N. Lussier and Anna Paretskaya. 2000. *The Republics and Regions of the Russian Federation: A Guide to Politics, Policies, and Leaders*. Armonk, NY: M. E. Sharpe.

Ostrow, Joel M. 2000. *Comparing Post-Soviet Legislatures: A Theory of Institutional Design and Political Conflict*. Columbus, OH: Ohio State University Press.

Petro, Nicolai. 2004. *Crafting Democracy: How Novgorod Has Coped with Rapid Social Change*. Ithaca, NY: Cornell University Press.

Petrov, N. 1995. "Vybory organov predstavitel'noi vlasti." *Mirovaia ekonomika i mezhdunarodnie otnosheniia* 3: 25–34.

Pipes, Richard. 1997. *The Formation of the Soviet Union*. Cambridge, MA: Harvard University Press.

"Podderzhki administratsii." 2 October 1993. *Sovetskaia Sibir'*.

Powell, G. Bingham. 2000. *Elections as Instruments of Democracy: Majoritarian and Proportional Visions*. New Haven: Yale University Press.

Power, Timothy, and Mark J. Gasiorowski. 1997. "Institutional Design and Democratic Consolidation in the Third World." *Comparative Political Studies* 30(2): 123–55.

Pridham, Geoffrey, and Paul Lewis. 1996. "Introduction: Stabilizing Fragile Democracies and Party System Development." In *Stabilizing Fragile Democracies: Comparing New Party Systems in Southern and Eastern Europe*, ed. Geoffrey Pridham and Paul Lewis. New York: Routledge, pp. 1–22.

Przeworski, Adam. 1986. "Some Problems in the Study of the Transition to Democracy" In *Transition from Authoritarian Rule: Comparative Perspectives*, ed. Guillermo O'Donnell, Phillipe Schmitter, and Laurence Whitehead. Baltimore: Johns Hopkins University Press, pp. 47–63.

Radio Free Europe/Radio Liberty. *Russian Political Weekly*. 10 June 2002.

———. *Russian Political Weekly*. 15 May 2003.

Rae, Douglas W. 1967. *The Political Consequences of Electoral Laws*. New Haven: Yale University Press.

Reddaway, Peter. 2002. "Is Putin's Power More Formal Than Real?" *Post-Soviet Affairs* 18(1): 31–40.

Reitblat, M. 1995. "Novosibirskaia oblast'." In *Rossiiskii sbornik*, ed. Ekaterina Mikhailovskaia. Moscow: Panorama, pp. 264–91.

Remington, Thomas F. 1994. "Representative Power and the Russian State." In *Developments in Russian and Post-Soviet Politics*, ed. Stephen White, Alex Pravda, and Zvi Gitelman. Durham, NC: Duke University Press, pp. 57–87.

———. 1999. *Politics in Russia*. New York: Addison Wesley Longman.

Remington, Thomas F., and Steven S. Smith. 1996. "Political Goals, Institutional Context, and the Choice of an Electoral System: The Russian Parliamentary Election Law." *American Journal of Political Science* 40(4): 1253–79.

Reynolds, Andrew. 1995. "The Case for Proportionality." *Journal of Democracy* 6: 117–24.

———. 1999. "Women in the Legislatures and Executives of the World: Knocking at the Highest Glass Ceiling." *World Politics* 51(4): 547–72.

Riedwyl, Hans, and Jürg Steiner. 1995. "What is Proportionality Anyhow?" *Comparative Politics* 27(3): 357–70.

Riker, William H. 1982. "The Two-party System and Duverger's Law: An Essay on the History of Political Science." *American Political Science Review* 76: 753–66.

Roeder, Philip G. 1993. *Red Sunset: The Failure of Soviet Politics.* Princeton, NJ: Princeton University Press.

Rokkan, Stein. 1970. *Citizens, Elections, Parties: Approaches to the Comparative Study of the Processes of Development.* Oslo: Univeritetsforlaget.

Rose, Richard. 2000. "How Floating Parties Frustrate Democratic Accountability: A Supply-side View of Russia's Elections." *East European Constitutional Review* 9(1/2): 53–59.

Ross, Cameron. 2002. "Political Parties and Regional Democracy." In *Regional Politics in Russia,* ed. Cameron Ross. New York: Manchester University Press, pp. 37–56.

Rule, Wilma, and Joseph F. Zimmerman, eds. 1994. *Electoral Systems in Comparative Perspective: Their Impact on Women and Minorities.* Westport, CT: Greenwood Press.

Russian Social Institute of Election Law (Rossiiskii obshchestvennyi institut izbiratel'nogo prava). http://www.roiip.ru/regions/index.htm. 26 May 2004.

Ryzhenkov, Sergei. 1997. "Saratovskaia oblast' (1986–1996): Politika i politiki." In *Regiony Rossii: Khronika i rukovoditeli. Tom 2. Rostovskaia oblast', Saratovskaia oblast'.* Occasional Papers in the Slavic-Eurasian World, ed. Kimitaka Matsuzato and Aleksander Shatilov, N34. Sapporo: Hokkaido University, Slavic Research Center, pp. 110–16.

Saideman, Stephen M., David J. Lanoue, Michael Campenni, and Samuel Stanton. 2003. "Democratization, Political Institutions, and Ethnic Conflict: A Pooled Time-Series Analysis, 1985–1998." *Comparative Political Studies* 35(1): 103–30.

Sakwa, Richard. 1990. *Gorbachev and His Reforms, 1985–1990.* Hemel Hempstead, Herts: Phillip Allan.

———. 1995. "The Russian Elections of December 1993." *Europe-Asia Studies* 47(2): 195–227.

———. 1996. *Russian Politics and Society.* New York: Routledge.

———. 2002. "Federalism, Sovereignty, and Democracy." In *Regional Politics in Russia,* ed. Cameron Ross. New York: Manchester University Press, pp. 1–22.

———. 2003. "Elections and National Integration in Russia." In *The 1999–2000 Elections in Russia: Their Impact and Legacy,* ed. Vicki L. Hesli and William M. Reisinger. New York: Cambridge University Press, pp. 121–41.

Samuels, David. 2004. "Presidentialism and Accountability for the Economy in Comparative Perspective." *American Political Science Review* 98(3): 425–37.

Saratov Oblast Electoral Commission. 8 March 1990. "Narodnye deputaty saratovskie oblastnogo soveta narodnykh deputatov dvadtsat' pervogo sozyva, izbrannye 4 marta 1990 goda." *Kommunist,* p. 2.

———. 21 March 1990. "Narodnye deputaty saratovskie oblastnogo soveta narodnykh deputatov, izbrannye ot otdel'nykh izbiratel'nykh okrugov pri povtornom golosovanii 18 marta 1990 g." *Kommunist.*

———. 24 April 1990. "Narodnye deputaty saratovskie oblastnogo soveta narodnykh deputatov dvadtsat' pervogo sozyva, izbrannye pri povtornom vyborakh 22 aprelia 1990 g." *Kommunist.*

———. 12 May 1990. "Narodnye deputaty saratovskie oblastnogo soveta narodnykh deputatov, izbrannye pri povtornom golosovanii 6 maia 1990 goda." *Kommunist.*

———. 27 June 1990. "Soobshchenie oblastnoi izbiratel'noi komissii ob itogakh povtornykh vyborov narodnykh deputatov saratovskogo oblastnogo soveta narodnykh deputatov, sostoiavshikhsia 24 iunia 1990 goda." *Kommunist.*

———. 1 July 1990. "Soobshchenie oblastnoi izbiratel'noi komissii po vyboram narodnykh deputatov saratovskogo oblastnogo soveta narodnykh deputatov." *Kommunist.*

Sartori, Giovanni. 1994. *Comparative Constitutional Engineering: An Inquiry into Structures, Incentives, and Outcomes.* New York: New York University Press.

Selivra, S. 12 April 1994. "Izbirkom nachal rabotu." *Pravda Buriatii.*

Semenova, L. 29 October 1993. "Novyi shag v reformirovannii predstavitel'noi vlasti na mestakh." *Sovetskaia Sibir'.*

Shevtsova, Lilia. 2003. *Putin's Russia.* Washington, D.C.: Carnegie Endowment for International Peace.

Shlapentokh, Vladimir, Roman Levita, and Mikhail Loiberg. 1997. *From Submission to Rebellion: The Provinces Versus the Center in Russia.* Boulder, CO: Westview Press.

Shugart, Matthew S. 1997. "Politicians, Parties, and Presidents: An Exploration of Post-Authoritarian Institutional Design." In *Liberalization and Leninist Legacies: Comparative Perspectives on Democratic Transitions,* ed. Beverly Crawford and Arend Lijphart. Berkeley: University of California Press, pp. 40–90.

Shugart, Matthew S., and Martin P. Wattenberg, eds. 2001. *Mixed-Member Electoral Systems: The Best of Both Worlds?* New York: Oxford University Press.

Shukin, Sergei. 1995. *Vlast' v zakone.* Izhevsk: Izhevsk Poligraficheskii Kombinat.

Shvetsova, Olga. 1999. "A Survey of Post-Communist Electoral Institutions: 1990–1998." *Electoral Studies* 18: 397–409.

Skilling, H. Gordon, and Franklyn Griffiths. 1971. *Interest Groups in Soviet Politics.* Princeton, NJ: Princeton University Press.

Slider, Darrell. 1994. "Federalism, Discord, and Accommodation: Intergovernmental Relations in Post-Soviet Russia." In *Local Power and Post-Soviet Politics,* ed. Theodore H. Friedgut and Jeffrey Hahn. Armonk, NY: M. E. Sharpe, pp. 239–69.

———. 1996. "Elections to Russia's Regional Assemblies." *Post-Soviet Affairs* 12(3): 243–64.

———. 2001. "Russia's Governors and Party Formation." In *Contemporary Russian Politics: A Reader,* ed. Archie Brown. New York: Oxford University Press, pp. 224–34.

———. 2004. "Governors versus Mayors: The Regional Dimension of Russian Local Government." In *The Politics of Local Government in Russia,* ed. Alfred B. Evans and Vladimir Gel'man. New York: Rowman and Littlefield, pp. 145–68.

Smirnov, William. 2001. "Democratization in Russia: Achievements and Problems." In *Contemporary Russian Politics: A Reader,* ed. Archie Brown. New York: Oxford University Press, pp. 517–29.

Smith, Steven S., and Thomas F. Remington. 2001. *The Politics of Institutional Choice: The Formation of the Russian State Duma.* Princeton, NJ: Princeton University Press.

Söderland, Peter J. "The Significance of Structural Power Resources in the Russian Bilateral Treaty Process, 1994–1998." *Communist and Post-Communist Studies* 36: 311–24.

Solomon, Peter H., Jr., and Todd S. Foglesong. 2000. *Courts and Transition in Russia: The Challenge of Judicial Reform*. Boulder, CO: Westview Press.

"Soobshaet press-sluzhba Prezidenta RF." 6 October 1993. *Sovetskaia Sibir'*.

Stepan, Alfred. 2000. "Russian Federalism in Comparative Perspective." *Post-Soviet Affairs* 16(2): 133–75.

Stepan, Alfred, and Cindy Skach. 1993. "Constitutional Frameworks and Democratic Consolidation: Parliamentarism versus Presidentialism." *World Politics* 46: 1–22.

Subbotin, A. 18 March 1994. "Kompromiss za schet konstitutsii." *Pravda Buriatii*.

Taagepera, Rein. 1994. "Beating the Law of Minority Attrition." In *Electoral Systems in Comparative Perspective: Their Impact on Women and Minorities*, ed. Wilma Rule and Joseph F. Zimmerman. Westport, CT: Greenwood Press, pp. 234–45.

Taagepera, Rein, and Matthew Soberg Shugart. 1989. *Seats and Votes: The Effects and Determinants of Electoral Systems*. New Haven: Yale University Press.

Teague, Elizabeth. 2002. "Putin Reforms the Federal System." In *Regional Politics in Russia*, ed. Cameron Ross. New York: Manchester University Press, pp. 207–17.

Territories of the Russian Federation, 2001. 2001. 2nd ed. London: Europa Publications.

Tiukov, N. 1995. "Respublika Buriatiia." In *Rossisskii sbornik*, ed. Ekaterina Mikhailovskaia. Moscow: Panorama, pp. 42–69.

Treisman, Daniel S. 1997. "Russia's 'Ethnic Revival': The Separatist Activism of Regional Leaders in a Postcommunist Order." *World Politics* 49(2): 212–49.

———. 1999. *After the Deluge: Regional Crises and Political Consolidation in Russia*. Ann Arbor, MI: University of Michigan Press.

Tsebelis, George. 1990. *Nested Games*. Berkeley: University of California Press.

Tubylov, V. K. 24 September 1993. "Postavlenie Verkhovnogo Soveta Udmurtskoi Respubliki." *Udmurtskaia pravda*.

———. 9 October 1993. "Postavlenie Verkhovnogo Soveta Udmurtskoi Respubliki." *Udmurtskaia pravda*.

Tucker, Robert C. 1995. "Post-Soviet Leadership and Change." In *Patterns in Post-Soviet Leadership*, ed. Timothy J. Colton and Robert C. Tucker. San Francisco: Westview Press, pp. 5–28.

Udmurtia Republic Electoral Commission (Izbiratel'naia Komissiia Udmurtskoi Respubliki). 10 March 1990. "Narodnye deputaty Verkhovnogo Soveta Udmurtskoi ASSR, izbrannye 4 marta 1990 goda." *Udmurtskaia pravda*.

———. 24 March 1990. "Narodnye deputaty Verkhovnogo Soveta Udmurtskoi ASSR, izbrannye pri povtornom golosovanii 18 marta 1990 goda." *Udmurtskaia pravda*.

———. 25 April 1990. "Soobshchenie okruzhnykh izbiratel'nykh komissii o rezul'tatakh povtornogo golosovaniia vyborov narodnykh deputatov Verkhovnogo Soveta Udmurtskoi ASSR." *Udmurtskaia pravda*, p. 3.

———. 2 May 1990. "Soobshchenie okruzhnykh izbiratel'nykh komissii o rezul'tatakh povtornogo golosovaniia vyborov narodnykh deputatov Verkhovnogo Soveta Udmurtskoi ASSR." *Udmurtskaia pravda*, p. 3.

"Ukaz Prezidenta Rossiiskoi Federatsii ob utverzhdenii osnovnykh polozhenii o vyborakh v predstavitel'nye organy gosudarstvennoi vlasti kraia, oblasti, goroda," 3 November 1993. *Saratovskie vesti*.

"Ukaz Prezidenta Rossiiskoi Federatsii o reforme predstavitelei organov vlasti i organov mestnogo samoupravleniia v Rossiiskoi Federatsii," 13 October 1993. *Sovetskaia Sibir'*.

"Ukazom Prezidenta Rossiiskoi Federatsii." 4 July 1992. *Saratovskie vesti*.

Urban, Michael E. 1990. *More Power to the Soviets: The Democratic Revolution in the USSR*. Brookfield, VT: Edward Elgar.

"V. P. Mukha—Glava administratsii oblasti." 28 November 991. *Sovetskaia Sibir'*.

Ware, Robert Bruce, and Enver Kisriev. 1999. "Political Stability and Ethnic Parity: Why is There Peace in Dagestan?" In *Center-Periphery Conflict in Post-Soviet Russia: A Federation Imperiled*, ed. Mikhail A. Alexseev. New York: St. Martin's Press, pp. 95–130.

Weaver, R. Kent. 2002. "A New Look at Federalism: Electoral Rules and Governability." *Journal of Democracy* 13(2): 111–25.

Wedel, Janine R. 1996. "Clique-Run Organizations and U.S. Economic Aid: An Institutional Analysis." *Demokratizatsiya* 4: 571–97.

White, Stephen. 1994. *After Gorbachev*. Cambridge: Cambridge University Press.

White, Stephen, Richard Rose, and Ian McAllister. 1997. *How Russia Votes*. Chatham, NJ: Chatham House Publishers.

White, Stephen, Matthew Wyman, and Olga Kryshtanovskaya. 1995. "Parties and Politics in Post-Communist Russia." *Communist and Post-Communist Studies* 28: 183–202.

Willerton, John P. 1992. *Patronage and Politics in the USSR*. Cambridge: Cambridge University Press.

———. 1994. "Yeltsin and the Russian Presidency." In *Developments in Russian and Post-Soviet Politics*, ed. Stephen White, Alex Pravda, and Zvi Gitelman. Durham, NC: Duke University Press, pp. 25–56.

"Zaiavlenie Prezidiuma Verkhovnogo Soveta Udmurtskoi Respubliki." 5 October 1993. *Udmurtskaia pravda*.

"Zakon Udmurtskoi Respubliki o vyborakh deputatov Gosudarstvennogo Soveta Udmurtskoi Respubliki." 27 December 1994. *Udmurtskaia pravda*, pp. 2–3.

Zharinov, A. 1 October 1993. "K variantu soveta s narodom." *Sovetskaia Sibir'*.

———. 21 January 1994. "Polozhenie est', ulozhenii ne trebuetsia." *Sovetskaia Sibir'*.

INDEX

www.ingramcontent.com/pod-product-compliance
Lightning Source LLC
Chambersburg PA
CBHW031548260326
41914CB00002B/318